No One Said Life Was Fair

How Bumpy Got His Name and Other Brief Encounters with
the Criminally Inept, the Emotionally Bankrupt and
the Sobriety Challenged Members of my Somewhat Twisted,
Albeit Lovingly Dysfunctional Family

A MEMOIR
MARY KATE DECRAENE

Copyright © 2013 Mary K. DeCraene
All rights reserved.
ISBN-10:1493765280
ISBN-13:978-1493765287

Dedication

To my family past, present, and future—may we all meet again
someday *under better circumstances.*

Acknowledgments

To my Mom and Dad—*I love and miss you both terribly. Thank you for showing me the importance of family, for never allowing me to feel sorry for myself and for making me who I am today.*

To my sisters, Patty and Kathy—*I love you both unconditionally and miss the times we had growing up together, crazy though they were. Thank you for helping me to look back fondly on our childhood, to see the humor beyond the tears and to share my version of our story.*

To Aunty Peggy, Aunt Evelyn, Uncle John, Uncle Pete, Aunty Lois, Uncle Bob, Aunty Shirley, Uncle Kenny, Patty, Kathy, and Dan—*I love you all! Thanks for helping me fill in the blanks. I could not have done it without you.*

To Cheryl, Deb, Jackie, Joyce, Judith, Julya, Karen, Vickie, Dan and Sarah, the members of T.W.I.G., and Writers in Progress—*Thanks for giving me honest feedback and the insight I needed to deliver the best story possible. I sincerely appreciate all your help.*

To The Doan's, The Duch's, The Hosmer's, The Kripner's, The McElroy's, The McMahon's, The Nakon's, The Ray's, The Rosinski's, The Sperry's, The Stack's, The Terlecki's, The Wagner's, The Waslo's, The Wheeler's, and The Zukowski's—*You welcomed us into your homes and gave us a safe place to stay when we were unable go home. Thank you for your kindness and for making my sisters and I part of your families.*

To my wonderful husband Dan and beautiful daughter Sarah—*I love you both with all my heart! Thank you for giving me strength to overcome any obstacles life throws my way and for allowing me to go on this journey into my past.*

Table of Contents

Preface

What you are about to read is based on family stories and faded memories distorted by time and emotion. Therefore, it may not be the whole truth, but only a reasonable facsimile thereof. Some of the names were changed to protect the innocent and the *not so innocent.*

For more than five generations, every member of my family has battled a vicious disease; a tradition passed down from parent to child through denial. It is in our blood, and it is an integral part of who we are. The disease is alcoholism, and there is no known cure. The only way to break with this tradition is to confront the truth. Lest our pain be in vain, we must not let history repeat itself.

Prologue

Can't Sleep

Restless night. Can't sleep again. Thoughts keep racing through my head. Not even complete thoughts. One begins and is soon interrupted by another, which is soon interrupted by another—an endless chain of incomplete thoughts racing through my head. I can barely keep my eyes open, but the fear of closing them, only to hear the inescapable thoughts racing through my head, keeps them wide open.

All of the soul-shattering memories I locked up in a box deep within the recesses of my mind have ignited, causing an explosion of emotion ever more powerful than a super nova. And after the explosion there is no real peace—only a whirlwind left to scatter the remaining debris throughout the corridors of my mind.

Anything can trigger it. Sometimes, all it takes is the sweet smell of rain on a cool autumn night, or a warm summer breeze motheringly blowing the hair away from my eyes, or a song on the radio that send chills down my spine. I become numb, stand dead in my tracks, and am flooded by flashbacks, memories, and nightmares of the past.

For a split second I relive them. My heart begins to race, and a tidal wave of pain comes crashing back. An incredible, inconsolable sadness overcomes me. The sadness is so great it suffocates me. I can barely breathe as a deluge of tears stream down my face. My hands become hot and red and tremble with fear. I try to control the shaking by clenching my fists, but I cannot make it stop.

I am alone. No one can help me. No one understands, and I am plagued by the senselessness of it all. Just for a split second, I am home again.

Why

Why? A question I find myself asking,
No answer will satisfy,
A thirst I cannot quench,
All logic it does defy,

Why? Haunting and relentless,
Consumes me with self pity and despair,
But then Mom's voice calls out to me,
Alas, "No One Said Life Was Fair"

Chapter 1

Black Toes
(Tuesday, March 7, 1995)

I stopped by Dad's house on my way home from work today. I was worried about him. The infection is getting worse.

As I descended the stairs into his makeshift bedroom in the basement, my senses were assaulted by a foot-and-a-half thick cloud of cigarette smoke, a wall of oppressive heat, and an obnoxiously loud television set. Dad was sitting on his girly white brass daybed next to the space heater which he cranked up to a stifling eighty-five degrees. He was watching the news, drinking Canadian Club Whiskey, and smoking an unfiltered Camel cigarette. The quart size of booze he purchased in the morning was three-quarters empty and the ashtray on the coffee table next to his bed was filled to the brim with ashes and cigarette butts.

"Hell-o!" I shouted.

"Hey, Mary Kat-rin. What's happening kid?" Dad greeted me with a smile on his face as he fumbled with the channel changer to lower the volume on the TV. "Grab a seat," he said pointing to the metallic gold folding chair he kept out especially for company.

"What you up to Dad?"

"Ah, nothing much. Just watching the paint dry."

"How are you feeling today?" I asked, trying not to look overtly worried—knowing if I did, it would set him off.

"Like horse shit ... and how are you?"

"Oh, I'm good."

The care basket I gave him for Christmas filled with triple antibiotic cream, antiseptic, and bandages was sitting on the floor next to his bed and was nearly empty.

"Hey, Mar' do you mind doing me a flavor? Kathy took the kid to the doctor. Can you change the bandage on my foot for me?"

"Sure Dad."

As I removed the bandages, revealing his blackened toes and an oozing wound on the bottom of his foot the size of a half-dollar, the pungent smell of rotting flesh hit me hard—like a baseball bat crashing against my skull. Instantly jarring me back in time, thirteen years earlier, when Mom lay on the couch wasting away in excruciating pain, unable to eat or drink.

Stunned silent, I searched for the right words to say. I needed to tread lightly or Dad might refuse to get help again.

"Well, Doc. Am I gonna live?"

I never did have much of a poker face.

"To be honest, I think you are going to lose a couple of your toes. It looks bad. Real bad."

"I see said the blind man to his deaf wife. Oh, don't worry about it. All I need is some antibiotics. I'll be fine."

"I've checked with all my friends, Dad. No one has any leftover antibiotics. You'll have to go to a doctor to get more. We can go tomorrow. I'll take you anywhere you want to go—except Cook County Hospital. I don't think I can go back there."

"You can't take me anywhere tomorrow. You have to work."

"I'll call in sick."

"You can't take me by yourself. What if I fall and I need help getting up?"

"Not a problem. Dan and I will call off work tomorrow and we'll both take you.

"Eh, I'll think about it."

Chapter 2

Too Sick to Go to the Hospital

God, I hate this place. How the hell did I let Dad talk me into coming here again?

Cook County Hospital is one of the best hospitals in the country, however, their emergency room is perpetually filled to maximum capacity because they offer free medical services to those who cannot afford to pay for them. Even individuals with severe medical emergencies are forced to wait their turn. Every time we go it is guaranteed to be a tedious all day event. It is where drug addicts are taken when they overdose. Where gangbangers go to when they get shot. Where Cook County prisoners wind up when they try to kill themselves.

No one in their right mind willingly goes to Cook County Hospital—not when they have other choices available. I begged him. I pleaded with him. I bribed him with my federal income tax refund check. I even offered to pay his hospital bill if he went somewhere, anywhere else. Yet he would not yield. He is, by far, the most stubborn and infuriating man I have ever known.

Forced to sit in this god forsaken waiting room for hours pondering Dad's fate, I cannot help but recall the months it took to get to this moment, this place. Months of trying to convince Dad the numbness he felt in his fingers and toes was not due to a stroke, but rather was the result of advanced alcoholism and untreated diabetes. Months of urging Dad to see a doctor, while he treated an open wound on the bottom of his foot with nothing more than bleach and water; a wound that became horribly infected and turned into an ulcer. Months of absolute agony, knowing someone I loved was possibly dying, and there wasn't a thing I could do about it but sit back and watch it happen. But, at last, we are finally here.

I honestly don't know what convinced Dad to go to the hospital. Maybe it was the fever from the infection or my sister Patty calling 911, twice, only to have him refuse treatment both times. Maybe he thought three strikes and he was out, or maybe it was because we let him choose to go to the hospital on his own terms, instead of forcing the issue.

Even after Dad decided to go to the hospital, it still took him

*a week to get here. His excuse was he was too sick to go. Have you
ever heard of such a thing? Too sick to go to a hospital? Maddening.
Absolutely maddening.*

*Once Dad felt well enough for us to take him to the
emergency room, we had to wait for him to catch up on his sleep.
Then we waited while he took a shower. The shower took too much
out of him, and we waited while he took a two hour nap. After he
awoke from his nap, he needed to eat. Eating made him sleepy. We
waited another hour, while he took yet another nap. When he woke
up, he announced it was "medicine time" then took a generous swig
of whiskey.*

"Come on Dad. Let's go." I whined.

*"One more for the road," he said then chugged another shot
back.*

Finally—at freaking last—we were on our way.

*Dad could only take a few steps before he had to stop to rest.
It took an eternity to get the man out the front door. When he opted
to rest on the front stoop, my husband Dan, whose patience was
completely worn thin, picked him up, and carried him to the car.
Dad was so weak from the infection he could no longer fight us.*

*We got to the hospital about noon. When the nurse took
Dad's vitals his blood pressure was 70 over 52. Not good. That was
seven hours ago. They just moved him from triage to the treatment
area. Now the real wait begins.*

Everybody Loves Ronnie

Everybody loves Dad. You can't help it. He has a wicked
sense of humor, is generous to a fault, and can throw one hell of a
mean curve ball. His love for his family, baseball and alcohol are
unparalleled, but it is Dad's irreverent personality that endears him
to those of us who know and love him.

A gifted story teller whose enthusiasm is contagious, Dad's
stories recount his infamous fights with Mom, pranks he pulled on
people he likes, and numerous times he got himself in and out of
trouble. His tawdry tales of mischief and mayhem are guaranteed to
end with me roaring with laughter, my stomach aching, and tears
rolling down my cheeks. I can always count on Dad to make me
laugh, no matter how bad things get. He is the comic relief in an
otherwise sad family melodrama.

Not one to hold a grudge, Dad seldom stays mad for long. Coupled with his alcohol-induced propensity for blacking out (he rarely remembers what transpired the night before), each new day begins with a clean slate. If Dad has a beef with someone, he has it out with them right then and there, and all is forgiven the next day, like nothing happened.

Above all else, Dad is loyal. Whenever a relative needs help, he is the first to lend a hand. He is well-known for taking in the strays of the family and has never once asked anyone who lived with us for a dime to help pay for food, rent, or utilities—no matter how long they stayed with us. Aunty Shirley, Uncle John, Uncle Kenny (and his girlfriends Esther and Cindy), and Cousins Deanna, Bobby, Jim, and Kenny all stayed with us at one time or another. For Dad, family comes above everything—well, almost everything but his "drinking time."

Party, What Party?

My father, Ronald Anthony Velesovsky, was born on September 25, 1943 in his parent's humble flat in Chicago's Pilsen neighborhood. The second-eldest of four children, he began smoking and drinking when he was twelve years old. His kryptonite is Canadian Club Whiskey, although, depending on his mood, he will drink any good alcohol, including Pilsner Urquell Beer and Du Bouchett Black Cherry Brandy. On special occasions (or rather when the opportunity presents itself), he is also known to smoke pot or snort cocaine. Freakishly proud of his less than stellar academic record, Dad treasures most the report cards in which the nuns gave him check marks for his unruly behavior. He dropped out of high school his junior year to join an interstate grand theft auto ring. Although he has had three brief attempts at sobriety, his alcoholism has steadily progressed throughout his adulthood.

Dad's father, George Velesovsky, was a functional alcoholic who never missed a day of work despite his disease. A beer drinker and former amateur boxer, he worked for a silk screening firm and was quite ornery, although he did soften up a bit in his old age. Dad's mother, Bernice (Bartoszek) Velesovsky, a self-proclaimed "wino," worked both as a waitress at Bishop's Chili and as a cleaning lady with her mother at several downtown Chicago high-rise buildings including the famed Sherman House Hotel.

At the age of twelve, Dad routinely hosted wild drinking parties for his baseball buddies in his parents flat without any regard to the consequences of his actions. His mother often came home from work to find empty beer bottles and rubbish strewn about the house. In classic enabling behavior, she cleaned up after Dad before his father returned home from work and, in essence, swept his drinking problem under the rug, too, pretending like nothing was wrong.

The Party's Over

My mother, Patricia Jean (Sheedy) Velesovsky was born on March 30, 1947 on the Lower West Side of Chicago. The youngest of five surviving children, Mom started drinking at the age of ten, began smoking at the age of twelve, and, by her own admission, was an alcoholic by the age of thirteen. Southern Comfort was her intoxicant of choice—although when she was desperate enough for a drink, any elixir would do. Despite having an IQ of 140, Mom dropped out of high school her freshmen year. She embarked on her battle to become sober when she was twenty-two years old. With three exceptions that I am aware of, she managed to stay sober the rest of her life.

Mom's father, Peter Sheedy, was a sailor in the U.S. Navy and served during World War II. An alcoholic for many years he eventually succumbed to the disease, and died of cirrhosis of the liver in November, 1968. Mom's mother, Eva (Tomsic) Sheedy, a homemaker, suffered from an undiagnosed mental illness. She drifted in and out of reality, often speaking to people who were not in the room.

Once, when I was little, I asked Mom why she drank, and she told me, "When I was young, kids picked on me and made fun of me. I was painfully shy. Drinking helped relieve the insecurities I felt about myself, and it provided an escape from the problems I had at home. When I drank, I had no fear. I was the life of the party, and I didn't care what other people thought about me."

It started innocently enough. Mom's brother Pete offered to pay her a dollar to clean up after a house party. A dollar was a lot of money to a kid in 1957. Mom looked up to her older brother and was eager to help. She rolled up her sleeves, grabbed the trash can from the kitchen, and went to work. After a couple of hours of cleaning, she got thirsty, and when no one was looking, she sneaked a sip of beer from one of the half-empty cans left on the coffee table.

Where did a young girl get her hands on alcohol? Her father always had alcohol in the house and never noticed a sip missing here and there. As Mom's dependency on alcohol grew, however, she was forced to find other means to support her habit. One way was by babysitting for her sister Evelyn's four boys at their home in the suburbs. The moment Evelyn and her husband, John, left the house Mom placed an order for a pizza and a six-pack of beer. Five minutes before the pizza arrived, she ran the shower and closed the bathroom door. When the pizza man rang the doorbell, Mom answered the door, claimed her sister was in the shower, and paid for the pizza and beer, herself. No one in her family knew about her drinking problem.

I guess if you are from a normal family, it is hard to understand how someone so young can get tangled up in the wicked web of alcoholism. When you come from a long line of alcoholics, it is easy to see how the insecurities of growing up are eased by the numbness alcohol can provide, especially when the only way you are taught to handle your problems is with a bottle.

Poor Mama

Mom's family was very poor. When she was a newborn, her sisters and brother came home from school to find the landlord tossed all of their belongings onto the front lawn. Suddenly homeless, her family gathered what possessions they could carry and walked to an aunt's home several blocks away where they stayed until they found another place to live.

Many of the apartments Mom's parents could afford were uninhabitable by today's standards. The worst had no working indoor bathroom. It did, however, have an outhouse in the backyard. During the winter, Mom traipsed outside in her pajamas and winter coat. In the summer, she avoided hornets and other bugs that made the outhouse their home. Fortunately, her family only lived there for a year.

From the time Mom was five until she was thirteen years old, her family lived in a ground-level flat off an alley, near 22nd and Drake Avenue in Chicago that had a forced-air, coal-burning furnace. When the heat ran, it left a thick layer of black dust everywhere, requiring Mom and her siblings to dust, sweep, and mop daily during the winter months.

While the apartment had a working toilet, the only bathtub was located in the rat-infested basement and was shared by everyone in the building. As a result, Mom bathed infrequently and suffered from head lice. The rat infestation was so great she could hear rats scurrying inside the walls on either side of the toilet whenever she used the washroom.

Each night before going to bed, my Nana (Grandma) Sheedy set a large trap on top of the stove in the kitchen. The next morning when the family woke up, they were greeted by another dead rat with its neck broken and blood dripping down the front of the oven. Occasionally, the rat was too large for the trap and was still alive and thrashing about.

Late one evening, Grandpa Sheedy came home drunk and noticed a paper bag lying on the floor in the living room. "These lazy goddamn kids can't even pick a lousy paper bag up off the floor." he shouted in a thick Irish brogue, and then angrily declared, "I suppose I have to do everything around here." As Grandpa reached for the bag to throw it away, a huge rat jumped out, startled him and sent him screaming out of the room.

The building Mom and her family lived in was sold about a year before they moved out. Shortly after the new landlords moved in, another infestation came with them—cockroaches. Whenever Nana got up in the middle of the night to get a drink of water, she turned the light on and said, "Look, a moving wall." The walls were covered floor to ceiling with roaches which scattered the moment the lights came on.

In the Outhouse

Grandma Velesovsky was an obsessive-compulsive cleaning fanatic. Without fail, she washed the floors, ceilings, and walls as part of her daily cleaning routine. She washed Whiskers, the family dog, so often with bleach he developed sores and lost most of his hair.

Once, during a visit to Grandma's house, Dad told me to help myself to a glass of "Ku-Ju" from the refrigerator. (Ku-Ju is short for "Kool-Aid Juice". When I was two years old my parents asked me what kind of juice I wanted and I said, "Kool-Aid". Dad thought it was funny as hell and still teases me about it to this day.) When I opened the refrigerator door, I was afraid to touch anything. It was immaculate, like a page out of a magazine. Leftovers were placed equidistant from each other on gold-rimmed dishes perfectly covered with plastic wrap.

I never understood why Grandma encased her leftovers in plastic, much like the couch in her living room, until she relayed the following story to me: Dad was sixteen years old and came home early one morning after a night of binge-drinking. Grandma was sitting at the kitchen table enjoying her morning coffee and a non-filtered Camel cigarette when Dad came stumbling in.

"Good morning, Ronnie. Are you hungry?" Upon seeing his inebriated condition, she added in a sarcastic tone, "*Or need a cup of coffee?*"

Dad turned to her with a glazed-over look on his face, and said, "I gotta take a piss."

Then he staggered over to his parent's 1940 General refrigerator, opened the bottom door, and proceeded to relieve himself all over everything inside.

"Ronnie, stop! You're peeing in the refrigerator!"

"Get the fuck away from me. Can't you see I am taking a piss?"

Mystery solved.

The Perfect Storm
(Two Wrongs Don't Make a Right)

The perfect storm is the convergence of two vast tropical storms culminating in a category five hurricane causing unimaginable devastation. My parent's tumultuous relationship was the perfect storm—two alcoholics uniting, destroying everything in their wake. The combination of Dad's Polish stubbornness and Mom's Irish temper proved to be a volatile combination, creating a tempest which wreaked havoc wherever they went.

In the spring of 1963, Dad was cruising around in his car and noticed Mom and a couple of her girlfriends as they sauntered toward the intersection he was stopped at. It was love at first sight. Dad was immediately enamored with Mom's vivacious curves, long jet-black hair, and crystal-blue bedroom eyes. Mom, no doubt, was attracted to Dad's *Rebel Without a Cause* looks, wicked sense of humor and insatiable charms. Whatever attracted my parents to one another also tore them apart. There was always a storm brewing on the horizon ready to erupt without warning.

Surely a sign of things to come, my parents never could agree on how they first met. Mom once told me she met Dad in a restaurant—however, Dad insisted the restaurant looked an awful lot like a bar. Even though Dad is known to stretch the truth on occasion, I am inclined to believe him *this time*. Mom purposely looked and acted much older than she was to obtain alcohol, and could have easily been served at a bar before she came of age.

The first time Dad brought Mom home to meet his family, they were both shit-faced drunk. They drove to Dad's parents flat in his convertible with the top down. Mom's hair was a mess. She got very upset when she realized she did not have a brush or a comb with her.

"I can't meet your family looking like this, Ron."

"Oh, come on. You look fine. Trust me. My family won't give a shit what your hair looks like."

"Maybe not, but I care. I want to make a good first impression," Mom pouted as she fussed with her hair in the rearview mirror.

Growing increasingly impatient, Dad decided if Mohammed wouldn't come to the mountain, he would bring the mountain to Mohammed instead.

"Well, fuck ya then!" he yelled as he marched toward his parent's house alone.

"Come back here right now, Ronnie! I mean it. We aren't finished talking about this yet."

Dad kept walking and never looked back. When Mom heard Dad slam his parent's front door shut, she let out a war cry, "Ooooooooo!" and kicked the windshield of his car.

A few minutes later, Dad unwittingly emerged from his parent's flat with his kid sister Shirley in tow. Momentarily confused by the shattered glass on the sidewalk as they approached his car, Dad paused briefly before he looked up and noticed the gaping hole in his windshield left by a woman's size five-and-a-half shoe. The perpetrator of said dastardly deed smiled sweetly at Shirley, then gave a friendly wave from the passenger seat.

"Hi, I'm Pat."

"Hi. I'm Shirley. Um, it's nice to meet you?"

Chapter 3

Waiting Room

Cook County Hospital is not like other hospitals. The security guards are real Chicago policemen and Cook County sheriff's police.

The hospital has no parking lot. It takes forty-five minutes or longer to find an open parking space on the street with a working parking meter in what I consider a safe spot (a well-lit, open area, within screaming distance of the hospital entrance). The parking meter costs fifty cents to park for half-an-hour, and that's all the time you are allotted to park before you get ticketed. It can take that long to get past the front desk.

A visitors pass is required to go anywhere beyond the waiting room. In order to obtain a visitors pass, you must wait in line and present two forms of picture identification. (Seriously, what photo I.D. do you keep in your wallet besides your driver's license?)

The waiting room is completely void of any warmth from its sterile white and green walls, to its institutional linoleum tile floors and its uncomfortable plastic bucket seats (most of which are broken in one way or another). All the televisions and magazines have been stolen. There are no vending or coffee machines. If by chance, you happen to find a working restroom, it is so vial and disgusting you are unable to use it for fear of catching a transmittable disease. Falling asleep is strictly forbidden and if you do you will be immediately escorted off the premises in a most unfriendly manner for vagrancy. Many of the rules observed in public transportation are also practiced in the waiting room. Like the rule no matter where you sit, an individual, who has not bathed in weeks, will sit next to you. This person typically suffers from some form of mental illness and engages in loud arguments with him or herself.

Using the stairs is strictly forbidden. Visitors are required to use the main elevator which can take ten or more minutes to arrive. The elevator has an armed guard who checks your pass. Once on the elevator, it takes longer to get where you are going then it did for the elevator to arrive. Call me crazy, but shouldn't hospital elevators be quicker than that? Isn't there a necessity to get patients up to surgery before they bleed to death?

Visitors are prohibited from entering the triage unit. Only patients are allowed in. A disgruntled Chicago police officer, who clearly hates his assignment, guards the triage unit. Unless the patient leaves triage, which, by the way, makes him lose his place in line, family and friends have absolutely no idea how the patient is doing.

If Cook County Hospital has taught me anything, it is how to shut up, be patient, and wait.

Drafted

"Greetings: You are hereby ordered to report for induction into the Armed Forces of the United States." –Words that changed young men's lives forever during the Vietnam War. At the induction center, Dad was given a physical exam and then a written test. When he was shown a picture of a hammer, he said it was a screwdriver. Out of one hundred questions, he got ninety-six wrong. Having failed the written test on purpose, Dad never did forgive himself for getting those four questions right.

Shortly after failing the exam, Dad and two other inductees, who also failed the test miserably, were pulled into an office by a sergeant. The sergeant looked at the test results, shook his head in disgust, and said to Dad, "Son, if you don't want to be in this man's army this badly, we don't want you. You're free to go." Then the sergeant pointed at the two other inductees and said, "The same goes for you two. Get the hell out of my office before I change my mind."

Officially, Dad was released from active duty because he was color blind. Unofficially, he was one lucky "S.O.B.".

Going to the Chapel

Desperately wanting to marry Dad before she turned eighteen, Mom begged her father for his permission, but he refused to sign the papers. My parents obtained their marriage license, against their better judgment, on April Fools' Day—two days after Mom's eighteenth birthday. They wed two days later, on April 3, 1965 at St. Michael the Archangel Church, on the south side of Chicago.

The reason why Mom wanted to leave home became abundantly clear when she went to say goodbye to her parents. She packed her bags, looked nostalgically around her bedroom, and stepped into the kitchen, where she found Nana Sheedy, sitting at the table.

"Goodbye, Mom. I'm leaving."

"They can't hurt me. I'm a five-star general." Nana declared.

Mom smiled, gave her mother a kiss on the cheek, and walked to the front room to say goodbye to her father.

"Goodbye, Dad. I'm going."

"Watch out for the tumble weeds, Patsy. They're out to get ya." Grandpa warned.

I guess I can understand why Mom married Dad. It was self-preservation. Little did she know she was jumping from the frying pan and into the fire.

Bathroom Brawlers Part I
The Bowling Banquet

When my folks were first married they belonged to a bowling league along with Mom's sister Evelyn and her husband, John. At the end of the season, the bowling alley hosted a banquet for all the teams. Dad consumed a bit too much alcohol and pizza, and excused himself from the table. He staggered toward the newly remodeled men's restroom, bouncing off the hallway walls like a wild gutter ball. Then he kicked the bathroom door open, took one step forward, and immediately fell down, leaving a head-shaped dent in the metal stall and a huge open gash on his forehead. In Dad's impaired condition, he did not notice the "Wet Floor" sign when he entered the room.

Suffering from a bad case of vertigo, Dad crawled over to the bathroom sink, pulled himself up, and washed the blood from his face. As he tried to dry his hands and face with the cloth towel dispenser, it jammed—which infuriated him to no end. Overcome with rage, he tore the towel dispenser from the wall, breaking several tiles along with it. Then he threw the towel dispenser at the mirror, shattering it, and sending shards of glass flying everywhere. Moments later, he exited the bathroom—battered, bruised and bleeding, with a train of toilet paper trailing behind him.

Perplexed, John asked, "What the hell happened to you?"

To which Dad replied, "You should see the other guy."

The bathroom was destroyed. The police were called. Dad

was escorted away in handcuffs and was asked never to return.

Son of a Bitch Bastard

A few months after my parents married, they adopted a dog from the Anti-Cruelty Society. Knowing them, they used the dog as a test to see if they were responsible enough to take care of a child. Not surprisingly, they disagreed on what to name the poor mutt. Dad nicknamed the dog Bastard because, according to Dad, "The dog's parents weren't married—therefore, he was a bastard."

Seriously, how can you argue with that logic? Thank God Mom had a hand in naming my sisters and me, otherwise, I shudder to think what names Dad would have dreamed up.

Bastard was a pup when my parents got him, and he liked to run. As a matter of fact, every time Dad took Bastard for a walk, he ran away. Smart dog.

Invariably, Dad ran up and down the street shouting, "Bastard! Come back here, you no good Bastard!" One day Bastard kept running, and never looked back. As a result of their experiment gone wrong, my parents elected to wait a couple of years before they had children.

I'll Pick You Up in the Alley

It was Christmas Eve, 1965—my parent's first Christmas together as newlyweds. Mom's brother Pete and his wife, Lucy, purchased a new home in Oak Lawn, Illinois, a southwestern suburb of Chicago. Their home was beautifully decorated for the holiday, and was immaculate—not a thing was out of place. They invited the entire Sheedy clan over to celebrate including all nine of their nieces and nephews, who were under the age of twelve. Mom's sister Lois invited her boyfriend, Bob, aka the Polish Cowboy, to meet the family for the first time.

At the height of the party, the children ran amok through the house. During their mayhem, they accidentally broke Pete and Lucy's new laundry chute. Exactly how the laundry chute broke and who was responsible, remains a mystery to this day. The men, including Grandpa Sheedy, congregated in the basement and were happily getting drunk. Nana Sheedy and the other women sought refuge from all the commotion in the kitchen. My parents were both drunk and having one of their world-renowned screaming matches in the recreation room. Mom wanted to stay at the party with her family, and Dad wanted to leave. *Ah, the joy of the holidays.* Dad demanded Mom get her coat and shoes on, and, as he exited the room, shouted, "I'll pick you up in the alley."

What Dad failed to realize during his drunken tirade was they were in the suburbs, and there were no alleys. Stubborn as he was, however, Dad did not let that stop him. He got into his car, revved his engine loudly, and gunned it. He created his own alley by tearing down whatever obstacles stood in his way—including fences, manicured lawns, and sod. The pristine white snow turned to mud as his spinning wheels flung dirt clods of grass high up into the air.

Dad's car came to a grinding halt as it got stuck in the mud behind the neighbor's house. My parent's private fight suddenly became very public as Dad kicked opened the car door, stumbled out, and exchanged a plethora of un-pleasantries with the neighbors. Right in the middle of Dad's rant, his foot got sucked into the mud like quicksand and knocked him off his feet.

Realizing he was unable to extricate his car out of the mud alone, Dad got up and marched toward Pete and Lucy's house for help. Unfortunately, all the cookie cutter houses in their neighborhood looked exactly the same. The only way Dad could tell them apart was by the address. Covered in mud from head to toe, he stomped up Pete and Lucy's front steps, flung open the door, and traipsed across the brand-new living room carpet leaving a trail of muddy footprints behind him.

"My car is stuck in the alley. Can someone help me push it out?" Dad asked then meandered back to his car.

Stunned party goers, in awe over the spectacle they witnessed, asked in unison, "What alley?"

Everyone at the party went running to the back window to see what happened. Lois's boyfriend, Bob, tried to distract the children by doing magic tricks and telling jokes. Mom, sensing Dad was about to explode, was determined to go outside and defuse him. She fought her way through the crowd and headed toward the back door. Her sister Peggy stopped her before she went outside.

"You can't go out there like that, Pat. It's winter. You'll catch a death of cold. Here, wear my shoes." Peggy took off her flats and offered them to Mom. As Mom fumbled to put on her sister's shoes, the argument outside came to a boil.

Uncle John is one of the few people who can reason with Dad when he is drunk. He and Dad are very close. They have known each other ever since they were kids and played baseball together. Curious to find out what Dad was ranting about, John followed him outside. "Are you crazy, Ronnie?" John screamed as he witnessed firsthand the carnage that was once the neighbor's backyard.

Dad turned to confront John and fell face first into the mud.

Much to Dad's chagrin, the police arrived on the scene right on cue. Peggy sent her husband, Frank, out to stop Dad before he did something he regretted. Mom attempted to slip out the back door with Frank, but her family urged her to stay inside and let the police handle matters.

As Dad tells it, "There I was, crawling through the mud, when I happened upon a pair of well-polished, patent leather shoes. I looked up and saw an angry Oak Lawn police officer glaring down at me."

Dad crawled between the police officer's legs and made a break for it. The officer turned around, grabbed Dad by the scruff of the neck, and pulled him back up to his feet. Dad steadied his footing and took a rounding swing at the officer. Not the soundest judgment, for it landed him and Frank in a heap of trouble.

"Ronnie, don't!" Frank pleaded, as he stepped in between Dad and the police officer.

Dad missed the police officer and hit Frank instead, right in the kisser then swirled to the ground. John pleaded with the officer to let his brothers-in-laws go, but he soon realized it was futile. Dad and Frank were arrested, charged with disturbing the peace, and spent the night in jail.

My parents had no money for bail. Luckily, Pete and Lucy came to the rescue and bailed Dad out of jail the next morning, so he could spend the rest of the holiday with his blushing, hung-over bride.

Two weeks later, Dad and Frank were scheduled to appear in court. Still bruised from the experience, Frank explained to the judge he was merely trying to prevent his brother-in-law from hitting the police officer. The police officer corroborated his story. The judge dismissed the charges against Frank and let him go. Dad, however, never showed up for court. The charges against him were dropped, and he got off scot-free.

The Blizzard of 1967
(The Faint Pitter Patter of Tiny Feet)

In January 1967, almost two feet of snow fell in Chicago. People were trapped in their homes by the ten-foot snowdrifts that formed outside of their front doors. During the blizzard, Mom went grocery shopping at a local A&P. She called her father from a pay phone near the front check-out lanes to see how he and her mother weathered the storm. The contrast of the brisk winter air, the toasty warm store, and Mom's thick wool winter coat proved to be too much for her, and she fainted mid-sentence. She was taken by ambulance to the nearest hospital where she was examined by a doctor.

"What is it, doctor? Do I have the flu? I have been feeling rather nauseous lately."

"No, it's not the flu, Mrs. Velesovsky. You are going to have a baby. Congratulations."

Mom nearly fainted again, when she learned she was pregnant with me.

Chapter 4

The Polish Interpreter - Part I

Three more excruciating hours have passed. After pestering the guard in front of the triage unit several times, Dan and I convinced him to let us in to inquire about Dad's condition. He has been here for ten hours now, and we have not heard a thing. When we peered into the triage unit window earlier, we saw they hooked Dad up to an IV drip, but that was all we were able to make out. The clerk at the triage desk directed us to the emergency room, where Dad was being treated.

The on call doctor, Dr. Wilson and his nurse, Rochelle could hardly wait to relay the following story to us: Every time Dr. Wilson tried to explain to Dad that he had diabetes, Dad yelled "Stroke!" in a Polish accent and pointed his index finger high up into the air. Dad did not let Dr. Wilson finish saying the word "diabetes" before he interrupted him by yelling "Stroke!"

"Diabetes."

"Ssstroke!"

"Diabetes."

"Ssstroke!"

Dr. Wilson checked Dad's chart and noticed his last name was Velesovsky. Thinking Dad spoke Polish, he requested an interpreter. Five minutes later, an interpreter was summoned to the room.

"Thank you for coming. Please explain to the patient his blood work indicates he is a diabetic. We will be administering an intravenous antibiotic drip to help fight the infection in his foot and will be giving him insulin to control his blood sugar levels. However, he will most likely lose a couple of his toes."

As requested, the interpreter translated Dr. Wilson's message to Dad in Polish.

Dad listened intently to the interpreter and said, "Hey, Doc. I don't know what the hell this guy is saying. Do you?"

The truth is Dad does not speak a word of Polish. The reason he kept saying "stroke" was he fell down the basement stairs about six months ago and heard a loud pop when his head hit the floor. Any reasonable person would know the sound he heard was his skull banging into the concrete. Dad, however, was convinced he had a stroke and the popping sound he heard was a blood vessel exploding in his head. That was why his fingers and toes were numb. It had nothing at all to do with him having untreated diabetes, or the fact he was a raging alcoholic for most of his adult life—nope, nothing at all. Clearly, the man is in bitter denial.

Dad's doctor and nurse were in tears from laughing so hard.

"Your father is absolutely hilarious." Dr. Wilson chuckled.

"We have never laughed this hard before in the ER," Rochelle said, as she wiped tears from her eyes.

"He made our day," they said in unison.

"Can we please see him?"

"Oh, sure, right this way."

Dan and I followed Dr. Wilson down the hall. He stopped by the door which led to the treatment area and said, "Please wait here."

Sure, why not. We've waited this long, what's five more minutes, right?

Twisted Sister

On Friday, April 21, 1967, a tornado struck Oak Lawn, Illinois. Several people died and hundreds of injuries were reported. All the telephone lines were knocked out by the storm, and Mom had no way of knowing if her brother Pete and his family were okay. The National Guard was called in to stop looting and prevent anyone from going in or out of Oak Lawn.

Mom grew more and more frantic as the hours passed. She felt completely helpless and pleaded with Dad to see if her family was all right. Without hesitation, Dad drove to Oak Lawn and risked his life by crawling past heavily armed National Guardsmen. Once he made his way into town, he "borrowed" a motorcycle and sped toward Pete and Lucy's home. Along his journey, Dad spotted looters at the Pick 'n Save, a grocery store near my uncle and aunt's house.

"What the hell is the matter with you? Get the fuck out of here before I kick your ass!" Dad shouted.

The looters stopped like deer in headlights, dropped the stolen items they were carrying, and ran for their lives.

Lucy could not believe her eyes when she saw Dad pulling

up to her front door. She welcomed him with a big hug and invited him inside where she and Pete recounted the details of their harrowing experiences from the previous day.

The tornado struck as the Friday night rush hour began. Pete was on his way home from work when a fellow motorist honked his horn at him and pointed up at the funnel cloud looming above them. The closer my uncle got to his home, the more worried he became. The tornado's destructive path littered his route home. Debris was scattered everywhere. Trees were torn out of the ground (roots and all), power lines were downed, and landmarks were no longer recognizable.

With each turn he made, Pete could still see the tornado in his rear view mirror. As he turned into his subdivision, he was overcome by the complete devastation a mere block away from his home. He pulled into his driveway, jumped out of his car, and frantically called out to his wife. Relieved, he found his family in the basement unharmed, where they eagerly awaited his arrival.

Before the tornado hit, the air was eerily calm, and the skies turned a pea soup green. Lucy took shelter in the basement with their newborn daughter, Lori, and dog, Tiger, seconds before the tornado roared by like a freight train. The force of the tornado was so powerful Lucy screamed to relieve the pressure in her ears. The storm knocked out the electricity and telephone lines, so they sat in the dark, in their basement, with a flashlight until the storm passed.

Uncle Pete and his family were very lucky. Several homes in their subdivision were completely destroyed. Their home, amazingly, was untouched, except for a single piece of wood that lodged in their garage door.

Once Dad was assured his in-laws were okay, he returned the motorcycle he "borrowed", crept past the National Guard unscathed, and drove home to let his worried sick, pregnant wife know her brother and his family were safe and unharmed.

Crank Calling the OB/GYN

Once while visiting Grandma Velesovsky, I flipped through one of her old photo albums. I came across a Polaroid of Mom and Grandpa Velesovsky I never saw before. In the picture, Grandpa has his arm around Mom, and they are both laughing so hard they have tears in their eyes. I had no idea Mom and her father-in-law were so close, so I inquired about the photo.

"What are they laughing about in this picture, Grandma?" Although it was not evident from the photo, Mom was pregnant with me. She went to her in-laws flat to ask Grandpa for a ride to her OB/GYN appointment in Berwyn. Dad had to work, so he was unable to take her. Since they had a couple of hours to kill, Grandpa offered Mom a beer. Before long, they were both drunk.

Mom's obstetrician, Dr. Goldman was a prominent white doctor who certainly disapproved of her drinking, let alone getting drunk while she was pregnant. Painfully aware she was slurring her words, Mom asked Grandma to call her doctor's office to cancel the appointment for her. Grandpa snatched the telephone receiver out of Grandma's hands as she finished dialing the telephone number. Much to his surprise, the doctor answered the telephone instead of the receptionist.

"Um, yea, my woman needs to reschedule her doctor appointment." Grandpa said pretending to be Mom's black boyfriend.

"What is the patient's name, sir?"

"Her name be Pat. Pat Velaslobski."

"And why can't she make her appointment this afternoon? Is she sick?"

"No, she ain't sick, doc. She be indisposed rightch ne-ow."

"Indisposed?"

"Yea, in-dis-posed. She be tending to my needs. You know what I mean? A man has certain needs…"

"Well I never!" Dr. Goldman said as he slammed down the telephone receiver in disgust.

The picture was taken moments later.

A Child Is Born

During the summer of 1967, Mom and Dad lived in a small attic apartment without air conditioning. It was a long, hot summer. Nine months pregnant and completely miserable, Mom anxiously awaited the birth of her first-born. According to Dr. Goldman, I was due to arrive on August fourth. Fifteen days later, when I still had not made an appearance, Mom all but gave up hope. She went to bed crying, "I'm never going to have this baby. God, I can't take it anymore." When she awoke the next morning, she was in labor. Dad nearly crashed the car getting her to the hospital. Thirty hours of hard labor later, I was born (fashionably late) on August 21, 1967 at 12:08 in the afternoon.

Back then, fathers were not allowed in the delivery room like they are today. They nervously paced back and forth, chain-smoking cigarettes in the waiting room with the other fathers-to-be until a nurse or doctor informed them their child was born. Then the new fathers were permitted to view their newborns through the glass window of the nursery. Dad, not fond of following rules, impatiently pushed his way into the maternity ward to see Mom and me, despite multiple objections by the hospital staff.

Moments after I was born, Dad burst into the delivery room and demanded, "I want to see my kid!"

"Here she is." Dr.Goldman proclaimed, as he proudly held me high in the air.

Covered in blood and afterbirth, Dad assumed the doctor dropped me, and lunged toward him with a closed fist screaming, "How could you drop my kid? I'll kill you mother fucker! Aaaaaahhhhhh!"

"Ronnie, stop!" Mom yelled. "Dr. Goldman didn't drop her. I just gave birth. They haven't had a chance to clean her up yet."

Christened in conflict, Mom and Dad welcomed me, kicking and screaming, into the world.

Mom once told me I was named after my great-grandmothers: Mary (Gorz) Bartoszek, Dad's maternal grandmother, who was of Polish descent; and Katherine (Huback) Tomsic, Mom's maternal grandmother, who was of Bohemian descent. The main reason Mom wanted to name me Mary Kathrine (note my middle name is spelled incorrectly) was because she wanted everyone to know I was part Irish. Well, I guess Mary Kate sounds Irish—that is, until you slap Velesovsky on the end of it.

Bathroom Brawlers Part II
Duck, Duck, Goose

After a wild night of partying, my parents returned home in the midst of a heated argument. They bickered from the time they left the bar, during the ride home, and up two flights of stairs. Their voices grew louder and echoed as they made their way down the hallway toward their apartment.

I was a newborn. Aunty Shirley, who was fifteen years old, was babysitting me when Mom and Dad burst through the front door, yelling and screaming at each other. Dad jokingly called Mom a fat ass, which he surely meant as a term of endearment. Mom, not appreciative of Dad's sense of humor, proceeded to let him know how she felt in the coolest, calm, and collected manner she knew how. After all, good communication is key in any marriage.

She stepped into the bathroom and found the perfect vehicle in which to convey her feelings. Unleashing her wrath of fury, Mom yanked the tank out from the toilet, yelled, "You son of a bitch!" and threw it at Dad. Water and shards of broken porcelain went soaring across the room as it made contact.

"What-the-fuck!" Dad roared as a huge fight blew up between my parents. Obscenities and fists went flying through the air. Although Mom was only five-foot-two, she stood up to Dad who was nearly eight inches taller and stuck her face in his grill like a mad junkyard dog, never backing down. Dad brawled with Mom like she was one of the guys at the bar.

Shirley grabbed me and ducked into my parent's bedroom to escape the fallout. A few minutes later, Mom and Dad appeared visibly scuffed up, with their hair a mess, and their clothes torn.

"Thanks for watching Mary," Mom said then nonchalantly took me from Shirley's arms.

"Come on, Shirl. I'll give you a ride home," Dad said.

Shirley gathered her belongings and walked out to the car with Dad. Still in shock, she was speechless as Dad acted like nothing happened, and made small talk with her on the ride home.

"Your mother held her own against your father," Shirley once told me. "She was incredibly strong."

Christmas in August

Uncle Bob paid Mom and me a visit for my first birthday. When he entered the front room he noticed an object covered by a white bed sheet sitting in the corner of the room.

"Hey Pat, what is that in the corner?"

"Oh, that? That's last year's Christmas tree."

That's when Bob became acutely aware of the ring of dried pine needles on the floor beneath the sheet.

"Dare I ask? Why hasn't anyone thrown it away?"

"Well…that's a long story Bob," Mom said like he hit a raw nerve.

Long story short, Mom was waiting for Dad to throw the Christmas tree out, and Dad was waiting for hell to freeze over. With my parents, it was always a war of the wills, and the winner of their disagreements always boiled down to whoever was more stubborn. And they both were quite stubborn.

It did not matter to either of them that there was a six foot tall fire hazard sitting in the corner of the living room. They were not even embarrassed this shriveled up tree was still there eight months later. All that mattered was the other should have thrown it out, and neither was going to budge, even if the apartment building burned down around them in the process.

Bob shook his head, walked over to the pathetic heap, and dragged it out to the alley for its long overdue burial. A trail of dried pine needles extended from our living room, down two flights of stairs, through the backyard, and out to the alley. Oh, what the neighbors must have thought.

Dad was absolutely furious when he learned what Bob did. He called him on the telephone and bellowed, "Pat was supposed to throw the Christmas tree out, *not you!*"

Hot Heads

One of the lesser known but none-the-less, legendary fights my parents had was one they rarely mentioned. Believe it or not, I think they were still bitter years later, and both had differing opinions as to what transpired.

It was a brilliant, yet bitterly cold day. The sun's deceptively warm glow masked the frigid winter air which bit through our jackets and stung our exposed faces and fingers. As the mid-afternoon sun melted the piles of freshly plowed snow, the asphalt streets glistened. Cars chugged along the streets decorated with random chunks of snow, while white plumes of exhaust trailed behind them, and their tires wicked away the moisture from the wet pavement. Not a fan of the cold weather, Dad cleared a small strip of snow from the front and back windows, and then quickly hopped back into the car visibly shaking, his teeth chattering loudly.

"It's colder than a witch's tit out here!" he announced.

We were bringing Mom and my newborn sister home from

the hospital. My sister, Patricia Ann, was born on February 12, 1969. I was one-and-a-half-years old. After a week in the hospital, Mom craved takeout.

"Oh, Ronnie, I am so sick of eating bland hospital food. Could we pick up something to eat on our way home?"

"Bishop's Chili?" Dad asked intuitively.

"Mmm. Yes!"

Dad drove us to the restaurant which was on 18th and Damen in his red convertible with white ragtop. As he exited the restaurant carrying two quarts of Bishop's Chili and dozens of packets of oyster crackers, he noticed the snow on the roof of the car was dislodging from the heat of the engine. To avoid having to brush the snow off the roof himself, he chose to put the ragtop down instead. It was a brilliant plan, until it jammed, and he could not get it back up again.

"Goddamn it, Ronnie! Can't you do anything right? It's freezing out here."

"How the fuck was I supposed to know the goddamn thing was going to break?"

We were on our way home when their argument fully erupted. I was sitting between my parents in the front seat. Mom had Patty cradled in her arms. Before long, hot chili went flying inside and outside the car, as we careened back and forth down the expressway.

Here is where my parents' stories differ. According to Dad, Mom tried to kill Patty by dangling her outside the car while he was driving in excess of fifty-five miles per hour. According to Mom, she was protecting her infant daughter from being scalded by molten chili. No matter what the intention, the result was the same.

An Illinois state police helicopter witnessed my parents' domestic squabble, and radioed a trooper on the ground to pull them over. When the trooper approached the car, he witnessed the culinary atrocity firsthand. Everyone was covered with chili. Steam literally rose from the car (and all its inhabitants) into the crisp winter air— thus giving a dual meaning to the term "hot heads". The trooper, having been married for a number of years himself, tried not to laugh as he let my parents off with a warning.

Chapter 5

The Drunk and Dis-Orderly

While we waited for the doctor to return, an orderly, who witnessed the doctor speaking to Dan and me, approached us.

"You're not allowed back here," he said in a stern voice.

"The doctor told us to wait here," Dan and I said in unison. "You asshole, you heard him tell us to wait here," was definitely implied in our tone.

"This area is for patients only!"

Dan barely uttered, "But the doctor said…" before he was rudely interrupted by the orderly again.

"I don't care what the doctor said. This area is for patients only."

Oh, no. That was the last straw. I could see it in Dan's eyes. My husband, who has always been the voice of reason and Zen-like calmness, was suddenly overcome by an uncontrollable rage. The madness that is Dad and Cook County Hospital, the countless hours of waiting, the lack of food and drink, and pure frustration finally took its toll.

To hell with reason and calmness, Dan was about to go postal. I saw him formulating his plan of attack on this utter nonsense. He took two steps toward the orderly, fully intending on putting his head through the wall.

Then, a rather large and mean-looking African-American security guard, who was standing nearby, said in a deep authoritative voice, "Sir, you need to leave."

Blind with anger, Dan turned to confront the security guard. From my vantage point, I saw Dan make a fist behind his back.

"Dan, stop! He's a cop!"

Thank goodness the police officer's gun gleamed brightly under the hospital's fluorescent lights and clued me in as to who he was before it was too late. Unfortunately, Dan was unable to get back to the task at hand—redecorating the wall with the remains of the orderly—as the police officer proceeded to kick him out the nearest door. Moments later, Dan found himself in the muddy alley behind the hospital. He trekked his way back to the main entrance, where he waited for me in the front lobby.

Luckily for me, the doctor reappeared as Dan was being escorted off the premises.

"Your father is down the hall."

"Do you mind taking me to see him? Security is pretty tight around here, and I don't want any more trouble, if you know what I mean."

"Sure. No problem. Follow me. To be honest, we thought your father was homeless. We don't typically see patients in your father's condition that have a safe place to live or families who love them. The infection in his foot is pretty bad and he most likely will lose a couple of his toes. We've got him on antibiotics to control the infection and insulin to control his blood sugar. He'll be our guest for the next couple of days or so."

Then Dr. Wilson pointed toward Dad's bed and allowed me to see him.

"I told you—all I needed was antibiotics!"

"You were right, Dad," I muttered.

"Hey, where's Danny boy?"

"Oh, he got kicked out when we tried to see you."

"Well, be sure to tell him I've gotten kicked out of far better places than this one."

"I will. The doctor said they will probably have to keep you here for a couple of days. If you don't need us, Dan and I want to head home. We both have to work tomorrow."

"I'll be fine. Go. Go home. You should have gone home hours ago."

"Alright then, I'll stop by after work to see how you're doing. I love you."

"I love you too. Goodnight to me says I to you."

"Goodnight Dad. Call me if you need anything."

I kissed Dad on his cheek and then went to find Dan who was eagerly awaiting my return.

Cook County Hospital is a forty-five minute drive from our home and we were both anxious to get on the road. It was a long, grueling day.

By the time we arrived home it was nearly eleven o'clock at night. I was physically and emotionally exhausted. It felt so good to lie in bed and snuggle under the covers. All the stress of worrying about Dad over the past few months seemed to magically lift from my shoulders. I breathed a sigh of relief, and fell asleep comforted by the fact Dad was going to be okay.

The Temptations

My parents rented a four bedroom, second-floor apartment above a business on Archer Avenue in Brighton Park. It had hardwood floors throughout and numerous windows which let in plenty of natural light. I have vivid memories of lying on the parlor floor and, from the gap underneath our front door, watching the landlady as she vacuumed the rug in the hallway. The vacuum looked like it was from the 1940's by its design, with its chrome art deco case, tapestry-like bag, and light which got brighter as the landlady banged the vacuum into the door.

It was the summer of 1969. Mom quit drinking. She joined Alcoholics Anonymous, attended meetings, and spoke with her sponsor regularly.

None too thrilled about losing his drinking partner, Dad often tempted Mom by saying, "Come on. One little drink isn't going to kill ya."

Each time Dad pressured Mom to drink, she firmly stood her ground. She was determined to fight for her sobriety. Nothing, and no one, was going to stand in her way, not even Dad.

Shortly after Mom quit drinking, Aunty Shirley and her eighteen-month-old-son Jim came to live with us. Shirley was sixteen when she got pregnant. Her shotgun marriage did not last, and she moved back in with her folks. Raising a child with her parents looming over her every move proved to be an intolerable situation. When Mom and Dad invited Shirley to stay with them, she jumped at the chance.

One day after work, Shirley, without thinking, brought home a six-pack of beer, placed it in the refrigerator, and then went out for the evening with friends while Mom watched Jim. When Mom opened the refrigerator to grab milk for us to drink with dinner, she saw the beer sitting on the shelf. It tormented her, knowing there was alcohol in the apartment, and she could not drink it.

As soon as Shirley came home, Mom pulled her aside. "Shirley, I know you didn't mean any harm, but could you please get rid of the beer in the refrigerator? Ever since I laid eyes on it, I haven't been able to think of anything else. I have been staring at it all night."

"I am so sorry, Pat. I completely forgot you quit drinking," Shirley apologized. "I'll dump it in the sink."

"No, please don't. The smell will drive me crazy. Could you take it out to the trash instead?"

"Of course, you know, you are doing such a good job staying sober. I am really proud of you."

"Thanks. To be honest it hasn't been easy but more than anything, I want to be a good mother to my girls—one they deserve."

Off the Wagon Part I
Someone's Knocking at the Door

My parents split up. They constantly broke up and got back together again. Most of their arguments involved money (or the lack thereof) and alcohol (or rather Dad or Mom's abuse of it). Mom moved Patty and me to a one bedroom, first-floor flat in an apartment complex in Blue Island, a suburb south of Chicago.

It is the first time I remember Mom drinking. She was sober for about three years before she relapsed. Even though I was only five years old, I sensed Mom was out of sorts, and was not acting like herself. She walked around the apartment all day without a stitch of clothing on. Pacing back and forth between the living room and the bedroom, she smoked cigarettes, cried, sang, and talked to herself. The glass tumbler full of ice and Southern Comfort she held in her hand clanked with every step she took, and spilled little droplets of liquor over everything in the apartment—like a priest flinging holy water at church.

Late in the evening, the doorbell rang, momentarily snapping Mom back into reality.

"Mary, go open the door, and see who it is," Mom whispered loudly.

Then she ran into the bedroom to get dressed and left me alone to answer the door. I was petrified.

Whenever an unexpected visitor rang our doorbell or knocked on our front door, my first instinct, as a child, was to run and hide. My imagination ran wild as I envisioned the boogie man lurking on the other side of the door. My hands shook uncontrollably as I fumbled with the locks, hoping desperately whoever was on the other side of the door went away long before I opened it. To my dismay, the doorbell rang once more followed by several loud knocks before I managed to get the door open. It was Dad. I was so relieved.

"Hey, kids! Want to go for a ride in my new used car?"

"Yes!" Patty and I shouted, as Mom, trying to appear sober, entered the living room wearing a sleeveless cotton nightgown and a matching terry cloth robe. Patty and I, in bare feet and dressed in our pajamas from the night before, were giddy with excitement as we climbed into the back seat of Dad's car. The freshly vacuumed carpet tickled the bottom of my feet and my pajama bottoms effortlessly slid across the newly waxed vinyl seats. Mom closed my door for me. As she grabbed the front passenger-side door handle, Dad hit the gas and laughed wildly. Then he slammed on the brakes, bringing the car to a screeching halt. He waited for Mom to stagger over to the car, and then took off again before coming to a complete stop.

"Ron-nie!" Mom whined loudly.

"What the hell are you waiting for? Get in."

Mom stumbled into the passenger seat, slammed the car door shut, and we were off. It was a beautiful breezy autumn night. Dad turned the heat on full blast and rolled down all the windows as we went for a cruise around the neighborhood. The cool night air rushed through my hair, and helped sober up Mom as we sped into the night. And just like that, my parents were back together again.

Snap Your Fingers

As much as Dad complained about how much work it was having pets, he was notorious for bringing home strays. He was working as a truck driver when he came across a large turtle lying on the side of the road. Thinking we might like it as a pet, he brought it home for Patty and me. It was literally the biggest turtle I have ever seen outside of a zoo. My parents got us turtles as pets before but they were the size of my palm, had markings on their bellies and I was not afraid of them. This turtle was as big as a dog, hissed, and scared me half to death.

Mom insisted Dad place the turtle in the bathtub before he went back to work. Shortly after Dad left, Mom called animal control.

"Hello? Yes. My husband found a stray turtle on the side of

the road and brought it home. It is huge. I have two small children, and I'm afraid it might bite one of them. Would it be possible to send someone by to pick it up?"

"Of course ma'am, we will send someone out right away."

Mom thanked the lady from animal control and gave her our address. About an hour later, an African-American gentleman dressed in a khaki jumper and a pair of black combat boots came knocking on our front door.

"Hello, my name is Jerome. I am with animal control."

"Thank you for coming so quickly."

"Now, where is this big turtle I've heard so much about?"

Mom pointed toward the bathroom and said, "I-I-It's in there."

Jerome gave Patty and me a wink as he walked confidently toward the bathroom. One look at our new pet and he ran out of the apartment yelling "Keep your children away from the bathroom!" A few moments later he returned donning a variety of personal protection equipment including a pair of thick gloves and safety goggles. He was carrying a wooden pole with a metal hook at one end and a large canvas bag with a draw string.

"That is a full-grown snapping turtle. Your husband brought home a full-grown snapping turtle. Why would he do that?"

"He saw it lying on the side of the road and thought the girls might like to have it as a pet."

"Is he crazy?"

"Yes. Yes, he is."

Even Superman Gets Sick

I was five and a half. My family moved to the second floor of a bungalow-styled brick two-flat in Gage Park, a neighborhood on the south side of Chicago. Patty and I shared the bedroom adjacent to the front room.

It was very late, way past our normal bedtime. I tossed and turned from the second I laid my head down on the pillow. I had trouble sleeping when Dad was not home, because I did not feel safe without him there. Dad often moonlighted at a local gas station to help ends meet, and he was rarely home at night. He was not home this particular evening, however, because he was watching the football game at a neighborhood bar.

Dad's car was in desperate need of a new muffler. It was extraordinarily loud and had a very distinctive sound. I heard him approaching from blocks away. The distant rumbling easily awoke me from my light slumber. It grew louder and more intense as he approached, and echoed wildly against the apartment buildings on our block. I knew, instantly, the moment Dad was home.

As Dad attempted to park, he banged into our neighbor's car. A deep metal-on-metal crash rang out into the cool autumn night. The sudden silence as he turned off the engine was only temporary. His rusted car door screeched open as he exchanged several ungentlemanly like words with the neighbor.

"Hey, that's my car! You hit my car." the neighbor angrily shouted from the safety of his front porch.

"Ah, shut the fuck up! You don't know what the hell you are talking about. Get back in your house before I kick your fucking teeth in!" Dad fired back as he slammed his car door shut.

Then Dad shouted one last obscenity, "Jag off!" before heading up our front steps.

He hiccupped loudly and his keys rattled as he fumbled to unlock the front door.

Patty and I squealed with delight, "Daddy's home!"

Stumbling into the hallway, Dad paused momentarily while he got his bearings then kicked the door shut behind him like a bucking bronco. His dress shoes tread noisily onto each wooden step, followed by a lion's roar of a hiccup and a loud thump as his shoulder slammed into the hallway wall. Step, hiccup, thud against the wall. Step, hiccup, thud against the wall. There were thirteen steps up to our apartment. It took him quite a while to reach the top landing.

Mom waited impatiently for Dad in our front room like a hot tea kettle about to boil over. Watching television in the dark with her arms crossed upon her chest, she angrily tapped her foot on the floor and blew her overgrown bangs away from her eyes with the side of her mouth.

"Go back to bed girls. You should be sleeping," she yelled.

As Dad reached the top of the stairs, he flung open the front door and said in a Jack Nicholson voice from *The Shining*, "Oh, girls. Daddy is home. Where are my girls? I'm hungry for dirty toes. Are there any little girls around here with dirty little toes?"

Patty and I ran out of our bedroom and squealed, "Daddy,

Daddy!"

"Where the hell have you been Ronnie? You said you would be home hours ago. You can't keep doing this night after night. You'll get fired if you show up for work hung over again."

"I can do whatever the hell I want. I am Superman."

Then he climbed on top of our wooden console television and yelled at the top of his lungs as he jumped off. "I am Superman! Da, ta, da, da!"

BOOM! Dad made a thunderous crash as he hit the floor, rolled on his back, and played dead like a dog.

Disgusted, Mom sneered, "You know what, Ronnie? You are a sick bastard. I am going to bed."

When Dad got drunk, he liked to get on all fours and pretend he was a dog. He followed Patty and me around the apartment barking and licking our hands if we put them too close to his face. Howling like a dog at the moon, Dad chased Patty and me into the kitchen on his hands and knees, and then passed out on the kitchen floor.

I thought, *"Hmm, Mommy called Daddy a sick bastard. Daddy must be sick."*

Suddenly, I had this great idea. I took one of the dinette chairs and pulled it over to the kitchen cabinets where Mom kept our favorite cure-all drink, Tang. *If it is good enough for the astronauts, it certainly will cure whatever is ailing Dad.*

"It will be more potent if we don't water it down," I told Patty.

Grabbing a tablespoon from the kitchen drawer, I took a heaping spoonful of the orange-flavored powder, and said confidently, "Here, Daddy, try this."

Patty and I spoon fed Dad half a jar of Tang. It was everywhere. Bright orange granulated crystals of Tang were in the crevasse of his neck, in his ears, and all over his face. He kept trying to moisten his lips and mouth with his Tang-riddled tongue—but to no avail.

Tang may not have been the cure for what ailed Dad, but Mom certainly got a kick out of it. Turns out he was more of a poor bastard than a sick one.

Off the Wagon Part II
Lady Godiva and the Plate Glass Window

I was awakened in the middle of the night by the sound of my parent's arguing. As quickly as the yelling escalated it subsided and I fell back asleep.

A short time later, my slumber was interrupted once again—this time by several loud knocks at our front door, and a man yelling "Open up, this is the police."

Dad answered the door while Patty and I looked onward from our bedroom. Two Chicago police officers brought Mom home. In her drunken desperation to get away from Dad, she ran down the street in nothing but her birthday suit and jumped through a neighbor's plate glass window. Staring blankly into space, she was draped in a plain white bed sheet which was covered with specks of blood. Minor cuts dotted her face, hands and legs from the shards of broken glass.

The elder of the two police officers looked about retirement age. His face was weathered, his gray hair was slicked back, and he carried a spare tire around his midsection. His partner was a good-looking rookie who was still wet behind the ears. He was average height, had a thin build, dark brown hair and hazel green eyes.

The cold from outside emanated from them both and chilled me. The smell of their black leather jackets, and the static and chatter from their walkie-talkies filled the room. Despite their "Officer Friendly" appearance, I was terrified of them. I thought they came to our house because I did something wrong.

"In order to preserve the peace and to ensure no one gets hurt, one of your parents has to leave for the night," the rookie police officer said.

Then the seasoned officer asked, "Which one of your parents do you want to spend the night with?"

It was the hardest thing anyone has ever asked me to do. How could they expect a five-year-old and a three-year-old to make such a decision? We could not decide and cried, "I don't know."

Feeling guilty, Dad volunteered to sleep in his car and promised not to come back until the next day. A few moments later, he and the officers left, and Mom, Patty and I went back to bed.

The plate glass window Mom jumped through belonged to an elderly lady who lived a couple of doors down from us. She was the type of woman who yelled at us if we played too loud and refused to let us get our ball if it happened to bounce into her yard.

The next day, our elderly neighbor stopped me in the alley.

"Was that your mother who came crashing through my front window last night?" she asked in a thick European accent.

"Yes," I responded in as an apologetic-sounding voice as I could muster.

She opened up her back gate, which she normally kept padlocked, and hugged me tightly with her matronly old lady arms. She was never mean to us again.

Under the Cover of Darkness

I learned at an early age there were nights when you didn't mess with Dad—nights when he was a mean drunk, looking for trouble and eager to get into a fight. Sometimes, it was best to avoid the beast whilst the moon was still out. Though Dad never laid a finger on me when I was little, other than a good spanking, he often got physical with Mom when they quarreled.

Late one night, I was awakened by the telephone ringing in the kitchen. Dad called Mom from the bar, and he was in a bad mood. By the tone of Mom's voice, and the way she slammed down the receiver, I knew trouble was a-brewin'. Dad was on the war path again. Wanting to avoid yet another confrontation, Mom called her sister Evelyn and asked her if we could spend the night. Five minutes later, Mom, Patty and I snuck down the back steps and into the cover of darkness.

Mom held our hands tightly as we scurried down the street constantly on the lookout for Dad. Struggling to keep up with her, my heart thumped loudly. I was fearful Dad would catch us. We walked to the corner of 51st and Fairfield where we hid in a dark doorway, nervously waiting for Evelyn to pick us up. The cool night air outlined my every breath as my body shook from head to toe—partially from fear and partially from the cold.

Twenty minutes later, Evelyn pulled up near where we hid. When the coast was clear, we cautiously stepped out of the shadows. Patty and I gladly piled into the back seat, while Mom slipped into the passenger seat. Evelyn's car was safe and warm. I knew we would be okay—at least for the night.

Chapter 6

Midnight Express

Anytime I get a call late at night, I am struck with fear something is wrong. Why else would someone call so late? It was midnight when my sister Kathy telephoned. Dan and I were asleep for less than an hour. The first ring shot through me like a lightning bolt. My heart beat so hard I thought it was going to pop right out of my chest.

Dan picked up the telephone and mumbled like a doctor looking at a set of bad test results. "Ah huh. Hmmm. I see. Okay. We'll be right there." Then he hung up.

"Kate, it's your dad. The infection has gotten worse. It's gangrenous. They have to amputate his leg and your dad is refusing to let them. Your sister is asking the entire family to go to the hospital to convince him to have the surgery."

"Didn't Dr. Wilson say Dad was only going to lose a couple of toes? How could this have happened so suddenly? I don't understand."

Dan and I jumped back in the car and headed toward Dad's house in Chicago. When we arrived, we were greeted by Grandma Velesovsky, Aunty Shirley, Uncle Bob, and both my sisters, Patty and Kathy. From Dad's house, we caravanned back to Cook County Hospital. Only two people at a time were allowed in to see Dad, so it took almost an hour before it was my and Patty's turn.

Everyone who came back to the waiting room after seeing Dad said the same thing, "He won't do it. He won't let them amputate his leg. He won't listen to reason. He is so stubborn. He keeps saying the doctors are wrong and all he needs are antibiotics."

Grandma grabbed my hand and pleaded, "Your father needs a reason to live, Mary. Go in there and give him a reason. Please."

Mr. French
(Dad Brought Home a Bear)

I was playing school with Patty in the pantry when I heard Dad walk through the front door.

"Daddy's home!" Patty and I shrieked as we ran out of the pantry to greet Dad.

That's when I saw it—a black, curly-haired baby bear slowly waddling its way towards me.

"Daddy brought home a bear! Daddy brought home a bear!" Patty and I yelled, as we ran back into the pantry and slammed the door shut.

"This isn't a bear. It's a dog. He's your new pet."

"Daddy, that's no dog. It's a bear." Patty and I yelled from the safety of the pantry.

"Come on and help me name this furry little guy," Dad said, trying to coax Patty and me to come out of hiding.

"Ronnie, are you sure he doesn't bite?"

"I am positive; he is very friendly and smart too. I think he is a French Poodle. I saw him while I was on my route. He was the leader of a pack of dogs. The dogcatcher came by and was going to take him away. He is very clever and dodged the dog catcher. I thought he deserved a second chance, and the girls might want to keep him as a pet."

Patty and I ran out of the pantry and pleaded, "Can we keep him Mommy? Can we? Can we, huh?"

"Alright, you can keep him," Mom answered reluctantly, "but you'll have to help me take care of him. That means feeding him, making sure he has milk to drink, cleaning up after him, and taking him for walks."

Then we uttered the lie millions of children before us have told, "Okay, Mommy, we promise."

Patty knew instantly what she wanted to name our new pet and shouted enthusiastically, "Let's call him Mr. French." Mr. French was a character from our favorite television show, *Family Affair*. Just in case you are unfamiliar with the show – Mr. French is an English butler for a wealthy New York divorcé, and essentially becomes nanny to his employer's three children when their mother dies.

And that is how Mr. French joined our family.

Mr. French was a wonderful family pet and, much like the character he was named after he took great care of us. Patty and I petted, hugged, and kissed him constantly, and he never growled or bit us. The only time he barked was if a stranger knocked at the door. When we took Mr. French for a walk, he looked both ways to see if a car was coming before he let us cross the street. Each night before going to bed, he made his rounds like a seasoned watch dog. Checking each room in the apartment to insure it was secure, he did a head count to confirm we were all where we were supposed to be. Then he went to sleep on the floor of our parents' bedroom, with one eye open.

Shortly after Dad brought Mr. French home, we had him groomed at a local dog parlor. We thought they gave us the wrong dog when we went to pick him up. Mr. French was easily a third of his original size. They shaved off most of his thick coat except for pompoms of fur around the bottom of his legs and tail. His nails were painted blue and they placed blue ribbons over both his ears. Patty and I thought the painted nails and bows meant Mr. French was a girl. We could not believe he was our dog. Dad assured us he was, and told us to call his name to see if he came to us. Sure enough, he did.

Unfortunately, as it turned out, Mr. French was lactose intolerant. We unknowingly fed him table scraps consisting of cheese, and Mom always had a fresh saucer of milk out for him. I think she thought he was a cat. The result was chronic diarrhea. Poor dog.

Hit Me with Your Best Shot

Dad was always play-fighting with me when I was little. He stuck out his chin and said, "Hit me with your best shot, kid." Most times, I was too afraid to hit him. On the rare occasion I did try, I closed my eyes and swung into the air, missing Dad all together, which caused him to laugh loudly at me.

I was seven years old the last time Dad and I play-fought. He got a little rough with me, and I got a little rough back.

"You shouldn't roughhouse with her like that, Ronnie. One of you is liable to get hurt," Mom cautioned him.

"What are you worrying about? Mary couldn't hurt a flea!"

Then Dad stuck his chin out and taunted me, "Go ahead, kid. Give your Daddy a knuckle sandwich. Show me what you're made of."

I made a fist and grunted as I punched Dad with all my might. To my surprise, my fist made contact with his right eye. Not quite the target I was aiming for, but mission accomplished, nonetheless. Much to Dad's surprise, my insignificant little girl punch gave him a black eye. Mom refused to let Dad punish me, because, after all, I was only doing what he told me to do.

Hair Raising Tales
(Rats Nests, Pixies, and the Bowl Buzz Cut)

When I was seven years old, I was expected to brush my hair every day before I went to school. Being I was only seven years old, I did not comply. Neither did Patty who was only five. As soon as we felt a tangle, we automatically stopped brushing our hair, because it hurt. As a result, we both had rat nests of tangled hair at the base of our heads. It was virtually impossible to get a brush to go through.

My parents gave us an ultimatum. If we did not take care of our hair, they would cut it all off. Mom painstakingly brushed our hair, strand by strand, until she got all the tangles out. It took the better part of an afternoon and required several breaks to get the blood flowing in her arms again. Patty and I were both in tears by the time she was done. It felt so good to be able to run my fingers through my hair again and not have all those nasty tangles.

Not five minutes after Mom finished brushing our hair; Dad piled us into the car and took us to a beauty school in the Garfield Ridge neighborhood. The haircuts were free, because they were given by students. The instructor greeted us at the door and asked Dad what kind of haircuts we wanted.

"Give them pixies. They both have a real problem with tangles. Cut it all off."

Mom begged Dad not to have our hair cut so short, "They will look like two little boys if you give them pixie haircuts."

Once Dad's mind was made up, there was no turning back. Patty and I sat in hydraulic beauty salon chairs with black vinyl cutting capes tied tightly around our necks. We watched helplessly as the student hairdressers chopped off our long, dishwater-blond locks, and, with it—our last shreds of femininity.

A few weeks later, our bangs grew out. Adding insult to injury, Dad trimmed our bangs himself instead of taking us back to the school. He had a brilliant idea—you see, he recently purchased a set of dog clippers to save money on grooming Mr. French, and was confident he could cut our hair straight with them. Mom was not thrilled with the idea. To be honest, neither were Patty and I, but our opinions did not matter in our household. Dad told us on many occasions, "This isn't a democracy I am running here."

To calm Mom's fears, Dad placed a bowl on top of Patty's head and cut her bangs from ear to ear—along with one of her eyebrows. Oh, Patty's bangs were straight all right—if she tilted her head slightly to the right.

I cringed in anticipation, knowing I was next. Sitting as still as a church mouse, I closed my eyes tightly and clenched my fists. The buzz of the clippers tickled against my forehead, as Dad hacked off my bangs one clipper length at a time. Although I was sparred my sister's fate and walked away with both of my eyebrows still intact, I, too, had bangs that spanned from ear to ear.

When Dad was finished, he admired his handiwork and said, "Not bad if I do say so myself. Do you still think they look like two little boys, Pat?"

"No. Now they look like two little Polacks."

Mother, Can We Go Out and Play

It was a beautiful summer day. The sun was shining, the birds were singing, and there was not a cloud in the sky. My parents were oblivious, however, because they bickered back and forth all morning long. As their argument drew to a close, Dad headed toward the front door.

"Where do you think you're going?"

"I'm going out to get a newspaper. I'll be back in five minutes," which was Dad's code for, "I'm going to the bar and I won't be back for hours".

"Bullshit! Admit it. You are going back to that damn bar aren't you? You are nothing but a pathetic liar!"

"Well, you are a no good Mother Fucker!" Dad yelled and then left.

Patty and I wanted to play outside with our friends, but we were afraid to leave our bedroom while our parents were arguing. When we heard Dad leave, we knew that was our cue. Patty pranced out of our bedroom, marched over to Mom and asked, "Mother Fucker, can we go outside and play?"

"What did you say?"

Patty cleared her throat and happily repeated herself articulately. "I said, 'Mother Fucker can we go outside and play?'"

I could not believe my ears. *Oh, was Patty in trouble now,* I thought. Sensing Mom would kill me if I laughed I went back to our bedroom and sat tight-lipped on the bed.

"That does it. I am washing your mouth out with soap." When Patty and I were bad, Mom often threatened to send us to Mrs. Meany's Orphanage or to sell us to the gypsies. This was uncharted territory. Mom grabbed Patty's hand and dragged her into the bathroom. The sound of water gushing out the bathroom sink faucet could not drown out the sound of Patty getting her mouth washed out with soap. All I heard was "gurgle, gurgle, gurgle."

When Mom was through, she said, almost hyperventilating, "There. How'd you like them apples?"

"Mmm. That tastes good. May I have some more?"

"Out. Out. Both of you get the hell out of the house! Go outside and play."

Trip to the Country

We never took vacations when I was growing up, because we did not have the money. Besides, my parents were not the vacationing type. Other than going to the bar, Dad has always been a homebody, and Mom never had any other choice.

It was a brutally hot summer day. The air was steamy, sticky and stagnant. As the temperatures outside soared, our second floor apartment became positively stifling. We did not own an air conditioner or a fan to get any relief. Dad, sharing in our discomfort, took the entire family for a long drive to the country to beat the heat. He headed north towards Wisconsin, driving up and down hilly rural roads.

Every once in a while, Patty and I spotted a horse or a cow, and screamed with excitement. The windows were rolled down, and the radio played softly as we watched the scenery pass by. Beautiful, lush, rolling green hills blanketed the landscape. Fresh fragrant air filled the car. Rows of vegetation seemingly stretched on for miles. Dad stopped briefly at a farm stand to pick up fresh tomatoes and corn before heading back to Chicago.

By the time we arrived home, the sun began to set, the humidity subsided, and the air cooled. Patty and I ran around our apartment like Tasmanian devils releasing our pent up energy from sitting in the car all day, while our parents unloaded the fresh produce they purchased. Mom discarded the packaging and carefully washed the tomatoes and corn.

The luscious red tomatoes were the size of grapefruits and were perfectly ripe. Dad sliced the tomatoes for us, like he was carving a Thanksgiving turkey. Then he fanned the tomato slices on a plate and lightly seasoned them with a pinch of salt. They were room temperature and the salt helped extract their sweet nectar. I eagerly awaited the spoils of our day, as Dad handed me a plate full. Each bite was more succulent than the last. Once the tomato slices were consumed, I drank the juice that pooled on the plate like I was sipping fine wine.

That was our dinner that evening. Whenever I think of summer, I think of the tomatoes we brought home from our trip to the country.

And Baby Makes Three
(Daughters That Is)

Since Dad struggled to hold down a steady job, we did not have health insurance when I was growing up. My parents only took us to the doctor if we needed shots for school, or if we were deathly ill. Preventative medicine simply was not in our vocabulary.

When Mom made a doctor appointment for herself and did not appear to be sick, Patty and I grew concerned. Dad attempted to ease our fears by telling us Mom was going for a routine checkup, but we knew better. Dad took Patty and me for a ride around the neighborhood, while Mom visited the doctor. About an hour later, Mom left the doctor's office in tears. When I asked why Mom was crying, Dad told me it was nothing for me to be concerned with.

Once Mom started showing, she told Patty and me about the bundle of joy she was expecting come summer. Patty was set to start kindergarten in the fall. Mom planned to return to work part-time while we were in school. When she first learned she was pregnant, she was tickled pink but was a tad disappointed to wait an additional five years to return to the workforce. Dad was out of work. The timing was terrible.

Between looking for gainful employment, working odd jobs to help ends meet, and drowning his sorrows at the bar, Dad was rarely home. To prepare Patty and me in case an emergency should arise, Mom placed a pillow beneath her shirt and pretended to faint in front of us to gauge our reaction. By the time Mom was ready to give birth, we were well versed on how to dial 911 for help.

It was a blistering hot afternoon. Mom was eleven days past her due date. Dad took us to the Sears Tower to kill time and escape the heat. Somewhere between the skydeck and the lobby, Mom went into labor. Dad dropped Patty and me off at Grandma and Grandpa Velesovsky's apartment before he took Mom to the hospital.

While we awaited the arrival of our new sibling, Grandma played connect-the-dots and tic-tac-toe with us and showed us her treasures, which consisted of a collection of hand-embroidered handkerchiefs, black and white photographs of her parents, and an old watch her mother gave her on her sixteenth birthday. The watch stopped working years ago, but Grandma did not have the heart to throw it away.

Patty and I sat on the edge of our seats as Grandma told us stories about her childhood like how she had platinum blonde hair until she was fourteen years old. Then one morning, she awoke, and she was a brunette—overnight. Or how the boys in the neighborhood she grew up in threw lit firecrackers at the girls' legs every Fourth of July and then she showed us the scars which were still visible on her shins.

Grandma's father, Stanislaw Bartoszek, was a violent alcoholic who kicked her mother and newborn brother out into the snow one cold winter's night shortly after her mother gave birth, because he didn't think the baby looked like him. Once when Grandma was seven, she and her brother Stanley got sick of their father getting drunk and fighting with their mother so they decided to do something about it. The next time their father sent them to the store to purchase a bottle of vodka, they switched out half of the alcohol with tap water. My heart sank as she told us how much trouble they got into when her father realized what they did.

My youngest sister, Kathleen Marie, joined our crazy family on July 24, 1974. I was seven years old and Patty was five. Mom acted like Kathy was made of fine china. We were specifically ordered to stay away from her, unless we had parental supervision. We were instructed, repeatedly, about how important it was not to touch the soft spot on the top of Kathy's head and, on the rare occasion Mom did let us hold her, how important it was we support her neck.

Shortly after Kathy came home from the hospital, we had to

say goodbye to our dog, Mr. French. It was too much for Mom to handle a newborn and a dog who suffered from chronic diarrhea—even if it was not his own doing. Dad placed an ad at the local supermarket. A woman came by to adopt Mr. French for her disabled sister, but ended up falling in love with him herself. According to Dad, the two sisters fought over who got to keep Mr. French. That made Patty and me smile, and we let out a little chuckle as we wiped the tears from our eyes. We were happy Mr. French was going to a good home, where they loved him as much as we did.

The summer flew by. Normally, I dreaded summer break coming to an end, but this time was different. Every year, our teacher asked us to write about what we did over the summer. Everyone in the class told amazing stories of the wonderful places they visited on vacation. Well, my family never went anywhere. This year I could talk about our trip to the country and my new baby sister. It was the most exciting summer I could remember, and I could not wait to share it with my classmates.

Chapter 7

Gang Green Gang

On our way to see Dad, Patty and I stopped to get an update on his condition and to find out what his options were. By the time we arrived, the shift changed and Dad had a new emergency room doctor on call. She was a stunning redhead with striking features, long curly hair and a creamy complexion models would be envious of. Her warm smile as she spoke to a patient nearby stood out in the otherwise cold, sterile hospital environment.

Patty and I waited patiently in the hall while the doctor finished making her rounds.

Much to my surprise, she approached us.

"Excuse me, but are you related to Mr. Velesovsky?"

(I don't know what gave us away - our strong family resemblance or the fact we stuck out like sore thumbs.)

"Yes, he's our father," Patty and I replied in unison.

"Hi. I'm Dr. O'Connor. It's nice to meet you."

"My husband and I were here a few hours ago, and Dr. Wilson said they might have to amputate a couple of my father's toes. What happened?" I asked.

"Your father's infection has gone from gangrene to a gas gangrene infection. A gas gangrene infection moves rapidly, is quite deadly, and can only be dealt with by immediate amputation. Your father, however, is refusing to have the surgery."

"How much time does he have?" Patty asked.

"He has less than twelve hours to live if he doesn't have the surgery. The longer he waits the more tissue we will have to remove. I'm afraid the infection may have spread past his hip, and it is only a matter of time before it reaches his heart."

Spit Fire Shoe Shine

A week after Mom came home from the hospital with Kathy, she went for a follow-up appointment with her doctor and left Dad in charge of watching all three of us—a rare occasion in our family. Kathy was sleeping soundly in her crib, which was in my parent's bedroom, directly off the kitchen. Patty was playing in the bedroom we shared. I went into the kitchen to grab a glass of cold lemonade. Dad was sitting at the table polishing his dress shoes for an interview he had at a trucking company the next day. He was listening to the Chicago White Sox baseball game which was playing on the television set in the front room. Unfortunately, the shoe polish he was using was old and friction alone was not warming it up enough to spread easily. Growing increasingly impatient, Dad placed the tin on a low simmer atop one of the gas burners on our stove, thinking a direct flame would speed up the process.

Harry Carey shouted, "Holy Cow!" and the crowd cheered loudly. Dad ran into the front room to see who scored and left the shoe polish unattended. While I poured the lemonade, I noticed the shoe polish on the stove come to a boil. As the black lava-like bubbles popped, they caught fire and splashed onto the linoleum below. Within seconds, the kitchen floor had several small tar-like fires.

Frightened, I yelled, "Daddy!"

"I'll be right there."

"But Dad—!"

"Just a moment," Dad said, annoyed I was interrupting the game.

The White Sox must have had the bases loaded with two outs at the bottom of the ninth inning, because I could not drag Dad away from that damn game.

"Daddy, the kitchen's on fire!"

"Oh, that's nice, honey. I'll be right there."

Now, Mom gave me strict orders to never to pick up my baby sister without supervision. I mean never—but this was a matter of life and death. I could not leave Kathy in my parent's bedroom while the apartment burned down around her.

I quickly darted past the mini fires and into my parent's bedroom where I gently picked up Kathy. She was sleeping peacefully, blissfully unaware of the mayhem about to ensue. I supported Kathy's head and neck the way Mom instructed me—the one and only other time I held her.

Rushing into the front room with Kathy nestled tightly in my arms, I shouted, "Dad, the kitchen is on fire!"

Dad ripped Kathy from my arms and ran into the kitchen, stomping out the fires within seconds. Of course, I was the one who got in trouble for picking up Kathy unsupervised and without permission. Dad assured me my sisters and I were never in any real danger, and the house was, in no way, going to burn down. Tell that to the dozen or so burn marks on the kitchen floor.

Farina Morning, Noon, and Night

There was a period of time during the early nineteen seventies when Dad struggled to find work. Mom helped him write his resume. She jotted down the different places Dad worked at (and a few he didn't) onto a loose-leaf sheet of paper. When she finished, she sandwiched a sheet of carbon paper between two sheets of typing paper and loaded them into her black Underwood typewriter.

Dad was wearing a short-sleeved, cotton dress shirt with a pale blue pin stripe, freshly pressed dark blue slacks and black dress shoes polished to a high sheen. His hair was slicked back and curled slightly above his forehead. He was clean-shaven and reeked of Aqua Velva aftershave.

Mom was wearing a navy-blue polyester ribbed tunic with matching pants. Her jet-black hair was shoulder-length, and her blunt-cut bangs hung above her eyebrows. The powder-blue eye shadow, black mascara, and eyeliner she wore made her look like Cleopatra.

It was amazing to see them working together. Dad stood over Mom's shoulder dictating what to type, and Mom clicked away at the keys without missing a beat. On the rare occasion Mom did make a mistake, she pulled the paper out of the typewriter and started all over again.

While Mom made a dozen or so copies of Dad's resume, Dad opened the telephone book and circled several trucking companies he wanted to work at. When Mom finished, Dad grabbed the stack of resumes and went door to door dropping them off and completing job applications.

Before long, the pantry was bare, except for a large box of Farina. Mom stretched the box of Farina for an entire month. I was unaware of how desperate we were at the time. I liked Farina, so it did not bother me we ate the same meal morning, noon, and night.

Then, things went from bad to worse. When the Farina ran out, Dad took Patty and me to St. Simon's Church. He parked the car on a side street next to the church and told us, "Wait here," while he went inside. Twenty minutes later, Dad emerged from the church with a priest. My family did not go to church. Patty and I never met a priest before. I was afraid. I associated priests with death and the giving of last rights from the old black and white movies I watched with Mom. The priest's black suit and calm demeanor unnerved me. He was a tall, thin young man with strawberry-blonde hair and big blue eyes. Bending down next to the car, he kindly smiled at Patty and me, gently patted us both on the head through the window, and said, "Don't worry, girls. Everything will be okay." And I believed him. Dad thanked the priest, shook his hand, and then got back in the car. Patty and I waved goodbye as we pulled away.

That afternoon, there was a knock at the front door. Since Patty and I did not know who it was we hid in our parent's bedroom near Kathy's crib. Volunteers from St. Simon Church came bearing a box full of canned goods and several bags brimming with groceries. Curious, Patty and I came out of hiding and stood in our parent's doorway as they thanked the volunteers for coming.

As soon as the volunteers left, Patty and I ran into the kitchen. It was like Christmas morning. We could hardly contain our excitement. The whole family happily rummaged through the box and bags to see what gifts they held. I was particularly excited about receiving a jar of Smucker's Goober Peanut Butter and Jelly and a box of Kraft Macaroni and Cheese.

School of Hard Knocks
(The New Kid *Again*)

Dad had trouble holding down a steady job and often struggled to pay the rent. As a result, we moved around a lot when I was a child. Whenever we moved, Dad insisted my sisters and I pack our belongings into plastic garbage bags. He claimed it was because we did not have enough boxes, but, given his track record, I should have known better. Coincidentally or not, each time we moved, a few of our bags went missing.

One of the times we moved, Dad got rid of Mom's dresser. It contained all her school pictures, wedding mementoes, and keepsakes. She was heartbroken. With each move, there were less and less of the possessions we held dear. Surely, Dad meant no harm. In his eyes, it was less stuff to lug up and down several flights of stairs.

When I was eight years old we moved again. It was the

middle of the school year. Adding to the trauma of starting all over again at a new school was the fact we moved to a rough neighborhood. My new school, Henry Wadsworth Longfellow, was located on 35th and Wolcott in the Brighton Park neighborhood. The school was built in 1886 and consisted of two three-story buildings connected by a crosswalk on the first floor. The school had two separate playgrounds, one for the girls and one for the boys. The gym was on the third floor in the second building and also served as the assembly hall.

On my first day, the meanest kid in class, a tomboy named Bertha, spotted me in the hallway between classes. She poked me hard in the chest with her dirty index finger and snarled, "Hey, new kid, I'll be waiting for you in the bathroom."

"Excuse me, but what does she mean by that?" I asked the girl standing next to me.

"It means she is going to beat you up if you go into the bathroom. I would not go to the bathroom if I were you."

Some welcoming committee, I thought.

I returned to class with the rest of the kids like a mindless zombie. Consumed with concern for my own personal safety, all I could think about was how Bertha threatened to beat me up and she did not even know me. At first I contemplated telling my new teacher, but then I reconsidered. I got the distinct impression class bullies were not exactly on her radar.

Mrs. Childers was an eccentric woman. She had platinum bleach blond hair, spoke with a southern drawl, which stood out like a fluorescent highlighter amongst us dull uninteresting Midwesterners, and she was perpetually cold. Each morning before we said the Pledge of Allegiance, Mrs. Childers dunked a handful of paper towels into ice water and covered the thermostat with them like paper mâché. Although the school engineer caught her red-handed, and reprimanded her almost daily, she was not dissuaded.

Personal hygiene was Mrs. Childers' passion, and she took it very seriously. She lectured the class daily on the benefits of bathing and using deodorant. After she took attendance, Mrs. Childers walked up and down the aisles with a can of Lysol at the ready, sniffing around the room like a bloodhound hot on the trail of a fox. Once she detected a hint of body odor, she took the can of Lysol and sprayed it on the unsuspecting offender. I was so grateful Mom made Patty, Kathy, and I take baths every night.

Since Mrs. Childers did not emit a warm and fuzzy vibe, and I did not know her well enough to trust her, I could not bring myself to go to her for help. Besides, I was afraid it would only make matters worse.

Ever fearful of getting clobbered by Bertha, I dared not use the bathroom while I was at school. I never fought with anyone other than my sisters, and I was not about to start. As soon as the bell rang at the end of the school day, I made a quick dash for the cloak room. Grabbing my back pack and coat with lightning speed, I darted out of the classroom and down the three flights of stairs to freedom.

I really hated moving.

Dizz Knee World

In November 1975, when I was eight years old, Uncle Bob took Dad, Grandma Velesovsky, Patty and me to Walt Disney World for two weeks. It was the one and only real vacation I went on as a child. Mom felt Kathy was too young to attend, so she elected to stay behind. To be honest, I think Mom was afraid to fly.

My heart raced, and my stomach turned cartwheels the moment I stepped onto the plane. It was my first time on an airplane. Dad did not help in calming my nerves, either. He held my hand so tightly during takeoff, it actually turned purple. To stop Patty and me from worrying during the flight, Bob took a quarter and balanced it on its side on my tray table.

"See," he said confidently, "air travel is so smooth you can balance a quarter on its end. I challenge you to do that in a car." Then he tried using logic on us, "Did you know you are more likely to get into an accident in a car than you are in an airplane?" Armed with this new information, I felt a little bit better. That is until we made our final approach. Dad squeezed my hand until it was numb and we were safely on the ground.

Bob spared no expense. He booked us at the A-shaped Continental Hotel right in the heart of Walt Disney World. We attended a real luau and visited The Magic Kingdom, Busch Gardens, and the Kennedy Space Center. Bob even rented a boat one day and let me drive it over a water bridge. On our final night, we watched fireworks from a rotating restaurant, while Patty and I sipped Shirley Temple kiddy cocktails.

Dad was on his best behavior. We had an amazing time. The

only thing missing was Mom and Kathy.

Some Like It Hot

Most of the apartments we rented either had radiant heat or large space heaters. On chilly nights Dad lit all the burners on the stove, turned the broiler up to 500 degrees and cracked open the oven door to heat the apartment. When I think back on it, we were lucky he did not burn the building down.

When we lived in Gage Park, I often awoke in the middle of the night from the cold. As the temperatures outside plummeted, our apartment became an ice box. Even though I wore footy pajamas to bed and was tucked in under the covers up to my chin, I shivered uncontrollably from head to toe and was unable to stop my teeth from chattering. Our apartment had two large space heaters, one in the front room and the other in the kitchen. The heater in the front room had a blower in the front. On cold winter nights, I snuck into the living room with my pillow and blanket and fell asleep in front of the heater. While the heater ran, I was toasty warm, but the moment the blower stopped, I was freezing again.

The apartment we lived in near McKinley Park had a radiator in every room that hissed loudly. The tenants who lived above us controlled the thermostat for the entire building and were very frugal. Dad came home late one evening after drinking black cherry brandy all night. Saint Bernard's carry brandy in small wooden barrels around their necks to warm up people they rescue in the Swiss Alps. Despite Dad consuming several small barrels' worth of alcohol, it did not take him long to realize the temperature in our apartment was less than 58 degrees.

Seeking to grab our neighbor's full attention and to ensure his message was clearly understood, Dad grabbed a large pipe wrench from his toolbox, walked over to the radiator in his bedroom, and pounded repeatedly on the pipes for half-an-hour yelling at the top of his lungs, "Turn up the fucking heat!" until the temperature in our apartment reached a toasty 72 degrees.

It was two o'clock on a Sunday morning. Dad woke up the entire building with his drunken outburst. To make matters worse, the little boy who lived upstairs had epilepsy and suffered frequently from grand mal seizures. His parents made him wear a hockey helmet to prevent him from injuring himself. Stress (like being suddenly awakened in the middle of the night by a loud noise) triggered his seizures.

Later that day, Dad ran into the gentleman who lived upstairs in the hallway.

"Is it warm enough for you, Ronnie?" he asked.

Dad replied politely, in a very civilized voice, "Why, yes, it is. Thank you for asking," as if nothing happened the night before.

Although Dad was never embarrassed by his behavior, I certainly was. I could have crawled up into a ball and died, but at least we were warm.

Off the Wagon Part III
Mom's Sick What Do I Do

One day after school, I was playing at a friend's house when Patty came knocking on the back door in a panic.

"Mary, Mom is very sick. You need to go home right away."

I was nine years old and panic stricken. Patty and I ran home. Mom was in her bedroom crying on the bed. She was surrounded by several bottles of booze with varying amounts of alcohol remaining in them.

"What's wrong, Mom?" I asked.

"I need help."

Mom motioned for me to come closer and held me tight. Then she placed two folded sheets of paper and a couple of dollars in my hand.

"Go to the tavern on the corner, give the bartender this note, and buy two packs of Viceroy 100 cigarettes for me. Use the leftover change to call my sponsor, Kelly, from the payphone in the bar. His telephone number is on the other piece of paper I gave you."

"What do I say to him?"

"Tell Kelly I fell off the wagon, and I need his help right away. He'll know what it means."

When I got to the tavern, the owner was hesitant to let me into his establishment, much less let me purchase cigarettes—*even though I had a note from my mom*. He did, however, allow me to get change to use the payphone to call Mom's sponsor. My hands trembled as I placed the quarter into the slot and dialed Kelly's telephone number. Unfortunately, Mom's sponsor was not home. I left a message with his wife who seemed less than enthused to hear from me.

Recalling the urgency in Mom's voice, I grew increasingly concerned, although I did not quite understand what was happening. What did Mom mean when she said she "fell off the wagon"? When Dad got drunk, it was normal. When Mom got drunk, it was scary.

I felt completely helpless until Dad came home from work. Dad did not think it was as serious as Mom made it out to be. He was angry with Mom because she used the grocery money to buy booze, but that was his only concern. The fact Mom got drunk when she should have been taking care of us girls did not seem to faze Dad in the least.

Mom later explained she was an alcoholic and said, "Once you're an alcoholic, you're always an alcoholic."

Although Mom might never drink again, she would always be an alcoholic—that was a hard concept for me to grasp. Dad was always drinking and getting drunk, but he was not an alcoholic. Mom rarely drank, but she was and always would be an alcoholic.

Chapter 8

Polish Interpreter Part II

As Patty and I inquired about Dad's condition, a call went out over the loud speaker requesting anyone who spoke Polish to please report to the ER. A patient broke her arm and the hospital needed a translator. Grandma Velesovsky spoke Polish, but had not practiced in many years. Aunty Shirley volunteered Grandma to translate for the hospital, thinking it would help get her mind off my father.

Grandma is legally blind. She suffers from macular degeneration and requires a magnifying glass (which she refers to as her "spy glass") to read even the largest of print. Her face is heavily wrinkled from a lifetime of worry. Her back is hunched over slightly from years of scrubbing floors on her hands and knees as a cleaning lady. Her hands are crippled with arthritis, and both her knees have been replaced, which causes her to wince in pain with every step she takes. She drinks two pots of coffee and smokes two packs of unfiltered Camel cigarettes every day.

Her old lady afro-permed hair looks like a gray football helmet on her head, which she lacquers daily with several layers of hair spray and protects with a sheer floral babushka. She wears pastel polyester pantsuits from the second hand store and flats with holes on either side to relieve the pressure from her bunions. Her purse, which she carries diagonally across her chest, always matches whatever shoes she is wearing.

Grandma loves her family intensely, is incredibly thoughtful and never forgets anyone's birthday. To say she has a flair for the dramatic, however, is a bit of an understatement. Distraught over her mother's passing, she leapt upon the casket as it was being lowered into the grave and she reportedly stuck her head in the oven when she learned her son Kenny was addicted to drugs.

A notorious worrier, she hates to be late. She starts cooking dinner at six o'clock in the morning and will wait (with her coat and shoes on and her purse in her lap) by the front door for her son Bob to pick her up a full two hours before he is due to arrive to take her to church.

When I was younger, Grandma used to say, "Don't grow old,

Mary. Everything hurts." On days when Uncle Kenny or Dad gives her grief, she says, "Never have children, Mary. They grow up and break your heart."

As Shirley and Grandma made their way through the ER, they saw Dad in passing. By the time they reached the examining room for the lady, who needed a translator, Grandma was in a state.

"Thank you for agreeing to do this. We really appreciate your help," the doctor said. "Please tell the patient the x-rays we took confirm her arm is broken. We will be placing her arm in a cast and then she can go home."

Before Grandma even uttered a word in Polish she burst into tears and embraced the patient tightly, openly sobbing into her shoulder. The patient's eyes became as wide as saucers and she looked like she saw a ghost. Confused, she stood helplessly as Grandma refused to relinquish her vice-like grip. I cannot even begin to imagine what this poor woman thought was wrong with her. Shirley apologized to the doctor and to the patient, collected her mother, and took her back to the waiting room. The patient was forced to wait another two hours before the interpreter came on duty.

Bummer

McKinley Park was a block away from our apartment. Spanning 69 plus acres, it had walking and bike paths, tennis courts, a swimming pool and a lagoon. Mom took us there practically every day in the spring, summer, and fall to "bum" cigarettes off complete strangers because Dad routinely forgot to leave her cigarette money before he left for work. No longer able to trust her with the grocery money, Dad kept Mom on a rather tight leash.

Mom paced back in forth in the apartment like she was a caged animal until she could no longer fight the nicotine cravings.

"Get dressed girls, we are going to the park" she announced. Then she packed a blanket, picnic lunch and Kathy's diaper bag and we were off to the park in search of kind, generous smokers. My sisters and I did not mind going to the park. It had an enormous playground, friendly squirrels that begged for food, and the fresh air was guaranteed to knock Kathy out for a couple of hours.

Suspicious Minds

Late one Saturday afternoon, Dad asked me if I wanted to accompany him to the grocery store. We needed milk and a few other necessities. I was nine and a half and was well into the "I am bored" phase of my life. I welcomed the opportunity to get out of the house with open arms.

During our little shopping trip, Dad confided in me, "I think your mother is cheating on me."

"What?" I said in total disbelief. "I don't think she is, Dad."

After all, Mom rarely left the house except to go to the grocery store or the Laundromat. As a rule, she never wore makeup or dressed nicely unless she was attending a family wedding or one of her weekly AA meetings. That is when it hit me. Mom spent literally hours getting ready for her weekly AA meetings. My mind began to race as images of Mom putting on makeup and curling her hair flooded my brain. A seed of doubt was planted, and I began to question Mom's fidelity.

"Mary, swear to me you'll never mention what we've discussed this afternoon to another living soul."

"I swear."

When we came home, Mom was in the bathroom getting ready for her meeting. Even though my stomach was turning cartwheels, I was determined to find out the truth. I sat down on the toilet and watched Mom intently as she stood in front of the medicine cabinet mirror, applying her powder-blue eye shadow and black eyeliner. She removed the curlers from her hair then sprayed half a can of Aqua Net onto her hairdo—all while a lit filtered cigarette dangled from her mouth.

"Close the door, Mary," Mom said, as she took a puff of her cigarette.

I closed the door and tried to muster up enough courage to ask Mom if she was cheating on Dad.

Before I uttered a word, she whispered, "I think your father is cheating on me."

"What?" I asked, as if I was experiencing a bad case of déjà vu.

I honestly have no clue why my parents both thought the other was being unfaithful. Perhaps they had guilty consciences or overactive imaginations. Substantiated or not, their suspicions continued to grow and it created a wedge between them.

One Flew Over the Coo Coo's Nest

My parents always broke-up and got back together again. It was a vicious cycle. They fought, Dad left, they got back together. Dad was gone anywhere from a couple of hours to a couple of weeks, but he always came back. This time Mom left. She and Dad had a huge blowout. Mom threatened to leave, and Dad called her on her bluff.

"If you don't like it here then leave and don't let the door hit you in the ass on your way out!" he yelled.

Mom was furious and angrily marched toward the front door. I tried to stop her by holding onto her arm and pleading, "Please don't go, Mom!" but she pried my fingers away and left, slamming the door behind her. I was devastated.

Weeks went by, and we did not hear from her. Then one day, we received a letter. Mom was in the psychiatric ward of a hospital. Her constant struggle to stay sober and the separation from Dad and us kids took its toll and she suffered a nervous breakdown.

Dad continually made crude, snide remarks like, "Here's another letter from your mother in the *nut house*."

My sisters and I were confused. Dad never explained to us why Mom was in the hospital or what a nervous breakdown was.

After she was released from the hospital, Mom found a job and rented a studio apartment in the suburbs. Shortly after she got settled she came to visit us. I did not know how to act around her. After all, I was still terribly upset she left us.

Mom was sporting a new hairdo, makeup, and business clothes. She looked amazingly confident and appeared to be doing fine without us. I thought *she is never coming back.*

Patty, Kathy, and I, however, all gained weight that summer. Dad was working regularly as a truck driver. He cooked seven-course dinners every night, including soup and dessert, and expected us to clean our plates.

I did not notice the weight gain myself until Mom mentioned it to Dad. "What happened to my girls? They look like three little piggies."

After some urging, Dad reluctantly agreed to let Mom take us to see her new apartment. It was far away and took several buses to get there. Mom's apartment building looked like a cheap hotel. Rows of numbered doors lined either side of the musky hallway. Her front door looked like Fort Knox. She unlocked two deadbolts and a lockset before revealing her studio apartment. When I heard "studio," I envisioned an artist's studio drenched in sunlight with a huge wall of windows. Mom's apartment was very dark, lacked windows, and consisted of a single room with a bed and an attached bath.

Giving us the grand tour, Mom pointed to the various corners of her room and said proudly, "Here is my kitchen (a small table with a chair), living room (television set), bedroom (a twin bed with no headboard), and bathroom."

A couple of weeks later, Mom visited me for my birthday and gave me a gold locket with my name engraved on it. The gift was lovely, but when I blew out the candles on my birthday cake, all I wanted—more than anything else—was for my parents to get back together. Dad's negativity tainted any joy or hope I felt.

He went on a bitter tirade after Mom left and said sarcastically, "Let me see that necklace. What a thoughtful gift. It looks like your mother spent a whopping twenty-five cents on you, Mar'. She must really care. How nice of her to stop by unannounced. We'll have to do it again some time."

Deadliest Catch

Mayor Richard J. Daley held an annual fishing derby at the McKinley Park lagoon. I think it was an impassioned effort to expose city kids to the outdoors and the joys of fishing. Each year the Chicago Park District filled the lagoon with fish. Kids of all sizes, shapes, and ages sat in the grass along the lagoon, hurled sharp hooks into the air, and went fishing for the first time. Seriously, what were they thinking?

Dad and Uncle John thought it was a fantastic way to spend a warm summer afternoon and lugged me, my sisters, and my cousin Cindy (Aunt Evelyn and Uncle John's youngest daughter who is the same age as me) out to the park to participate. Uncle John loaned us a few of his fishing poles. As a fan of the *Andy Griffith Show*, I saw Opie fishing plenty of times and thought there was nothing to it. John helped me place a worm on the hook and told me to cast my line into the water. I wound up the fishing pole like it was a lasso, swung it backward, and then flung it forward toward the water like a fly fisherman.

Much to my surprise, I caught something right away—Patty's left hand. She immediately let out a bloodcurdling scream and started to cry.

"Stop being such a goddamn baby," Dad scolded, as he ripped the hook out from the palm of Patty's hand before she could protest.

Oh, boy was I in for it. Luckily for me, there were too many witnesses for my sister to retaliate right then and there. Needless to say, it was the first and last time I ever went fishing. Considering my klutzy nature and the safety of those around me, it is probably best not to place me in close proximity of sharp objects of any kind.

Don't Tell Mom I Wish the Babysitter Was Dead

We had the worst luck with babysitters the summer my parents split. One (I will call her Satan since I cannot remember her name) pretended to be nice to us in front of Dad and treated us horribly the moment he left. She told us repeatedly how she was going to marry Dad and be our new mother.

Satan owned two rather large, ill-tempered German shepherds she treated as if they were her own children. Twice daily, she forced me to walk them in the gravel alley behind her house. Invariably, the dogs spotted a cat or squirrel and chased after it, dragging me through the gravel until my knees were bloody scabs.

To be honest (as the nickname implies), Satan was a mean person, but she was an even worse cook. Every day was a new trip into culinary hell. Satan made food her dinner plates were ashamed to serve. One dish Patty and I particularly disliked (an understatement) was her pepper soup. As soon as Patty tasted it, she gagged and vomited all over the kitchen floor. Luckily, Kathy ate baby food and was spared Satan's gastronomic poison.

After Patty got sick, she refused to finish eating the rest of her pepper soup. This infuriated Satan. She flew into a rage and yelled, "If you think I am going to slave over a hot stove all day for you ungrateful, spiteful children, only to have you waste my food, you have another thing coming."

Then our sadistic babysitter insisted I eat Patty's uneaten

portion, as well as my own. Instead of fighting with her, which was futile, I opted to bite the bullet and get it over with. Tossing a spoonful of the unsavory green concoction into the back of my throat, I swallowed hard to avoid it making contact with my tongue and, thus, spared myself from actually having to taste it. Within minutes, both bowls were empty, and I was allowed to leave the table.

Unfortunately, I was born with a cast iron stomach. It was not until hours later that I got sick, while on my way in to Comisky Park to see a White Sox game with Dad, Uncle Bob, and his four children Deanna, Julie, Bobby and Danny. I gratefully excised my demons into a large metal garbage can near the front entrance of the park.

The next babysitter we had was the wife of one of Dad's co-workers. I will call her Angel. Angel was a devoutly religious woman who insisted we pray with her before each meal. Since we had no clue what to do, my sisters and I mouthed along the best we could. When Angel learned we did not belong to a church, she made it her personal crusade to educate us about the Bible and even dragged us to her church once with Dad's blessing. A Sunday school teacher who also taught vacation Bible school, Angel amassed a large collection of religious education materials to share with us, including a children's Bible. Then she did the unthinkable—the unforgivable. She gave us reading and homework assignments—the last thing a kid on summer vacation wants to do. The woman had to go. Luckily, Dad agreed.

Dad found Angel's replacement in the classified section of the Brighton Life newspaper. She lived in Archer Heights near Archer Park. A kind woman in her late thirties, her long black hair, blue eyes, and heavyset build reminded me of Mom. Her name was Pat, and her husband's name was Ron—the same as my parents' names. Even though Pat and Ron loved children, they could not have any of their own.

My sisters and I liked Pat. The home she shared with her husband had a huge playroom filled with toys for us to play with. Pat loved music and tried to incorporate it into our playtime every day. She played "The Hustle" on her record player, and sung "Do the Hustle" as she danced around the room with us. When the weather permitted, we walked to Archer Park. Patty and I loved playing on the various slides and monkey bars, while Pat pushed Kathy in the baby swings. Then one day, out of the blue, Pat told Dad she could no longer babysit us. We were all terribly disappointed.

When we got home, Patty and I went outside to play with a girl named Kelly who lived down the street. When her mother, Jennifer, called her to dinner, Dad seized the opportunity and asked Jennifer if she might be interested in watching us until he could find a more permanent solution. She was reluctant until Dad explained to her how desperate we were and told her about our unfortunate history with babysitters.

Jennifer watched us for a couple of weeks, until we went back to school in the fall. That's when Uncle Kenny and his girlfriend, Esther, moved in with us. They took care of Kathy while Patty and I were at school and watched us until Dad got home from work. I missed Mom terribly, but I would never admit it because I was so hurt she left.

Home for the Holidaze

When Mom left, I was destroyed. When she did not come home right away, I felt abandoned. I thought she did not care about us anymore. Images of her prying my fingers away as I pleaded, "Mom please don't go." haunted my every thought.

Six months passed. It was the day before Thanksgiving when Mom returned home. It was late and I fell asleep on the living room floor watching television. Mom bent down, gently kissed my forehead, and said. "Hi, honey. I'm home. When you wake up in the morning, I'll make you and your sisters a wonderful Thanksgiving dinner with all the trimmings."

I was angry with Mom for leaving. All the hurt and pain I bottled deep inside came pouring out that night in a dream. I held nothing back and told Mom exactly how I felt. By the time I awoke, I was convinced I said aloud what I felt inside.

Uncertain as to whether or not the dream was real, I remorsefully crept past the living room and peered into the kitchen. It was like Mom never left. She was making Thanksgiving dinner like the previous six months were all a bad dream.

Chapter 9

Checking Out

Dad was moved to a room on the fourth floor. He was not pleased, to say the least, when he opened his eyes and saw another pair of concerned family members hovering over him. Perturbed at the prospect of being bothered yet again, he snarled, "Why can't you two leave me the fuck alone? Can't you see I am trying to get some goddamn rest here? This is a hospital isn't it?"

"Dad, this is serious. If you don't have this operation we are going to lose you. Please, don't do this," I implored him.

"Hey, I'm three times seven I can do whatever the hell I want."

"But Dad..."

"Look, I have had it already. Grandma, Shirley, Bob, Kathy—I can't take it anymore. I'm not going under the knife. I've got the antibiotics I need, and all I want to do is get some rest. Please, just leave me alone."

"Dad, you will die without this operation," Patty pleaded.

"I don't give a fuck! They are not hacking off my goddamn leg and that is final!"

"So you're just going to lie there and die. Is that it?"

"Yeah, I am. Guess I'm checking out today. It's been a slice. Now get the fuck out of here so I can get some goddamn rest already!"

"Dad!" Patty and I cried.

"Do I have to call security to drag you two fuckheads out of here?"

The Christmas Present

Even though my parents were married for a number of years, they did not exchange Christmas presents.

"Christmas is for kids," Dad used to say.

This Christmas was different. It was a like a homecoming for Mom. Dad went Christmas shopping for the first time in years and purchased a gift for her. Mom's present came in a big box, which he beautifully wrapped in festive paper, and tied up with a shiny red bow and a big tag that read, "Don't open until Christmas!" One of the first jobs Dad held as a teenager was wrapping gifts in a department store and he excelled at it. Knowing it would drive Mom mad, he placed the wrapped present beneath the tree a couple of weeks before Christmas.

The next morning, Mom walked by the Christmas tree and discovered the present. Honestly, she could not miss it. It took up nearly half the tree skirt, the branches on the bottom of the tree rested upon it, and it was nearly two feet high.

"What's this?" A present—for me?" she said in awe, as her eyes welled up with tears of joy.

I watched Mom as she walked by the tree several times, like a kid eyeing a candy jar, trying to figure out what goodies awaited her inside.

When Dad got home from work, she pestered him, "What did you get me, Ronnie?"

"Oh, you'll have to wait for Christmas, along with everybody else, to find out."

Day after day, Mom pondered what the gift could be. Curiosity got the best of her and one day after Dad to left for work she launched a formal investigation into the box's contents. Although she shook it, measured it, and weighed it, she still did not have a clue as to what it was. She even placed the box by the front window to see if the sunlight permitted her to read the lettering beneath the wrapping paper, but not a single word was visible.

A week before Christmas, Mom could no long take the temptation. She carefully opened the present and then meticulously rewrapped it so Dad would be none the wiser. He figured it out anyway. It was not the most romantic gift, but it was something she needed—a new set of nonstick pots and pans.

Elvis Has Left the Building

Patty and I were watching the "Wizard of Oz" on television in the living room when the telephone rang.

Mom answered. It was Aunty Lois. She listened intently and then gasped, "Oh, no!"

Patty and I crept toward the kitchen to find out what happened.

Then Mom cried, "What happened? I cannot believe he is

gone. He was so young!"

Tears welled up in our eyes. Patty and I hung on Mom's every word, anxiously waiting to learn who passed away.

Mom told Aunty Lois she loved her then hung up the telephone, collapsed on to one of the kitchen chairs and openly wept into her hands. Patty and I ran to Mom's side and placed our arms around her while tears streamed down our faces.

"Who died, Mom?"

"El-vis. Elvis died! Boo-hoo-hoo-hoo!"

"Who's Elvis?"

Near Christ Mess

After Uncle Pete and Aunty Lucy moved to Colorado, Aunty Peggy and Uncle Frank took over the duty of hosting the Annual Sheedy Christmas Party and Grab Bag. It was great. Just when Patty, Kathy, and I thought the fun of Christmas was over—after all our presents were opened and played with to the point of boredom—we drove to Aunty Peggy's house and got to open more gifts. We looked forward to going every year. All of our cousins were there. The older sect hung out in the basement drinking beer, smoking cigarettes, and shooting pool, while the younger cousins played in the rest of the house, eating junk food, loading up on sweets, and running up and down the stairs like maniacs until we passed out from pure exhaustion.

It was late Christmas night. We were on our way home from the party. Dad was drunk (big surprise). Mom was in the passenger seat biting her tongue. Patty, Kathy, and I were in the backseat holding all the presents and goodies our aunts gave us to take home.

It was so cold inside the car I could see my breath. I snuggled inside my winter coat, trying to keep warm, when I noticed we were quickly approaching a stopped squad car. Dad's reaction time was significantly slowed due to his inebriated condition. My anxiety mounted as we drew closer. *"Daddy, please stop!"* I screamed inside my head as we continued to race toward the brake lights in front of us. I closed my eyes tightly, braced myself, and prayed for Dad to engage the brakes.

Dad slammed on the brakes moments before impact. The brakes locked, he hit a patch of ice, and the car spun out of control. Although Dad missed the Illinois state trooper, he did hit a light pole with the driver's side of the car. The force of the spinning and subsequent crash sent our goodies flying through the back seat and all over my sisters and me. I do not know what upset my sisters and me more—the fact we were in a car accident or that all those luscious Christmas goodies were splattered everywhere.

My heart was beating so hard I thought it was going to pop out of my chest. I was fearful Dad was going to be arrested, and we would be spending Christmas night in jail. Fortunately, the trooper took pity on us, and let Dad go with a warning.

My parent's arguments peaked during the holidays. Most car trips to and from family functions were made in hostile silence none of us girls dared break for fear of triggering an all out war. Good times always went hand-in-hand with the bad. It was as if we could not have any joy without enduring a little pain, too.

Runaway

When Mom and Dad announced we were moving again, I was stunned. Each time we moved, we went from a bad to a worse situation. We recently got settled. I made friends. The class bully stopped threatening to beat me up on a daily basis. We lived near a great park and the best sledding hill ever.

"How could you do this to me *again*?" I cried as I ran to my bedroom, plopped down face first onto my bed and sobbed loudly into my pillow.

Through my muffled tears I overheard Dad say to Mom, "Don't worry, she'll get over it. Kids are resilient."

I was frustrated with my parents. Unable to bear the constant upheaval or the thought of going to another new school and having to start all over again, I ran away.

It was a bitterly cold January night. I ran out past the entryway of our brick apartment building and slid across the freshly fallen snow. As I stood there contemplating my fate, the snow sparkled sweetly under the yellow street lights. Hot tears ran down my cold, red cheeks and into the corner of my mouth where I bit my lip earlier. The sting of my salty tears was a bitter reminder I had no choice. I had no say. I had absolutely no control.

Like it or not, I was forced tag along on this train wreck of a ride. Being the child of an alcoholic is like being the only person awake in the back seat of a car, while the rest of the occupants sleep peacefully—the car careens out of control and flies off the side of a cliff.

That's Your Brother

I've got a riddle for you. What do you get when you put two drunk Polacks and a Jew in an Irish bar? Answer: Trouble.

It was winter. Dad, Uncle Kenny, and their friend Roy, aka "The Nose," got comfortably numb at one of their favorite watering holes, an Irish pub in Lyons, Illinois a southwest suburb of Chicago. Dad was in a particularly foul mood. Poor Roy quickly became the target of his pent up rage. Dad is the type of drunk who can go from happy to sinister without warning. He went from playfully joking with Roy about the size of his nose to wanting to bash Roy's nose in. Thinking quickly, Kenny wedged himself between Dad and Roy before Dad was able to land the first punch.

"You don't want to fight with Roy," Kenny pleaded. "Remember, we like Roy. He's our friend."

"Problem? No problem." Dad said in a Polish accent.

Roy, who was more than familiar with Dad's switchblade mood swings, took his cue, and immediately exited stage left before Dad noticed he was missing. Once the coast was clear, Kenny said, "Come on Ronnie, it's time to go."

Dad reluctantly got into Kenny's car with a little persuading. By the time they reached Central Avenue and the Stevenson Expressway, however, they were arguing loudly. Dad was pissed Kenny prevented him from pummeling Roy, and demanded he stop the car and let him out. You see, Dad looks at bar fighting like it's a competitive sport. It is great exercise, he gets all his aggressions out, and it's cheaper than breaking the furniture.

"I can't drop you off on the side of the road, Ronnie. It is ten degrees outside. You'll freeze to death."

"Let me the fuck out of this goddamn car RIGHT NOW!"

"Fine!" Kenny shouted as he slammed on the brakes, threw the car into park, and engaged in an old-fashioned fist fight with Dad smack dab in the middle of the street. Two guys who drove by saw them fighting, stopped their car, and attempted to break them up. "Hey, stop! What are you doing?" they cried.

"Mind your own goddamned business." Dad growled, as he and Kenny switched their aggressions toward the good Samaritans.

A few dozen well-landed punches later, the men had enough, jumped back into their car, and sped away.

"Come on, Ronnie. Get in the car. Let's go home."

"Fuck you! I'd rather walk."

"Fine, then. Walk home and freeze to death, you stubborn bastard. See if I give a shit," Kenny shouted as he sped off and left Dad to fend for himself.

"Oh you no good Mudda Plucka! I'll kill you if I ever get my hands on you Kenny," Dad shouted.

Kenny left Dad on the corner of 47th and Central Avenue—which was about two and a half miles away from our new apartment. The area can be pretty desolate after midnight. There are several trucking companies scattered along either side of 47th street, which are essentially deserted after business hours. To add to the creepy ambiance, the entire area is pitch-black at night because there are no street lights.

Fuming mad and ranting loudly to himself, Dad slowly made his way back to our (and Kenny's) neighborhood. Each breath he took came puffing out of him like an angry steam locomotive. Did I mention at the midway point home, around 47th and Cicero, there are several rows of low income housing and, along with them, a certain, let us say, undesirable element? A group of teenagers, who were up to no good, observed Dad walking alone, and made the mistake of messing with him. Dad got into a huge fistfight with a couple of them and scared them off.

Furious, Dad headed towards Kenny's apartment on foot like a stark raving lunatic with one goal in mind—revenge. He kicked down Kenny's front door, dragged him out of bed (while was making love to his girlfriend Esther), and beat the crap out of him—even though he is fifteen years Kenny's senior. When Dad felt Kenny had his fill, he yelled, "Pister on your sister. You're not so muckin futch," and then headed back toward our apartment, a block and a half away.

Kenny, quite understandably, did not appreciate getting sucker punched in his birthday suit in front of Esther. He quickly got dressed and sped off in hot pursuit of Dad. By the time he caught up with Dad he was in front of our next door neighbor's house. Blind with anger, Kenny jumped out of the car without putting it into park and ran toward Dad with fists-a-blazing. He took one swing at Dad, slipped on the ice, and broke his leg as his car slowly crashed into a parked car. Injuries requiring immediate medical attention were not enough to deter them from fighting, however. It only briefly interrupted them, as Kenny adjusted to punching Dad on one foot.

A neighbor across the street heard the commotion and said in a thick German accent, "Stop! What are you doing? You're friends. Friends should not fight like that."

"Friends? We're brothers!" Dad and Kenny shouted in unison.

"Oh, I see," the neighbor said, and slowly closed his front door.

That's What Happens When You Get in the Way

Our new apartment was on the second floor of a two flat in Archer Heights. Mom rarely had friends over to our apartment. Let's be honest—she never had friends over. A teenage girl named Darcy who lived across the street liked to ask Mom for advice about her love life. Although Mom was happy to assist, Darcy always came over unannounced, usually while Mom was cleaning the house or cooking dinner.

It was late afternoon. Dad brought Uncle Kenny home for dinner. They stopped for a couple of beers on their way home from work and were laughing and joking around. Once Dad found out Mom had company, he could not resist messing with her.

"Get me my dinner woman, and make it snappy." he demanded. Then he giggled as he winked at Kenny and me. "What the hell is taking you so long? Hurry up! I'm hungry," he yelled.

"He wants his dinner, huh? Oh, I'll give him his goddamn dinner alright." Mom mumbled from the kitchen as she angrily slammed food down onto a large dinner plate.

Moments later, Mom stormed into the front room holding the plate above her head with her left hand like a waiter. "You want your dinner, Ronnie? Well, here it is!" And with that, she threw a plate full of hot food at him.

Homemade meatloaf, baby peas, and mashed potatoes with brown gravy went flying everywhere, and with it, so did their fists. I made the mistake of stepping in between them to break them up, and got one of Dad's lefts in my right eye.

"Stop it!" I screamed.

Mom's uninvited teenage guest darted past me like a bat-out-of-hell. I don't think Darcy ever asked for my mother's love advice again. I can't say as I blame her.

"Why do you two have to fight all the time? I can't take it anymore!" I cried then ran out the back door and downstairs to the basement where I hid next to the washer. Our landlord's apartment was on the first floor. Is it a wonder why we moved as often as we did?

Once the dust settled, and my parents came to their senses they went looking for me. I could hear them calling for me outside, but I ignored them. Relishing a few moments of peace and quiet in the basement, I managed to have myself a good cry before Kenny found me.

"Are you okay Mare?"

"Yes, but I do not feel like talking about it right now, *if that's okay with you.*"

"You can't get in the middle of your parents' arguments like that. You could get seriously hurt."

Then Kenny helped me up and accompanied me back to the apartment.

Dad took one look at my black eye and said, "That's what you get for getting in the way, kid. Didn't I teach you how to duck?"

The Love Boat and Fantasy Island

Every Saturday night Dad watched us while Mom attended her weekly AA meeting. One day without warning, he refused to watch us any longer. Mom was bitterly disappointed. The truth is Mom never went anywhere socially. She needed AA in order to stay sober and preserve her sanity. When I learned what Dad did, I offered to babysit my sisters so Mom could go. Even though I was only ten years old and was not "legally" old enough to watch my sisters, Mom took me up on my offer.

While Mom attended her meetings, Dad went to the bar and got drunk in protest. I resented Dad for not watching us and leaving my sisters and I home alone. I was frightened from the moment Mom left until she came home. Dad had this rule about turning all the lights off at night to save money on our electric bill. The only lights we were permitted to have turned on were the bathroom and the kitchen and only if we were using them. Otherwise, it was lights out. We lived in an old drafty building that made all sorts of eerie noises whenever the wind blew. Every creak I heard sent me into a panic.

I rarely ventured outside the safety of our living room for fear of what was lurking in the darkness. *The Love Boat* and *Fantasy Island* were the only television shows my sisters and I could agree to watch, and we watched them every week. Our television set was a beacon of light on those dark scary nights. It gave me comfort knowing as soon as the shows ended, Mom would come walking through the front door.

Up in Smoke

Mom needed a partial. She and Dad had a fistfight and she lost. Luckily, I have no recollection of how it happened, other than Mom was very upset it took the dentist nearly a month to create her dental appliance.

While brushing her teeth one night, Mom discovered a few white patches in the back of her mouth. Although she did not feel ill, she became alarmed as the patches grew larger in only a matter of days. Thinking it was nothing, she reluctantly mentioned it to her dentist at her next appointment. He diagnosed Mom with a precancerous condition which was directly attributed to drinking alcohol and smoking both marijuana and tobacco cigarettes.

"I've got good news and bad news for you Mrs. Velesovsky. The good news is—if you stop smoking, the white patches in your mouth will go away and will significantly reduce your chances of getting mouth cancer. The bad news is—if you continue to smoke, there is a one hundred percent chance the white patches will become cancerous."

Mom tried everything she could to stop smoking, including hypnosis. Uncle Bob gave Mom a huge box of hard candies to help her quit. He figured if she had something to put in her mouth, she would be less likely to crave a cigarette and it worked. I was relieved.

The word cancer can be so scary when you first hear it. To a ten-year-old, cancer is synonymous with death. My elation, however, did not last long. One day after school, I came home and found Mom smoking a cigarette at the kitchen table. Overwhelmed with emotion, I could not speak. Mom greeted me with her usual, "Hi, honey. How was school?" Like nothing happened.

I started crying as I walked toward her, and said, "Mom, how could you do it?" That's when I learned no matter how hard she tried, Mom could not stop smoking. She was sneaking cigarettes all along. The thought of getting cancer made her so nervous she went from smoking two packs of cigarettes a day to smoking three packs of cigarettes a day.

Chapter 10

Dead Leg

Dad was moved to a semi-private room on the fourth floor and was assigned a new doctor. Dr. Livingston was a prominent well respected internist who split his time between Cook County Hospital and Rush Presbyterian St. Luke's Medical Center.

"Oh great! Another doctor to poke and prod me. Why can't you guys go to hell and leave me the fuck alone?" Dad shouted.

Unaffected by Dad's charms, Dr. Livingston flipped through his chart and said, "Good morning, Mr. Velesovsky."

"Listen Doc, I've got the antibiotics I need now. Can't you please leave me alone so I can get some rest?"

"I don't think you understand the levity of the situation. If you do not have this operation immediately, you will die."

"Stop being so goddamn melodramatic, all I need is a couple days of good rest."

"That is what I am trying to tell you. You will not be here in a couple of days if you do not have this operation."

"I know what you guys are all about. It's the money isn't it? You want me to have this operation so you can stuff your pockets full of money and go golfing. Well, I am not going to do it, and you can't make me!"

"Mr. Velesovsky, your leg is dead. We cannot save it. Your dead leg is killing you. If we don't remove your leg, you will certainly die. Do you understand?"

"Well then, I guess I am checking out today." Dad shouted then gave him a one finger salute.

Dr. Livingston left Dad's room in a huff. I stopped him in the hallway.

"Excuse me, doctor, but isn't there anything we can do?"

"It is your father's decision, and he has obviously made up his mind. The only way to save him now is if a psychiatrist found him to be incompetent, and allowed you to sign the papers on your father's behalf for the surgery. Unfortunately, your father is completely aware of what is going on. There is nothing I can do. I'm sorry."

On the Wagon Part I
Health Kick

Once Mom was diagnosed with a precancerous condition, Dad went off the deep end—Mom got sick, despite giving up drinking eight years earlier, while Dad continued to drink alcohol, smoke pot, and snort cocaine. Thinking he was doomed, he went on a major health kick. He stopped drinking and quit smoking—cold turkey. Dad dropped fifty pounds in a couple months' time. His beer belly became nonexistent, and his Adam's apple protruded like he was a teenage boy.

All that clean living took its toll on our family. Dad was absolutely miserable, and there was no living with him. He had a short fuse and zero tolerance for what he called "bullshit." Flying off the handle at the drop of a hat, Dad was angry all the time. It was the most stressful six months of my young life. It got to the point I wished Dad would go to a bar, drink beer, smoke cigarettes, and eat pizza.

Bats in My Belfry, Moths in My Hair

One day, shortly before my sisters and I returned home from school, Mom noticed what appeared to be the remains of a mouse hanging from the curtain of our back porch window. Uncle Kenny happened to stopped by, and Mom asked him to dispose of it for her. Kenny gladly came to Mom's aid, grabbed a broom from the pantry and smacked the dead mouse with it. The mouse emitted an eerie screeching sound, opened its *wings*, and *flew* towards Kenny and Mom. Yes, flew. Startled, they both ran back into the apartment screaming loudly and slammed the back door shut.

Mom immediately grabbed the yellow pages and called an exterminator. The exterminator arrived a couple of hours later, thoroughly checked the porch and attic and then explained to Mom, "Ma'am, for your information, mice rarely climb up curtains to die—just in case you stumble upon another sleeping bat."

I often awoke to bloodcurdling screams in the middle of the night, followed by Mom begging me to kill a moth, spider, or some other poor insect. She had a paralyzing fear of moths and was terrified one might fly into her hair and get stuck.

"Mary! Mary! Get up!" Mom yelled in the wee hours one morning.

I jumped out of bed from a sound sleep, my heart beating like a heavy metal drum solo, until I realized what was happening. Then Mom handed me a rolled up newspaper and trembled as she pointed to where the creature was hiding. She immediately ran to the furthest corner of the room, kneeled, and held a pillow over her head until the savage beast was slain. After the deed was done, she cowered back toward me, said "Thanks Mary," and kissed me goodnight.

Hole in My Heart

During a routine kindergarten physical, the pediatrician noticed an extra sound when he listened to Kathy's heartbeat. She was diagnosed with a heart murmur and was referred to a pediatric cardiologist to determine the severity of her condition and whether or not she required surgery to correct it. The specialist was completely booked, and Mom was unable to get an appointment for over a month and a half. It was an agonizing wait for my parents. They were both worried sick.

Late one night, I overheard Mom talking to her sister Lois on the telephone. Mom was crying. "My little girl is too young to die. Please, God, let me trade places with her. Take me instead."

Unable to bear the thought of losing Mom or my sister, I cried myself to sleep. A few days later, my parents received word from the specialist that Kathy would most likely grow out of her condition. The entire family breathed a simultaneous sigh of relief. Our jubilation was short-lived, however.

In light of Mom's recent health scare, I choose to do my school science project on cancer and wrote to the American Cancer Society for information. Along with several brochures, they sent me a top ten list of the warning signs for cancer. Mom had them all. A trip to the doctor and a biopsy confirmed her suspicions. Her precancerous condition was now cancerous. Mom's doctor immediately scheduled her for surgery to remove as much of the cancerous growth as possible.

Hungry Eyes

Shortly after Mom's diagnosis, we moved to an old

converted farmhouse directly across the street. It was my idea. The family who lived there purchased a new home and put their old one up for rent. We never lived in a house before, and I thought it might be nice for Mom to recuperate from her surgery in a larger space. The house was set way back on the lot. The front of the house lined up with the back of the houses on either side. The front yard was huge. It had a row of white peonies planted along the chain-link fence to the right, a couple of t-shaped metal clothesline posts which ran parallel the front walk to the left and two crab apple trees by the front sidewalk. The backyard was the size of a postage stamp and backed up to the alley.

The kitchen was enormous and took up half the basement. Dad set up the front half of the kitchen like it was a lounge, complete with a stereo and a couch. The pale yellow walls and mushroom curtains only added to its ambiance.

Late at night, long after my sisters and I went to bed, Dad, Mom, and Uncle Kenny smoked pot and listened to Beatles records in the kitchen. They locked the kitchen door and blocked out the window so we could not see what they were up to. The three of them talked and laughed all night long. The next morning there was not a lick of food left in the house.

My bedroom was located directly above Dad's makeshift den. Countless nights I fell asleep listening to Dad bellow out Beatles' tunes like "Michelle" and "With a Little Help From My Friends." Although, when Dad sang "Michelle," it came out more like, "Me-Shell." In between the songs, deeply philosophical conversations echoed up through the vent in my bedroom, dispersed with random roars of laughter, and whiffs of marijuana smoke.

On rare occasions, my parents allowed my sisters and me to hang out with them while they partied. The kitchen table brimmed with food. It looked like a Thanksgiving Day feast with a cloud of cigarette and marijuana smoke hovering above it. Dad's eyes were bloodshot and half open from smoking pot. My sisters and I teased him and told him he had "hungry eyes."

The song "Hungry Eyes" has a completely different meaning for my family.

Blacky

Blacky became a member of our dysfunctional family when

90

Kathy was in kindergarten. A family who lived across from the street from her school owned a dog that gave birth to a litter of puppies. On their way home from school one day, Mom and Kathy saw the puppies frolicking in the front yard. Kathy immediately fell in love with Blacky. Mom could not resist bringing Blacky home, despite knowing full-well what Dad's reaction would be.

Although Dad loves his animal shows and firmly believes no animal should ever be caged in a zoo, he, under no circumstances, wanted to have another dog—no matter how cute and cuddly it was. I will never know if Mom got the dog to please Kathy or to spite Dad. Either way, he was a cute little mutt. Blacky looked like a miniature Labrador retriever, with a shiny black coat that was as smooth as silk, and a tail that curled upward like a question mark.

However, his bark was truly worse than his bite. When Blacky barked, he sounded like a much larger ferocious dog. People were shocked when they met him for the first time. He barked so fiercely at the front door whenever the door bell rang they assumed he was a Rottweiler.

As we opened the door, unsuspecting visitors said in a frightened tone, "Please, hold back your dog." Once they saw Blacky, they said, "That little dog was making all that commotion? I don't believe it."

I loved snuggling with Blacky. He was a sweet, loving dog who listened intently to every secret I revealed to him. Ever playful, he loved running around in figure eights in our front yard, playing fetch and jumping high in the air to catch balls that were tossed to him.

Every blue moon, Blacky ran away with the Doberman pinscher from down the block. Like a couple of playboys, they went on the prowl together looking for female dogs. Once I watched as Blacky returned home at five in the morning. He stopped by the crab apple trees in our front yard and appeared to say goodbye to his wing man. Then he ran up the front walk and whined for me to let him back into the house. I swear those two were responsible for all of the new litters of puppies in the neighborhood.

Blacky was a gentleman and never humped our legs like our friend's dogs did—with the exception of my girlfriend, Dee Dee. Dee Dee came over once to play Atari by our house. She made the mistake of wearing a black, rabbit fur coat. Blacky mistook Dee Dee's elbow for a dog's posterior and had his way with her. We laughed so hard we could not utter a single word. Dee Dee thought we were making fun of her poor game play. She was so captivated by the game she did not notice Blacky banging away at her elbow. Once Dee Dee figured it out, however, she was utterly disgusted. Come to think of it, I do not think she ever wore that coat again.

Chapter 11

White Lies

After Dad's doctor angrily departed, a nurse carrying a clipboard came into Dad's room. She asked him all sorts of questions, and he was being difficult. I stepped in to see if I could assist her.

"Mr. Velesovsky, what is your date of birth?" she asked. Dad gave her a dirty look, crossed his arms upon his chest, and turned the other way.

I answered quietly, "It's September 25, 1943."

"Mr. Velesovsky, do you smoke?"

"He smokes about three packs of cigarettes a day."

"Mr. Velesovsky, do you drink?"

"He's an alcoholic."

"How much does he drink a day?"

"About a quart of whiskey, every day."

"Have you ever been suicidal Mr. Velesovsky?"

Dad was about to bellow a resounding "No," when I interjected, "Yes, he has."

"Absolutely not," Dad hollered.

"Well, what the hell do you call this then Dad?"

Attempting to appeal to an unbiased party, I said, "The doctor gave my father less than twelve hours to live if he does not get his leg amputated, yet he refuses to have the surgery. I'd say that was pretty suicidal. Wouldn't you?"

"Have there been any other instances when he was suicidal recently?"

"Yes." I was telling a bit of a white lie here. I have never been a good liar, but Dad's life was at stake after all.

"Mary, what the hell are you doing?"

"How did your father indicate he was going to take his life?"

I stood out of Dad's line of vision and pointed my hand like a gun to my temple.

"Oh, I see," said the nurse, as she feverishly wrote in Dad's medical chart.

"Mary, what line of bullshit are you feeding this woman?"

About thirteen years ago, Dad was very depressed. He stated on several occasions he wished someone would shoot him and put him out of his misery. So it was not a big lie. I omitted one small insignificant detail—an oversight really.

Luckily, Dad's nurse believed me and agreed there was sufficient evidence to put in a call to the hospital's staff psychiatrist. However, he did not come on duty for a few more hours.

Same Bat Time, Same Bat Channel, Part I
Goose Egg

I acquired my "lucky" bat, during my brief softball career when I hit my one-and-only homerun with it. Since softball season was over, and no one wanted to play with me, I went to the school yard, tossed my yellow, glow-in-the-dark, sixteen-inch softball up into the air, and hit it against the brick school wall.

Through my peripheral vision, I saw Patty approaching.

Concerned she might get hurt, I yelled, "Watch out! I'm practicing here."

Patty foolishly refused to heed my warning and proceeded to walk towards me, yammering on about something I did earlier in the day that royally pissed her off.

Ignoring her negative rant, I decided to concentrate on the task at hand. I tossed the softball high up into the air and swung the bat with all my might, never taking my eyes off the ball. As the bat made contact, I closed my eyes tightly. Then I heard a loud thump. When I opened my eyes, I saw the softball bouncing on the ground next to my feet. My heart sank. From the corner of my eye, I saw Patty slowly fall to her knees.

My sister has a very bad temper. To slap this girl in the face is the kiss of death. What I did, though, could not be compared to a slap in the face—even if it was an accident. This was the same sister who, while we were growing up, had the hardest head in the universe. When we bumped heads when we were little, I was the one who reeled in pain and cried while Patty laughed hysterically. Let's say I got head-butted a lot as a child.

The largest goose egg I have ever seen began to protrude from my sister's forehead. Seriously, you could not miss it. She looked like a damn unicorn for crying out loud. But Patty was extraordinarily calm. Not one tear. She was fine. I did not see the need to draw her attention to the big lump on her head. It might upset her.

"I'm sorry! I'm sorry! Are you okay?" sprung immediately from my lips.

Then, like out of a surreal nightmare, my friend Dee Dee, who witnessed the entire event, came running over and shouted, "Oh, my God. That is the biggest bump I have ever seen in my entire life."

Tears, screaming, upset. Yes, at this point, my sister became visibly upset. However, she was in too much pain to hit me at the time. We limped our way home, and my parents immediately rushed Patty to the hospital. I was convinced I killed my sister. The doctor examined her, and instructed my parents to watch her overnight to see if she exhibited any signs of a concussion. No signs. No concussion. *I told you she had a hard head.* Rest assured, I paid for this incident at a later date—a sort of "beat you up later" rain check.

Brace Yourself

In the seventh grade, our family dentist told me I needed braces. Dad took me to see my Cousin Julie's orthodontist. He was a kind, family man in his early forties, who made the transition to becoming a metal-mouth a little less painful. However, shortly after I started seeing him, he was diagnosed with cancer, and his partner took over his practice.

His partner was a young man who was just starting off and, quite understandably, liked being paid in a timely manner. I had a little yellow appointment book I took with me on every visit. Each time I went to the orthodontist, I was supposed to pay fifty dollars. The receptionist, in theory, would record the payment in my appointment book and schedule my next appointment.

Dad eventually stopped giving me rides to the orthodontist. He insisted I go on my own with no money, and told me to say, "My dad said he would pay the next time I come in." Except, it was no different the next time I came in. Time and time again, I showed up by myself with the same lame excuse. I had no money and ended up with another blank in the payment column of my little yellow appointment book.

Each time I went to the orthodontist, he threatened not to work on me and harassed me about my past due account. I was only supposed to have my braces on for two years. Three years later, when my father made the final payment, my braces came off. Coincidence? I think not.

Blood Poisoning, Obviously

Jellies (plastic sandals) were very popular in the early nineteen eighties. Since they were inexpensive, only $1.99 on sale, they were one of the few fashion trends I participated in while it was still considered "fashionable". I soon, however, paid the price for my vanity. Not only did the shoes make my feet sweat profusely, but they caused a terrible blister to form on the big toe on my left foot. The blister got badly infected and, within a day, throbbed intensely. A red line slowly climbed up my leg from the infected blister on my big toe.

The red line was halfway up my calf when I happened to mention it in passing to Mom. "Hey Mom, isn't this weird?" I asked pointing to the red line on my leg.

"You have blood poisoning."

"What is blood poisoning?"

"Blood poisoning is what happens when an infection, like the one on your big toe spreads to a vein. The infection will continue to climb upward until it reaches your heart."

"What happens if it reaches my heart?"

"You could die. But, don't worry. It is easily treated with antibiotics. We need to get you to a doctor before it spreads any further. Your father will take you when he gets home from work."

We did not have any medical insurance, credit cards or even a checking account—let alone any money to go to a doctor. When Dad got home from work, he and I went in search of a medical professional who did not require immediate payment or health insurance. We went to five different doctor's offices. Each one turned us away before a doctor even looked at me.

When we returned to the car, I started to cry.

"Dad, what if we can't find a doctor that will help me? The red line is almost up to my knee."

"Don't worry Mary. The next doctor will see you one way or another. I guarantee it."

When the receptionist at the next doctor's office asked how we were paying for the visit Dad told her with cash. Because we did not have an appointment, we were forced to wait to see the doctor.

Forty-five minutes later, a nurse led us to an examination room and took my vital signs.

"The doctor will be in to see you as soon as he is available," she said then left the room.

Dad and I both fell asleep waiting. Another hour passed before the doctor came to the room. He diagnosed me with blood poisoning, wrote a prescription for an antibiotic and instructed Dad to settle our bill with the nurse in front before we left. Dad thanked the doctor and gave me a wink.

As Dad exited the examining room he whispered, "Get dressed kid. Not to worry, Daddy will take care of everything."

After I got dressed, I met up with Dad who was eagerly waiting for me in the hallway. He grabbed my hand and giggled wildly as we ran out the back door of the doctor's office. My heart, head and blister pounded in unison while Dad drove me to the nearest drugstore to fill my prescription.

When we got home, Mom asked, "What took you so long?"

As Dad finished telling Mom the whole sordid story, the telephone rang. It was the doctor's office calling to see why we did not pay the bill before we left, except they made the mistake of asking for me instead of Dad.

"She went to take a shit and the rats ate her." Dad yelled, and then hung up the telephone. "Serves them right trying to collect a debt from a twelve year old," Dad laughed.

The doctor's office called back again. This time they asked for Dad. Dad did arm lifts with the telephone receiver and said, "I – think – we've – got – a – bad – connection." Then he tapped the receiver until they got disconnected and laughed aloud.

The next time the telephone rang Dad answered it by yelling, "Good-bye!" loudly then slammed the telephone receiver down.

My father, a grown man, was reverse crank-calling the doctor's office. I was in awe. And his laughter was infectious. I could not help but laugh too, although I did feel a bit guilty.

The nurse at the doctor's office was very persistent and called back several times. Dad messed with her every single time. She grew angrier, and more hostile with each telephone call she made. By her last call, we were all teary-eyed and rolling on the ground, holding our stomachs in pain from laughing so hard. Dad told us all to be quiet then he answered the telephone by saying, "Chello. "Twat did you say? Tits alright, I cunt hear you anyway.

I've got an infuction in my ear."

Infuriated the nurse yelled, "Obviously, you have no intention of paying this bill, do you, Mr. Velesovsky?"

"OB-VI-OUS-LEE!" Dad shouted like he was Jim Carey. Then he unceremoniously ended their conversation by unplugging the telephone from the wall. We were stunned speechless until Dad relayed back to us what the nurse said, breaking the silence with a simultaneous roar of laughter.

Lone Star of Texas

"Pack yer bags, little ladies, we're movin' ta Texas." Dad bellowed like he was John Wayne.

"We're what?" Mom, my sisters, and I asked in disbelief.

"No way," Patty protested.

"We just made friends here, Dad," I whined.

"We can't move to Texas. Our entire family lives here, Ronnie." Mom said.

"Well, you better kiss your family and friends goodbye, because I can't find a decent job here, and I've got a line on a really good paying job with benefits in Texas. We can find a place to rent and register the kids at their new school before the next school year begins in the fall. The best part is we'll never have to deal with below zero temperatures or shoveling a foot of snow again. Isn't that awesome?"

Dad truly despises the cold. He complains from the moment the first snowflake falls until the first flower blooms, come spring. I suspect it stems back to his early childhood when he was unable to play baseball during the brutal Chicago winters.

My sisters and I were stunned. We moved plenty of times before but always within a ten-mile radius. Texas was several states away. We did not know a living soul there. As much as we hated doing it, we told our friends and family we were moving.

Not wanting Dad to throw away any of my treasures again when we moved, I found a cardboard box the size of a small hope chest. Inspired by Penny from the Disney movie *The Rescuers*, I wrapped the inside and outside of the box with contact paper that resembled wood grain, then placed my most prized possessions in it and taped a large sign on it which read, "Do not throw away!"

A week after Patty, Kathy, and I made our final farewells to our friends, I asked, "So, Dad, when is the big day?"

"What big day?"

"You know. The move."

"What move?" he asked, like he had no clue what I was talking about.

Annoyed Dad was toying with me, I blurted out, "Dad, when are we moving to Texas?"

"Texas? We aren't moving to Texas. Where the hell did you get that idea?"

"You. Remember, you said you had a good job lined up?"

"Oh, yeah. Well, that fell through, kid. Looks like we're staying put—for now."

If I wasn't so relieved, I swear I could have killed him.

Shopping for School Clothes

When we were young, Mom and Dad insisted on dressing Patty and me like we were twins (a rather cruel form of parental torture if you ask me). One winter, they purchased us a hideous pair of matching, reversible winter jackets with splotches of blue, purple, and orange. They were waterproof, came with a drawstring white faux-fur lined hood, zipper closure, and elasticized wrists and waists. The sleeves were so big and puffy we could barely touch our arms to our sides.

People constantly stopped us as we walked down the street and shouted, "Look, twins." Patty and I were both mortified.

A couple of years later, Dad found a pair of matching polyester pantsuits for Patty and me to wear for our annual school pictures. Patty's was navy blue and mine was a deep maroon. The pants had an elastic waist and high inseam. The jacket had an oversized collar with a gold button front and two huge rectangular panels of white *faux* fur with matching tuffs on either side of the buttons. No matter how much we pleaded, our parents were adamant we wear them.

For these and numerous other reasons, I dreaded shopping for school clothes. I mean—I dreaded it. Come early August, my stomach churned in anticipation. In addition to my parents' eclectic taste in clothing, I was a hard fit and always seemed to be in-between sizes. Nearly everything I tried on was either too big or too small, or it was too long or too short. Shopping for clothes was guaranteed to be a painful all day-long ordeal, in which we aimlessly went from store to store in search of an outfit that did not make me wince in horror when I stepped in front of the mirror.

To make matters worse, we had a very limited budget. Finding items that fit and were within our budget always trumped anything remotely "in style." Ask any of the snooty girls at my grammar school who went out of their way to point out to me I was not making the cut fashion wise.

Dad's philosophy when it came to buying school clothes was to find something that fit and then purchase the next size up. He thought the clothes would last us longer if we had room to grow into them and if they were too big, he could always shrink them in the dryer. We never owned anything that fit us properly on the first day of school.

When I was in eighth grade, designer jeans were in. Levi's were okay, and I would not be ostracized for wearing them in public, but Sassoon and Chic-brand jeans were highly coveted amongst the teenage sect. After Patty and I begged Dad repeatedly to buy designer jeans for us, he eventually gave in and said he knew of a place that sold jeans we could afford. He called it "Jew Town."

"Ronnie, don't call it that." Mom scolded. "You'll have the girls talking just like you."

"Jew Town," as Dad so lovingly referred to it, was a row of storefront businesses on Halsted Street near the University of Illinois at Chicago campus more commonly known as Maxwell Street.

Maxwell Street was an area of the city like nothing I have ever seen before. A string of discount clothing and shoe stores, as well as several small fast food restaurants, dotted either side of the street. The air hung heavy with the smell of grilled onions, Polish sausage, and cigarettes. The streets were littered with garbage, chewed gum and cigarette butts, and were full of people looking for deals. The rumble of the crowd was drowned out by traffic cops blowing their whistles and cars beeping their horns. The plump owners of the shops donned in black business suits with crisp, white dress shirts and ornately embroidered yamakas, stood outside of their businesses yelling, "You can't afford to miss this sale." and "Such a deal."

We parked the car and walked down the street in awe. "This way, follow me." Dad said. My sisters and I followed closely behind Dad, afraid of the numerous strangers who vied for our attention and crowded around us trying to sell us their goods and wares. As we stepped into the store, we were overwhelmed by the sheer volume of designer jeans before us—literally piled up to the twelve-foot-high old tin ceiling.

I smiled quietly, taking in the spectacle, like a kid in a candy store. "Wow" was all I could utter.

The store did not have air conditioning and was stifling hot. The old-fashioned metal fan placed near the cash register did little more than blow the hot air around the store. The salesgirl, who I suspect was the daughter of the owner due to a strong family resemblance, asked Dad if we needed any help. She was a thin, petite girl, with long, dark brown hair pulled back into a pony tail, beautiful blue eyes, and a rather large nose. The gold Star of David necklace she wore twinkled beneath the fluorescent lights. Dad told her we needed jeans for school.

"What size do you wear?" the sales girl asked.

Patty and I looked at each other, shrugged our shoulders simultaneously and said, "I dunno."

The salesgirl smiled and said in a thick Yiddish accent, "No problem." She pulled out a yellow measuring tape from her tattered canvas apron and proceeded to measure our hips, waists, and inseam. I was already uncomfortably hot and sticky, and was definitely not prepared for the inseam measurement. *Whoa! Hold your horses, lady. My mother doesn't even touch me there.* I thought to myself.

After the salesgirl finished measuring Patty and me, she told us what sizes we were and then grabbed a couple of pairs of jeans from the shelves.

"Here try these on," she said as she pointed to the dressing rooms at the back of the store.

I closed the curtain and put the jeans on as quickly as I could, knowing what an impatient man Dad was.

Much to my surprise, the jeans fit nicely, once I got them up past my sweaty thighs. That is until I looked down and realized they were easily six inches too long. The familiar pangs from previous bad shopping trips came crashing back. I was riddled with disappointment, as I stepped out of the dressing room and showed Dad and the salesgirl how the jeans fit.

"What's with the long face? They fit you like a glove." she said. Dad nodded his head in agreement. I looked at the both of them like they were crazy, and pointed to the train of denim behind me.

"Oh, that's nothing—a simple hem job," the clerk smiled, gesticulating her arms.

"Don't worry about it kid." Dad assured me. Then Dad asked the salesgirl, "How much are the jeans?"

She stroked her chin, paused hesitantly, and said, "Well," then she gave Dad her sales pitch, eventually telling him how much the jeans cost.

"How much?" Dad shouted in disbelief. Dad's frugal nature reared its ugly head as he haggled with the girl on the price. They negotiated back and forth until the girl crossed her arms upon her chest and said firmly, "I am sorry, sir. I cannot let them go for any less than that."

"Ah, come on now. Can't I Jew you down any more?"

Oh, my God. The salesgirl looked like she came right out of the movie, *Fiddler on the Roof,* for crying out loud. My face immediately turned beet-red, and I thought I was going to die of embarrassment—right then and there. Oh, yeah. That was Dad, Archie Bunker in the flesh.

Without missing a beat, the sales girl managed to come to a mutually agreed upon price with Dad, and the sale was complete. I could hardly wait to escape the store and make my way toward the car. Much to my disappointment, though, our trip into shopping hell was far from over. The tailor was located on the second floor of the same building. We lugged the jeans we purchased up the stairs and into an even hotter space. Sweat oozed from our pores. Eager to put an end to our misery, Patty and I quickly put the jeans back on for the tailor to pin our hems in place.

When we got home, we discovered how the vendor on Maxwell Street could afford to sell designer jeans at such low prices. The jeans we purchased were castoffs and had small defects of one kind or another. Some defects were more noticeable than others—like one pocket you could fit your hand into and the other pocket, only a couple of fingers. Such a deal, my foot.

Sorry Wrong Number

I awoke one night to Dad violently shaking me. He covered my mouth to prevent me from screaming and whispered, "Someone broke into the house. Go downstairs and call the police. Take your sisters with you."

"What about Mom?"

"Do as I say. Don't worry about your mother. I'll take care of her. Now go."

Dad, Patty, Kathy, and I quickly tiptoed down the stairs into the kitchen. Dad grabbed a large knife from one of the kitchen drawers and handed it to me.

"Here, use it if you have to."

I was scared to death. My heart thumped hard against my chest, and my hands shook uncontrollably, as Dad darted back upstairs to wake Mom. A few seconds later, I heard a bloodcurdling scream as Mom tumbled down the stairs in terror, frantically trying to get away from the unseen intruder. We all huddled together in the kitchen, anxiously waiting for the police to arrive.

Luckily, there was a unit in our neighborhood when the call went out, and the police responded within seconds. The flashing lights ricocheted back and forth across the buildings as Dad, in a hushed tone, told the police officers where the intruder was. I shook from head to toe as policemen with drawn weapons crept up our attic stairs. There was a brief scuffle and some yelling before it was all over.

It turns out a drunken old man was sent home in a cab by well-meaning friends. The cabbie, unfamiliar with the area, thought his fare lived at our address—right address, wrong street. The man lived in an attic apartment of a house with a deep front yard similar to ours. It was late and in his inebriated condition he thought he was home. To further complicate matters, our front lock was broken. Mistakenly thinking he opened the door with his key, he let himself in and passed out on the attic floor. The police officers kicked him several times to wake him up. It took so long for the man to respond, they thought he was dead. False alarm.

Chapter 12

Charm School

We were fighting a losing battle against the clock. According to Dr. O'Connor, Dad had less than four hours left to live. Growing more frantic with each passing moment, I pleaded with every hospital employee I could find to page the staff psychiatrist. They all shrugged their shoulders and said the same thing, "I'm sorry, but he doesn't come on duty for a few more hours. There is nothing I can do."

Just as I thought all hope was gone, a cute blonde-haired, blue-eyed medical student came on duty in the triage unit. Patty spotted him from a mile away. She smiled and whispered, "I've got this."

Gifted with an uncanny ability to charm people to do whatever she wills, Patty can walk into a room, focus in on her prey, and make her unsuspecting target instant putty in her hands. If I am the sweet one in the family, Patty is definitely the sweet talker. It is amazing to watch her in action.

Standing at five-foot two-inches tall, Patty sauntered up to the front desk like she was a six-foot tall lingerie model. She said seductively, "Hi, there." Then she flipped back her shoulder-length, dishwater-blonde hair, lit up her million-dollar smile, and went in for the kill.

Their eyes locked and the medical student barely squeaked out "Um...Hi!" before the papers he was carrying went flying up into the air. He cleared his throat and asked, "Can I help you?"

"Yes, please. It's a matter of life and death. My father needs an operation to save his life, but is refusing to authorize the surgery. The only way we can save him is by having him deemed mentally incompetent. Can you please page the staff psychiatrist to go to his room immediately?" Patty implored, as she batted her big hazel-green eyes at him.

"I would be happy to assist you. What room is your father in?"

I am so glad Patty was with me. I do not think I could have gotten anyone to respond as quickly as she did. It was a long shot, but it was our last chance to save Dad from his terminal stubbornness.

What You Crave
(Broken Dreams and Sprained Ankles)

Mom desperately wanted to earn money of her own. When she confided in us that she was interested in working again, Patty and I offered to watch Kathy for her. It was years since Mom held a job, and she found it difficult to join the workforce again. She had little experience and was thrilled when White Castle hired her as a cashier. For a fast food restaurant, they had excellent benefits, plus she received a discount on hamburgers, so my sisters and I were also thrilled.

The night before Mom was supposed to start her new job, I walked with her to a nearby gas station to purchase a pack of cigarettes. She was so excited about her new job; it was all she could talk about. On our way home, Mom tripped over uneven pavement, fell, and twisted her ankle. She lay on the ground rocking back-and-forth in pain, while I stood helplessly by her side. Once the initial shock wore off, I helped her get up and she slowly limped her way home.

By the time we walked through the front door, Mom's ankle was so badly swollen she could hardly get her shoe off. It was sprained. Heartbroken, she cried all night. The next morning, Mom called her manager and told her the unfortunate news, fully expecting to lose her new job. Luckily, the manager was understanding and allowed Mom to start work after she healed.

Mom was only able to work for a couple of months before she learned the cancer spread, and she required further treatment.

I Don't Want You to Die

It was a long, bad day. I plopped my school books down by the front door and made my way toward the kitchen for a well-deserved afterschool snack. The midday sun streamed in through the windows casting a warm glow on the sink full of dishes waiting for me. I took a deep breath and sighed audibly, "Hi, Mom."

"Mary, I need you to help out more around the house with the chores," Mom said, with a twinge of urgency in her voice. It was becoming increasingly more difficult for her to do everyday tasks.

The cancer was consuming her. Her jaw locked, she could barely open her mouth and tumors blocked her throat. Even swallowing water took tremendous effort and caused unimaginable anguish.

Since I was the oldest, it felt like the weight of the world always fell upon my shoulders. "What about Patty and Kathy? Why can't they help out more? Why do I have to do everything?" I whined.

We were not even talking about it—the unspoken fear that plagued me ever since the night I overheard Mom telling Dad she was diagnosed with a precancerous condition. I was afraid if I verbalized my fears, they might come true. I could not bear the thought of losing Mom. I loved her so much.

Mom instinctively grabbed me and held me tight.

We both cried and I blurted out, "I don't want you to die."

Mom held me even tighter and whispered, "I don't want to die either."

As we stood in the middle of our artificially cheerful yellow kitchen comforting one another, I thought *who will wrap their arms around me and comfort me when I am sad? Who will make me feel safe? Who will love me as much as Mom does, if she dies?*

Then Mom grasped my hands and said, "If anything happens to me, I want you to promise me you'll never hit your sisters. Most important of all, I want you to keep the family together."

"I promise."

Nothing came easy for Mom. She struggled her entire life. Raised by an alcoholic father and mentally ill mother, she survived poverty, a 20+ year bout with alcoholism, and a tenuous marriage to Dad. The pain she endured from the cancer was excruciating. It did not seem fair she was given such a large cross to bear.

Half Pints

The more Mom deteriorated, the less Dad was around. It was simply too hard for him to sit back and watch her waste away in pain. Instead, he chose to escape by frequenting several different neighborhood bars where he drank himself into oblivion each night.

Whenever Dad needed a good laugh, he and Uncle Kenny went to the Midget Club on 63rd and Pulaski. It was owned by a little couple. The husband was one of the original Munchkin soldiers from the movie, *The Wizard of Oz*. The bar's surreal "Alice falling down the rabbit hole" look and feel appealed to Dad's wicked sense of humor. It had a huge painted mural of Munchkin Land behind the lowered bar. The bar stools were only a couple of feet off the ground and the telephone booth was child-height, as were the toilets and urinals in the bathroom.

Dad stepped up to the bar like a cowboy at an old fashion saloon, plopped a couple of dollars down and ordered a drink. After he downed a shot of whiskey, he asked the bartender for a refill and change for the jukebox. He took a quarter, placed it into the slot and snickered as he made his selection, "Short People," by Randy Newman. The mechanical motion of the jukebox as it retrieved the record was amplified in the stone silent pub until the needle touched down onto the vinyl and played the first few notes of music. Before Dad knew it he and the other patrons broke out into song, singing those all too funny lyrics, "Short people got no reason. Short people got no reason. Short people got no reason to live."

Veterans Day

It was early morning, Veterans Day, 1981. My sisters and I had the day off from school. Mom was scheduled to have a biopsy the next day. I was grateful we had a three-day weekend to spend with her before she checked into the hospital. Mom always got overly nervous before each hospital stay and I thought it might help calm her nerves to have us around.

Ever since Mom got sick, she slept on the couch in the living room. From my bedroom, I could hear her mumbling something. The mumbling grew louder and more intense. I quietly peered into the living room to sneak a peek.

Mom was jogging in a tight circle and chanting me and my sister's names over and over again, "Mary, Patty, Kathy, Mary, Patty, Kathy, Mary, Patty, Kathy." Even though she made eye contact with me and appeared to recognize me, Mom kept jogging in circles and repeating our names louder and louder, "Mary, Patty, Kathy, Mary, Patty, Kathy."

It was spooky.

"What, Mom?" I asked.

"Mary, Patty, Kathy, Mary, Patty, Kathy"

"What, Mom? What is it?"

"Mary, Patty, Kathy, Mary, Patty, Kathy"

"What's wrong with her?" Kathy asked.

"I don't know Kathy. Mom, please snap out of it. Patty, Kathy, and I are all here. Everything is going to be all right. You had a bad dream or something."

"Mary, Patty, Kathy, Mary, Patty, Kathy," Mom repeated louder and louder, as she jogged around in tight circles with her fists clenched.

"Dad! Dad, wake up! There is something wrong with Mom!" Patty yelled.

Dad jumped out of bed and started barking orders, "Patty and Kathy, go back to bed. Mary, help me get your mother downstairs."

I did not want my sisters to see Mom like this. As Dad and I took Mom downstairs, she went into a mad tirade. She yelled profanities at us and flailed her arms wildly. It was a struggle to get her down each step. Considering how little Mom was able to eat and drink, she was unbelievably strong. Thankfully, Dad and I managed to get Mom into the basement and onto one of the recliners in Dad's den in the kitchen.

Dad and I both knew Mom needed to go to the hospital. The problem was we could not afford the ambulance ride. There was no way Dad could drive Mom alone to the hospital in her current state. She might grab the wheel or get out of the car while it was moving. Dad had no choice but to call Mom's brother-in-law John to help.

The instant Mom realized Dad called John, she went totally ballistic. Overcome by a Tourettes syndrome-like madness, Mom fought bitterly with us and screamed bloody murder, interspersed with sailor-like vulgarities. No matter what we did, we could not calm her down.

John lived about a half hour away.

"It's okay Mom. Everything is going to be all right. Dad and Uncle John are going to get you help, but you have to keep it together. Please, Mom, do it for your daughters. We need and love you very much."

I continued talking, something I excelled at being a teenage girl. With every word I spoke, Mom became more coherent. By the time John arrived, she was relaxed and cooperative. Mom did not utter a single word as Dad and John walked her, arm-in-arm, to the car, and then drove her to the hospital.

At the hospital, the emergency room doctor informed Dad Mom was suffering from malnutrition, and was severely dehydrated.

As a result, her electrolytes were off balance, thus causing her agitation and confusion. Due to her inability to swallow, she was surviving on a diet of Seven-Up and Jell-O.

Mom remembered everything that happened and told Dad how proud of me she was. I sincerely hoped she be spared any memory of the "nightmare like" incident.

Jaw Breakers

Once the doctors operated on Mom, the cancer spread like wildfire. Before long, it metastasized in her jawbone. Her oncologist urged her to have part of her jaw removed to prevent the cancer from spreading further. Unable to fathom living like what she perceived as a "sideshow freak", Mom flat-out refused to have the surgery.

To help ease her mind, Mom's doctor arranged for her to meet with one of his male patients whose jaw was removed recently and was adjusting well. Mr. Johnson and his wife came to visit Mom while she was at the hospital. He spoke with an electronic device which he held up against his throat. His speech was slow and sounded robot-like. Horrified at the prospect of her possible fate, Mom could barely utter a word.

Unfortunately, Mr. Johnson's words of encouragement fell onto deaf ears. All Mom could think about was how deformed his face looked without his jaw. In her mind's eye, he resembled a jellyfish. Tears streamed down Mom's face as she sat upright in her hospital bed, consumed with fear. If she did not have the operation, she faced certain death. If she did have the operation, she faced living with a devastating facial deformity with no guarantee such a monumental sacrifice would save or even prolong her life.

Mom was so distracted by Mr. Johnson's looks when she went to thank him and his wife for coming to visit her, she inadvertently said, "Thank you, Mr. Jellyfish." Freudian slip. Mom was mortified. She immediately corrected herself and apologized profusely to Mr. and Mrs. Johnson, who graciously assured her that her *faux pas* went unnoticed.

The Day the Snowman Came Crashing Down

Every day Mom took three buses to Northwestern Memorial Hospital to receive her radiation treatments, and then took three more buses to get back home. She did it all alone and never once complained. The radiation treatments took a lot out of her and made her very weak.

Old man winter arrived in Chicago with a fury, blanketing the city in a layer of pure white snow. Mom was due home any minute. The snow was coming down pretty hard outside and was perfect for packing. I thought it might be nice to surprise Mom by shoveling the sidewalk for her and making a friendly snowman to greet her as she came up the front walk.

Mom's friend from AA and her two sons came to visit and were waiting for her in the house. I let Blacky out to frolic in the snow while I built Mom's snowman. He ran in circles around me like a maniac while I rolled three snowballs across the front lawn forming the head and body of the snowman.

Patty came home as I was placing the finishing touches on Mom's snowman. The next thing I knew, I was pelted with a snowball. At first I ignored Patty's childish game, but, when the next five snowballs came whizzing by, I could no longer stand idly by. The snowball fight soon escalated into an unhealthy exchange. In order to avoid fist fighting in front of our company, I ran up to the bathroom and tried to collect myself.

A few minutes later, I went back outside to shovel the sidewalk for Mom and witnessed Patty stomping all over the snowman I made. I was absolutely furious. All the good snow was ruined and there was not enough time left to build another one. So instead of coming home to a welcoming snowman, Mom came home to a stomped-on pile of snow, an un-shoveled walkway, and Patty and me arguing, *again.*

Chapter 13

Like Sand Through the Hour Glass, So Are the Days of Our Lives

Whenever I am presented with a potentially tragic event in my life, I always prepare myself for the worst and hope for the best.

Waiting for the staff psychiatrist to arrive was unbearable. My mind ran rampant as I prepared for the possibility of losing Dad. Before long, I found myself planning his funeral. The details flooded my every thought. From the music to the photographs to the words said at his eulogy.

The playlist, selections from Dad's "Music Day" favorites, included The Beatles, Roy Orbison, Pink Floyd, Billy Joel, The Electric Light Orchestra and Meatloaf. And for the pièce de résistance, Frank Sinatra singing, "I Did it My Way."

No one photo captures Dad's wild personality better than a Polaroid Kathy once took of Dad. His eyes are crossed, his hair is messed up and is standing on end, both of his middle fingers are extended, and he has an absolutely wicked smile on his face. My sisters and I would prominently display it near the casket for all to see, it is classic Ronnie and screams, "Fuck You World!"

For Dad's eulogy, I thought it would be appropriate to recite a few Ronnie-isms, talk about Dad's likes and dislikes and tell stories reminiscent of his infamous escapades.

Even if the staff psychiatrist deems Dad unfit, we are so close to the sand running out of the twelve-hour hourglass given to us by the emergency room doctor, there is little hope of Dad surviving the surgery. I am convinced we are fighting a losing battle, despite our gallant efforts.

Band of Gold

One day, I noticed Mom was no longer wearing her wedding ring. When I confronted her about it, she confessed, "I took it to a pawn shop the other day and exchanged it for something I've always wanted." Seeing the look of disappointment on my face, she added, "I discussed it with your father beforehand and he said, 'It's your ring. Do with it as you please. I do not care if you sell it'. So I did."

Mom used the money she got from selling her wedding ring

to purchase a black leather jacket and matching boots.

I know it was only a band of gold, but it had so much more meaning than that to me. I vividly recall the pattern it had. Dad could not afford to buy Mom a real diamond ring, but he did manage to scrounge up enough money to purchase her a 14 carat solid gold wedding band. It was a yellow gold 1960's modern styled ring with engraved flecks in it that mimicked diamond starbursts all around it.

If that ring was a symbol of their love, and Dad did not care if Mom sold it, and Mom did not have any sentimental attachment to it, did that mean my parents did not love one another? What else was I to think? It was not hard to fathom, considering all the horrible fights my parents had over the years, the terrible things they said to each other, and the numerous times they broke up. And when my parents did get back together, they always blamed my sisters and me for their reconciliation saying they stayed together for the "kids' sake."

Experimental Chemotherapy

When three different operations and six weeks of radiation failed to stop the progression of Mom's cancer, her oncologist offered a glimmer of hope. A clinical study was being conducted of an experimental chemotherapy Mom qualified for. Brutally honest, he explained the chemotherapy would not save her life; however, it might prolong it.

Mom was a science geek, a side of her personality she rarely revealed, except during episodes of Carl Sagan's *Cosmos*, or when she and Dad watched Mutual of Omaha's *Wild Kingdom*. Since Mom planned on leaving her body to science anyway, she volunteered to be a participant.

Though we tried not to let it, the experimental chemotherapy raised our hopes. Maybe, just maybe, a miracle would occur, and Mom would be okay after all.

Shrink-e-dink

Chemotherapy made Mom very ill. She lost one hundred pounds in a couple of month's time. Whenever someone commented about Mom's weight loss, she made a sound like a balloon deflating and demonstrated with her hands how her breasts shrunk. Then she smiled and shrugged her shoulders.

The doctors and nurses joked with Mom and said, "Look how much weight you lost. You can wear an itsy bitsy teeny weenie yellow polka dot bikini now."

When Aunty Shirley came for a visit and witnessed Mom's dramatic weight loss for the first time she responded, "Wow, Pat. You've lost so much weight. You look so good."

"Yeah, this isn't how I wanted to lose it."

Mom looked like the incredible shrinking woman to me. It did not seem possible her sudden weight loss was the least bit healthy or helping keep her strength up to fight the cancer which continued to wage war against her.

Warm Beer

I came home early from school and caught Mom drinking a warm beer. The remainder of the six-pack was on the floor next to the couch where she slept. A knot formed in the pit of my stomach. I did not know how to react. Part of me was crushed Mom was drinking alcohol again. Even though she only drank a few sips at a time and did not consume enough to get drunk, it was like she was betraying a promise she once made to us. Part of me was convinced it was another sign she was going to die. Even Mom's sobriety did not matter to her any longer. If she was going to die, she wanted to die happy. Mom wanted one last beer, so she had one.

With all the suffering she was going through, who was I to deny her anything that brought her joy?

Last Time Home

We all grew accustomed to the sound of Mom getting sick in the middle of the night. It became second nature to us, like my sister Patty talking in her sleep, or Dad snoring. Mom once told me she wanted to die peacefully in her sleep. I often found myself watching her intently during the night to see if she was still breathing. In a selfish way, it comforted me to hear her vomiting. It meant she was still alive.

It was early the morning of July 5, 1982, the summer before my sophomore year in high school. We went to Aunt Evelyn's house the day before to celebrate Independence Day, and Mom came with us. She was too ill to attend several previous family functions, and it meant a great deal to have her there, especially since she was scheduled to have surgery the next day. Her doctors planned to remove as much of the tumor as possible to unlock her jaw and permit her to open her mouth again.

I was reluctant to disturb Mom when I heard her getting sick. She did not like us to interrupt her or to ask her if she was okay, because she wasn't. Besides, she did not like us to worry, but this time was different.

Sensing something was wrong, I asked, "Mom, are you okay?" There was a dead silence that lasted for five devastating seconds, followed by a weak, frightened, "No!"

Shaking uncontrollably, I slowly rose from my bed, and saw Mom's hunched over shadow quivering on the front room floor. As I drew near, the bathroom light blinded me. All I could make out was a frail silhouette in a halo of bright dancing light. Then suddenly, brutally, as my eyes focused in, I saw Mom covered with blood. She was throwing up blood, lots of blood. The bathroom sink was full of it. The green and blue muumuu she was wearing was drenched with it. The couch in the living room where she slept was soaked with it. It looked like a vicious murder scene. Blood was everywhere.

For Mom's sake, I had to remain calm. I had to call for Dad without sounding afraid. I took a deep breath, and "D-d-dad!" trembled from my lips in an urgent, frightened tone. "Dad, we have to take Mom to the hospital," sounded much less scared, but just as urgent.

I cannot remember which one of my sisters called for the ambulance. I vaguely remember Dad's reaction. All I can remember is how calm Mom was. How at peace she was. She kept giving me the same loving look she gave me when I tried on my eighth grade graduation dress. I am sure it was the same look.

"Come on, Mom. Let's get you cleaned up. You can't go looking like this," I said. I quickly dashed into my bedroom, and grabbed an old goldenrod-colored T-shirt and a pair of brown corduroys for her to wear. None of Mom's clothes fit her anymore. She weighed ninety-six pounds. The entire time I helped Mom dress she kept giving me that look. Chaos was blurring around us, but she was as calm as the eye of a storm. The peace she radiated infected me with the touch of her hand. I felt as if everything would be all right. Mom comforted me in her time of need.

The sirens grew louder with each heartbeat and were suddenly silenced by the screeching of brakes. Red lights flashed across the bricks of our neighbors' homes, and streamed in through our front window and across the living room. The ambulance finally arrived.

Dad rushed down the front steps and met the paramedics mid way. As he explained Mom's condition to them, Dad's voice echoed against the buildings. One of the paramedics upon seeing Mom, gasped and said, "Oh, my God." It was not necessarily what he said, it was the way he said it. A lightning bolt of fear struck my heart. "Please God, don't let her die," I prayed.

From the top of our porch, I watched as they rushed Mom to the ambulance. She looked up at me and simply waved goodbye.

I Don't Want Them to See Me Like This

Although Mom was in the hospital for quite a while, she begged Dad not to bring me or my sisters to visit her. She did not want our last memories of her being on her deathbed in a hospital hooked up to a bunch of scary machines. She preferred us to remember her like she was before the cancer.

Against Mom's wishes, Aunt Evelyn took me to the hospital, because she knew how much Mom and I needed to see one another. Mom was upset for about the first five seconds. Once I stepped toward her and got close enough to hold her hand, she was elated. I wanted desperately to hug her, but I couldn't. She had several monitors attached to her arms and chest, an IV in her arm, and a clear tube with oxygen below her nose.

I stood at the side of her bed, holding her hand, and said, "I am sorry, Mom. I couldn't stay away. I miss you so much. I don't care that you are in the hospital and are hooked up to all these machines. It honestly doesn't bother me. I love you, Mom."

We did not stay long. The last thing Evelyn and I wanted to do was upset her. I leaned over, gently kissed Mom on her cheek, and we left.

Chapter 14

Amazing Grace

    The faint sound of gospel music and soulful voices softly echoed down the corridor as I nervously paced back in forth in front of Dad's room waiting for the staff psychiatrist to arrive. Uncle Bob put his arm around my shoulder and asked, "Mary, would you like to pray with me?"

    Bob has been a born again Christian ever since his son Bobby died of an aneurism at the age of 22. He preaches twice a week, every week, to the prisoners at Cook County Jail. On his way to preach, Bob always stops by Dad's house to check-in on him and Grandma Velesovsky. During his brief visits, Dad teases Bob, calling him a "Holy Roller" and refers to the Bible as the "Book of Lies." Then, as Bob leaves Dad shouts, "Be sure to give my regards to God."

    Since I figured Dad needed all the help he could get, I agreed to pray with Bob. I did not know Cook County Hospital even had a chapel. As we entered the sanctuary, I was taken aback by the beautifully carved pews and pulpit. It looked as if they built a hospital around a sweet little church in the middle of the city. Several African-American women of various shapes and sizes sat in the front row with their hymnals open. They were wearing vibrant multi-colored blouses that looked like stained glass. One of the women led the prayer.

    Bob and I sat down in a pew and bowed our heads in prayer. I prayed to God to save Dad's life and asked him to give Dad an epiphany.

    "Dear God, Please help my father, for he knows not what he does. He is a stubborn man. A very stubborn misguided man, but he needs your help. Please spare his life and save him from himself. I know he probably doesn't deserve it, but his family needs and loves him very much. Despite his many faults, he is a good man. Please don't take him away from us, not yet. Amen."

    After the prayer, the women invited us to join them in song. We were instructed to open our hymnals to "Amazing Grace." I only knew one gospel song at the time and "Amazing Grace" was it. It also happens to be Bob's favorite. As we sang those old familiar lyrics, I began to tear up. My fears of losing Dad slowly faded away with each word we sang, and I felt a ray of hope fill me. I started to think Dad might pull through.

When I heard the fat lady sing in the front row, I chuckled and envisioned Dad saying to me, "It ain't over until the fat lady sings, kid."

Obsessive Compulsive Crank Callers from Hell

Mom was in the hospital. Dad left us home alone while he drowned his sorrows at the bar. It was a quiet rainy afternoon. That is, until we were barraged with dozens of crank telephone calls from Cassandra, a girl I went to high school with.

Cassandra and her two younger brothers, Marvin and Doug, were bored. If an idle mind is the devils workshop, then Cassandra's mind was the devil's playground. I have to admit it was funny the first couple of times she and her brothers called us but it got to be annoying after a while. The moment we hung up the telephone, it rang again. As a matter of fact, we received so many calls from them; I grabbed a sheet of loose leaf paper and a pen and recorded them. I kept tallies going for toilet flushes, farts, burps, heavy breathing, hang-ups, strange noises, various swear words, and one-liners. My sisters and I logged over one hundred and fifty telephone calls from my deranged classmate and her little brothers.

The telephone rang non-stop. I was tempted to take it off the hook and put an end to their afternoon of fun, but I couldn't in case the hospital tried to reach us. I was fuming mad.

The next time the telephone rang, I yelled, "Listen, you sick fucks, stop calling here. My mother is very sick and I have to keep this line open in case the hospital calls." Then I hung up. One minute later the telephone rang again. This time Patty answered. She was about to give whoever was on the other line a piece of her mind, until she realized it was the hospital calling.

Mom was unable to speak. She missed my sisters and me terribly and wanted to hear our voices. After Patty and I hung up on Mom several times, she flagged down a nurse and asked her to relay the following hand written message to us; "Your mother wants you to know she loves and misses you. Since she is unable to speak, she will tap the telephone—once for yes and twice for no. Okay?"

"Okay. Thank you." Patty said then she handed the telephone

to me. I was in a panic. *Oh, my God, Mom busted me swearing on the telephone.* I thought to myself.

"Mom, I am so sorry. I didn't know it was you calling. I love you." I blurted out.

Mom assumed we thought she was an obscene phone caller and we did not get in trouble for swearing or hanging up on her.

Surprise

My friend Dee Dee threw a surprise birthday party for me five days before my fifteenth birthday.

We went shopping together the day before at a local department store. I window shopped because I did not have any money to purchase anything. Dee Dee paid close attention to all the items I showed an interest in. I guess my mind was elsewhere, because I never noticed her placing every single item I looked at into her shopping cart. When she got home she placed everything she purchased in a box, wrapped it with colorful paper and gave it to me as a present at my birthday party. It was the sweetest, most thoughtful thing anyone has ever done for me.

I was at the party for about half an hour when Dad and my sisters came to pick me up. Dad received word from the hospital Mom probably would not make it through the night.

Say Goodbye

We piled into Dad's car and headed over to Northwestern Memorial Hospital. As the Chicago skyline drew closer, my anxiety became unbearable. We drove up and down the streets near the hospital frantically looking for an open parking space. Every minute we spent searching was another precious moment wasted. It took nearly forty-five minutes before we found a parking spot—which is one of the reasons Dad seldom visited Mom.

We hurriedly walked six city blocks in the sweltering summer heat to the hospital. The insufferable humidity made us all sweat profusely. After we made our way through the old-fashioned brass revolving door, my sisters and I ran across the heavily patterned kelly-green rug to the elevator. Even though Patty and I got there first, we let Kathy press the elevator button.

The elevator took forever to arrive. We waited impatiently

while the antiquated floor indicator painstakingly counted down to the lobby, floor by floor. A cool breeze blew directly on me from the vent above, which felt amazing—at first. Five minutes later, however, the cold air sent chills up and down my sweat-soaked spine. As the elevator's ornate Victorian cherry and brass trimmed doors crept slowly open, Dad, my sisters, and I dashed in. The elevator doors closed shut, Kathy pushed the button to Mom's floor, and my mind began to race.

It was all so surreal. Dad's words hung over me like a looming black cloud. One minute I was at my birthday party; the next I was about to say goodbye to my mother—forever. This was not the first time we were told Mom would not make it through the night. She was in the hospital for a month and a half and always pulled through before. What changed?

At Mom's request, my sisters and I were purposely kept in the dark about her condition. I am certain it was her way of protecting us. She did not want us to worry. Dad reluctantly revealed to us the cancer spread again. Mom had another tumor—this one was in her brain. The doctors were unable to treat the tumor because it was surrounded by an infection. None of the antibiotics were working, so Mom only had a few hours left to live.

Those thoughts, however, quickly dissipated when we arrived on Mom's floor. I did not know how to act or what to feel. I was in shock. The severity of the situation did not sink in when it occurred to me Mom did not see me since I got my braces off. I could not wait to show off my new smile to her. Significant events like getting my braces off would never be the same without being able to share them with Mom. How would anything ever have meaning in my life again?

When we reached Mom's hospital room, her sisters were at her bedside. I stood outside the room, hesitant to enter at first. After a few moments, I mustered up enough courage to walk in and was overcome by the brilliant sunlight which filled the room. Mom could no longer speak. She communicated through a series of nods, taps, and the pen and yellow legal pad she kept next to her bed.

When I spoke to Mom, it was not a goodbye. No words of wisdom were shared with me. No regrets, no worries, no last wishes. It was a light conversational exchange. In retrospect, there are so many things I wish I had said to her.

I visited with Mom briefly then Dad announced it was time

for us to go. I kissed Mom goodbye, told her I loved her, and waited in the hallway for Dad. Dad said his goodbyes and then had a brief exchange with Mom's sisters. From the hallway, my sisters and I watched as Mom waved goodbye.

Unable to sleep, I spent the night lying on the living room floor watching television with the telephone by my side. A local station broadcast a computerized lineup that looped and played popular music, provided news and weather updates, as well as zodiac fortunes and movie trivia. It broke the silence of the night and provided relief from my raging thoughts and rampant emotions.

About five o'clock in the morning, as I drifted to sleep, the telephone rang. It was Aunt Evelyn, and she asked to speak to Dad. From the tone of her voice, I immediately knew why she was calling. Grief-stricken, tears flooded my eyes, and I trembled from my head to my toes.

"Dad, Aunty Evy is on the phone." I cried. Then I paused momentarily, handed the telephone to Dad and mumbled, "M-mom …died."

I was not ready to lose her.

"It's too soon! It's too soon!" I screamed in disbelief.

Mom got her wish. She often told me she wanted to die peacefully in her sleep, and she did. Shortly after we left the hospital, Mom lapsed into a coma and died. Her sisters were with her to the bitter end. I regret not being with Mom when she died. Oh, how I wish I was there for her.

August 17, 1982

That eve I could not sleep,
Awaiting the call long I dread.
How hard I did weep,
When I learned you were dead.
Unrelenting feelings of guilt,
Relieved you were no longer in pain.
Struck down by the harsh reality,
Our lives would never be the same.
Heavy does my chest feel,
From the sorrow left in your wake.
An open wound never to heal,
Oh, how my heart does break.

Robbed, cheated, how we did suffer,
Left to go on without our mother.
Taken too soon by cruelest of fate,
That ripped you away from us this date.
'Twas a beautiful sunny day,
We laid you down to rest.
Your love reached out to warm us,
Surely you did mourn us,
Those cold final days.

The Wake

Mom's wake was held at a funeral home down the street from my high school. It was a rectangular, mint-green building with a white marble relief sculpture of a tree on the front facade. The window to the right of the main entrance had an aluminum framed sign with Mom's name, PATRICIA VELESOVSKY, spelled out in white plastic letters on a black background.

The funeral home was packed with relatives and friends when I arrived. Even though it was summer, several of the teachers from Patty and Kathy's elementary school stopped by to pay their respects. Many of Mom and Dad's friends and neighbors from the old neighborhood also attended the wake, including Mom's childhood friend, Peggy. Mom told us many stories about her, and it was an honor to finally meet her.

As I stepped in to the viewing room, I was drawn to the beautiful fragrant flowers that lined either side of Mom's casket. The sweet smell of roses, carnations, and lilies permeated the room. Mom's body was lying peacefully in the coffin, and she looked as if she were sleeping. She was wearing a powder-blue dress and a black wig her sisters purchased for her. I kept waiting for Mom to wake up and say it was all a big mistake. But she never did.

The funeral director took me aside and asked me to keep a close eye on Mom's body and to notify him immediately if there were any signs of decay. The chemotherapy Mom was given before she died counteracted the effects of the embalming process and caused rapid decomposition. To help prevent this, the funeral director set the air-conditioning in the room at 65 degrees. The cold only intensified the numbness I felt.

Dad was missing in action for the majority of the wake.

Overcome with grief, he dealt with Mom's death the only way he knew how—by getting comfortably numb at the pub across the street from the funeral home.

Death and funeral parlors give Patty the heebie-jeebies. She could not bring herself to enter the room where Mom was laid out, so she sat on a couch in the lobby. After much urging from family and friends, Patty slipped into the rear of the viewing room and sat quietly in the back row.

Kathy turned eight years old about a month before Mom died. She was running around the funeral home with our cousins and playing "it" with her friends, oblivious as to why we were there. I did not see the harm in letting her enjoy the last few moments of a normal childhood. How do you explain to an eight-year-old her mother is never coming home again? It saddened me Kathy was too young to remember what Mom was like before she got sick.

Not the Sharpest Pencil

My friend Jason and his friend Kevin stopped by after Mom's wake to see how I was doing. They knew what block I lived on, but had no clue which house I lived in. They went door to door and asked, "Does Mary Velesovsky live here?" until one of my neighbors directed them to my house.

Touched they came to visit, I invited Jason and Kevin into the basement. Technically we were not allowed to have any friends over, but Dad was at the bar. What he did not know could not hurt me. Kathy and I were chatting with Jason when we noticed Kevin cranking the arm of the pencil sharpener which was mounted to the side of the wooden shelves in the basement. He cupped his hand along the side of his mouth and spoke into the pencil sharpener in a spooky voice, "Patty, I see you. I know what you're doing. Boo!"

Jason, Kathy, and I looked at Kevin like he was crazy.

"What are you doing?" I asked.

"Dude, I'm messing with your sister Patty on the intercom."

Kevin was a pothead who acted perfectly normal when he was high as a kite and totally air-brained when he was sober. I cannot explain it other than to say, "Just say no." Some people need every last brain cell they have.

Chapter 15

Crazy for Loving You

It took the staff psychiatrist, Dr. Ashok, over an hour to arrive. A very distinguished looking gentleman, he stood 5' 8"tall, had short black hair with flecks of silver and spoke with an Indian accent. Before proceeding with his psychological assessment, he consulted briefly with Dad's team of doctors. After the consultation, Dr. Ashok took my sisters and me aside and explained there was little chance he was going to find Dad incompetent. Dad was fully aware of what was going on; he knew his name and what day it was. Although Dr. Ashok agreed to speak to Dad as a courtesy to us, he warned us not to get our hopes up.

"Good morning, Mr. Velesovsky. I am the staff psychiatrist here at Cook County Hospital."

Dad shook his hand firmly and responded, "Damn glad to meet you. I'm the pope."

And then the door closed shut.

We could not hear the conversation that went on between Dad and Dr. Ashok after that. Time ticked by very slowly while we waited for the doctor to complete his assessment. However, what felt like an eternity, did not take but five minutes. Dr. Ashok exited Dad's room looking like he was about to deliver bad news.

"I am sorry...," he said then paused.

My heart sank. "Oh, no," I thought.

"...but your father obviously cannot make this decision for himself. I will sign the papers allowing his family to make this decision for him."

"Oh, thank you, doctor. You have no idea what a relief this is. Thank you so much," I cried as tears of joy streamed down my face.

"Now all we need is Mr. Velesovsky's wife to sign the papers authorizing the surgery."

"Our mother died a long time ago."

"Well then, I guess one of his children will have to sign."

"I'll do it. He'll probably hate me for it, but I'll sign."

Tears poured from my eyes and my hands trembled as I signed the photocopied hospital forms. I felt pangs of guilt, knowing

Dad was being his typical, comedic self, and Dr. Ashok mistook Dad's smart-ass remarks for the truth—but we were running out of time. With every moment wasted, the doctors would have to amputate more of Dad's leg. It was less than three hours to "D-time".

After I signed the papers, I handed them back to Dr. Ashok and asked, "How long before we can get my father into surgery?"

"The next available time in surgery is ten o'clock, and it will take about an hour to prep him. They should start prepping him right away."

The Funeral

I did not have anything remotely appropriate to wear to Mom's funeral. Aunt Evelyn generously offered to take me shopping for a dress. I felt bad taking her money, so I chose the least expensive frock I could find. Since it was the end of the summer, the only dresses on sale were sundresses. Instead of wearing traditional black to Mom's funeral, I opted for a bright yellow sleeveless sundress with a large orange, lime-green and white floral pattern.

Adding insult to injury, I got my hair cut at a nearby department store. Unfortunately, I was too distraught to pay attention to what the beautician was doing. The result was as close to a pixie as you can get. It looked as if I went through a chop shop. I had no hair left to hide behind. Nothing was going right.

I got dressed and did the best I could with my hair. When I stepped into the closet to grab my dress shoes, I came across the teal dress Mom wore to Cousin Sandy's wedding. It dawned on me Mom would never wear it again. I hugged the dress and started to cry. A faint hint of Mom's scent was still present. It took everything I had to finish getting ready for Mom's funeral.

The day Mom died it was gloomy and raining. It was as if the heavens themselves were saddened by her passing. It was a beautiful sunny day when we laid Mom to rest. Her Mass was held at St. Bruno's Catholic Church, only a couple of blocks away from the funeral home. The sun streamed in through the stained glass windows of the church and warmed my bare shoulders. I felt completely exposed in my painfully short hair and bright yellow sundress. All I wanted to do was to fade into the background like camouflage. Tried as I might to put up a brave stoic front, I completely fell apart.

The church service made Mom's death all too real for me. Church made it official. Mom was never coming home. We were never going to see her again. She was finally out of pain—and not just from the cancer. The pain of life was behind her now. I felt such relief at her passing, I felt incredibly guilty. I did not want Mom to die, but I did not want for her to suffer, either. Tears poured out of my eyes.

How were we going to live without her?

Humble Heirlooms

Mom left few tangible things in this world when she died. She rarely purchased anything new for herself. Our closet, aka our back door, was empty, except for a few wire hangers, Mom's winter coat, and her teal polyester dress. The two pairs of shoes Mom owned; her everyday shoes and a pair of dress shoes were placed next to each other on the closet floor. In my parents' bedroom, Mom shared a dresser with Dad. Her clothes were stacked neatly in the second drawer from the bottom. The bottom drawer contained her personal items.

The only jewelry Mom owned was her gold wedding band, which she pawned before she died, and the gold-plated necklace with matching clip-on earrings she wore to her niece's wedding. The necklace had a square white enamel pendant with a gold butterfly on it.

Other than a few scattered pictures, the only real evidence of Mom's existence is her birth certificate, her three daughters, and the few memories we hold of her.

After Mom died, Dad cleaned out her dresser drawers and closet, took her handful of clothes and shoes, and threw them away. My sisters and I were allowed to keep one thing each from Mom's bottom drawer. To be honest, there was not much to choose from. I kept Mom's old red cigarette case which contained a couple of her brass sobriety medallions from Alcoholics Anonymous. Each medallion has on the front a triangle with the words "To thine own self be true" in the middle surrounded by the words recovery, unity, and service and the Serenity Prayer on the back.

Denial is More Than a River in Egypt

The facade of normalcy I so desperately tried to project began to crumble soon after Mom died. Until then, I was a straight-A student, and school was my haven. I guess it was part of my denial there was anything wrong at home. It became harder and harder for me to keep up this image as time went by.

Denial is more than lying to yourself and everyone around you. It forces you to store all the hurt and pain deep down inside your soul. It's deceptive in its comfort, and gradually, bit by bit, you begin to believe it yourself. You are normal, and there is nothing wrong at home, when, in actuality, you are reeling with pain, unable to ask for help, and terrified someone might find out the truth and break up what is left of your family.

Holloween

It was an eerie, lonely Halloween. The dancing candlelight of the jack-o-lantern my sisters and I carved scarcely illuminated the darkness that consumed the living room. The mystery and exuberance of life eroded away and lost all meaning for me after Mom died.

Disillusioned and lost, I rebelled against what I considered the plasticness of teenager-dom. The numerous cliques at school and the infinite fakeness that surrounded me completely repulsed me. Tired of living a lie and carrying the burden of denial, I was no longer able to mask the pain I felt inside. Anguish was bursting out of my pores, whilst the masquerade cruelly lived on.

The pagan ritual of dressing up for Halloween became a bitter reminder for me. People pretending to be someone they were not, haunted my every thought.

For solace, I read the letters from friends and boyfriends I collected since the seventh grade—letters that used to make me laugh and bring me comfort. I thought they were all lies—every last one of them. I questioned whether anyone ever genuinely liked me or meant anything they ever wrote or said to me.

I took the jack-o-lantern up to the attic along with a book of matches and my collection of letters. I read each letter one last time. Then I tore them up, placed the pieces inside the pumpkin, and watched them burn. Burning the letters did not provide any relief or the cleansing feeling I hoped for. All it did was erase any written proof against the crushing melancholy that was eating me up inside.

Time Travel

Patty and I were dating brothers. They were from New York, spoke with a Brooklyn accent and were easy-on-the-eyes. I was dating Anthony, the second-born, cigarette/pot-smoking troublemaker, while Patty was dating Dominic, the youngest, athlete/honor student. I guess opposites do attract. Just kidding!

Anthony was grounded—*again*. Unable to leave his block, he asked me to come to his house and keep him company. It was late, almost curfew, and I was afraid to go by myself. Since Kathy was spending the night at a friend's house, I asked Patty to join me. Besides, I figured if Patty came with she was less likely to squeal on me if she was out past curfew also.

Even though we did not expect Dad home for hours, Patty and I concocted a backup plan just in case he arrived earlier than anticipated. We set every clock in the house back two hours, so we could stay out until midnight. That way if Dad happened to come home to check on us before we returned, he would think it was still before curfew.

Anthony and Dominic lived six blocks away. We hopped on our bikes and peddled out to their house as fast as we could. Neither one of us wanted to miss a word Anthony said. It was rare to find someone who helped us forget about our troubles for a while.

Anthony always had something funny to say. He was very animated and used his hands when he spoke. I often joked while we were dating if you tied his hands up, he would be unable to speak. Patty and I were having such a good time; we did not notice how late it was. It was almost midnight by the time we left. Not wanting to push our luck, we high-tailed it back home. As we approached our block, I saw Dad waiting for us on the corner. He had his arms crossed and was angrily tapping his right foot on the sidewalk. I whispered "Uh oh." then hit the brakes like a guilty driver caught in a speed trap.

"Hi, Dad. What's up?"

"The next time you two fuck heads try to set the clocks back, you ought to check to see if I am wearing a watch first. Now, get in the goddamn house. You're both grounded."

Then he chuckled, beaming with pride that we even attempted to do something so devious.

Needless to say, our experiment with time travel went horribly wrong. Who would have guessed Dad was sober enough to check the clocks in the house against his watch? I did not see that one coming.

Contradiction Addiction

Despite our sparse, humble surroundings, Patty, Kathy, and I yearned to bring our friends home. Whenever we asked for Dad's permission he said, "No. Absolutely not. Look at this pigsty. If you want your friends over, you'll have to clean the house first. And I mean clean. Understand?"

Patty, Kathy, and I spent hours cleaning the house, yet it never met Dad's high standards. We swept, mopped, dusted, and vacuumed. We cleaned our rooms, made our beds, threw the garbage away, washed the dishes, did the laundry and disinfected the bathroom. Heck we even scrubbed the walls. After weeks of bleaching every surface in the house, Dad officially gave us his "Seal of Approval." We were so excited we immediately asked him if we could invite our friends over.

Dad's response: "No. Absolutely not. Look at this place. It is spotless. You can't have your friends over here. They'll wreck the joint."

We often heard from Dad, "Don't do as I do. Do as I say." *Say what?*

Chapter 16

Who Stole My Leg

Dad was in surgery for hours. The waiting room near the surgery wing was much smaller and slightly nicer than the main waiting room in the hospital lobby, but, there were no magazines, and the room no longer had a television. All that remained were a couple of empty magazine racks and the broken television stand where a television once stood. We all sat silently wondering if Dad would survive. It was awful. No one ever contacted us to let us know how Dad's surgery was progressing.

Then, instead of expecting the worst and preparing for a life without Dad, I thought of scenarios in which Dad survived the surgery, got a false leg, and learned to walk again. How would Dad react? What would he say? What would he do?

I envisioned Dad's first day home from the hospital. My husband, sisters, nephew, nieces, and I are all gather around Dad on his daybed. Always the prankster, Dad looks up at us with that shit-eating grin of his, hides his false leg, and says to my nephew, "David, where did my leg go?"

New Year's Eve 1982

It was New Year's Eve 1982, the first holiday season since Mom died and the warmest I can remember in the Chicago area. The temperature reached sixty degrees. It was a beautiful night. I thought the unseasonably warm weather was a sign from Mom letting us know no matter how cold and dark things got, her love would always be there to warm us.

After Mom died, the rules of the house were seldom followed or became non-existent all together since Dad was rarely home to enforced them. Dad gave my sisters and me free reign. His motto was, "So long as you tell me where you are going, and what you are doing, you don't have a curfew, but the first time you lie to me, we've got a problem."

My friend Valerie and I spent the night at her boyfriend Nick's house. Nick's parents were visiting family in Greece for a month, and his older brother, Alex and sister, Donna threw an absolutely fabulous New Year's Eve party while their parents were away. I made certain I told Dad all about the party before I left.

It was an interesting evening to say the least. My boyfriend, Anthony drank too much and passed out on the living room floor. I had fun hanging out with Donna and her best friend Elaina, despite my sleeping Romeo. Elaina thought it was shameful my date fell asleep on me before midnight and decided to give him what she referred to as a "wakeup call." Tiptoeing into the kitchen, she took a tray full of ice cubes from the freezer, unzipped Anthony's jeans with her sinfully long crimson nails, and dumped the entire tray of ice into his Calvin Klein designer underwear. Then she zipped his pants back up while Donna held Anthony's hands behind his back. Anthony went from peacefully sleeping to hysterically screaming, "My dick is cold! My dick is cold!"

Everyone laughed as Anthony frantically tried to escape from Donna and Elaina's wicked grasp. Luckily, he broke free and saved his family jewels before they became permanently frostbitten.

The next day when I came home Dad was drunk and absolutely furious. We got into a huge argument over me staying out all night, even though I specifically told him who I was with, where I was going, and what I was doing before I left for the party. Dad ripped the telephone out of the wall and threw it at me. Fortunately, I ducked in the nick of time, and the telephone went crashing into the wall behind me. When Dad lunged toward me, I escaped out the kitchen door, and ran back to Nick's house for the cleanup party.

When I returned home the next morning it looked like someone dropped a bomb on the kitchen. The refrigerator and stove were knocked over, and their contents were scattered all over the floor. The table was flipped upside down and chair fragments were everywhere. Dad walked in behind me, stood in bewilderment at the door as he assessed the damage, and asked, "What the hell happened here?"

"Well, Dad, by the looks of things, it appears you were a bit angry last night."

"Better the furniture than you, kid. Hey, how was the party?"

She Stole My Diet Pills

Patty became obsessed with her weight after Mom died. It was her way of controlling something in our otherwise completely out of control lives. I worried about her. She starved herself, exercised for hours at a time, and became extraordinarily thin.

Early one afternoon, before Patty came home from school, I snuck into her room to take back a cassette tape she "borrowed" from me without asking. That's when I discovered them—diet pills. They were lying out in the open on top of her dresser. I could not, in good conscience, sit back and do nothing. If Dad found out Patty was taking diet pills, he would kill her for sure. If I threw them out, Patty, no doubt, would dig them out of the garbage. So I hid her diet pills in my room where I thought she would never find them. Quietly protecting her, I never acknowledged taking them, nor did I reveal I knew her secret.

Instead of destroying them, I held onto Patty's diet pills as evidence just in case I needed Dad to intervene. It was a great plan, until my suspicious sister went snooping in my room a few days later. She ransacked my room and tore apart everything I owned, looking for those damn diet pills. Patty suspected me right from the start but dared not confront me for fear I was not the one who took them.

When I got home from work, I found my room in shambles and instantly knew who was to blame. Before I could react, Patty rushed into my room blind with anger—like a mad WWE wrestler—and a terrible brawl ensued. Dad returned home from the bar at the height of our battle. When Patty realized Dad was home, she pushed me onto my bed and raced downstairs to tell him about my thievery. Not wanting her to rat on me, I ran after her in hot pursuit.

"Dad, Mary stole my diet pills!" Patty yelled as Dad walked through the front door.

"Mary is this true? You stole from your own sister? From now on, keep your hands off your sister's shit! What the hell is the matter with you?" I was dumbstruck as Dad reprimanded me. Then Patty's words hit him like a delayed thunderclap following a lightning strike. Furious, he turned toward Patty and shouted, "She stole you're what?"

Grabbing Patty by her shirt, he lifted her up off the ground, slammed her up against the kitchen wall, and bellowed, "Are you fucking nuts? Look at you. You don't need to take that shit." The look on Patty's face was priceless. She thought she finally got me, Ms. Goodie-two-shoes, in trouble. Oh, boy was she in for a reality check.

Dad let go of Patty, tossed a twenty-dollar bill at me and shouted, "Here's twenty bucks. Take your sister to Brighton (a family restaurant three blocks from our house) and feed this kid."

Sobering Solitaire

My Cousin Deanna came to live with us about a year after Mom died. We did not have much, but Deanna had no place left to go. She was struggling with an addiction to a powerful hallucinogenic called PCP (more commonly known on the street as Angel Dust). They say you have to hit rock bottom before you can turn your life around. I was certain this was Deanna's rock bottom.

Still beautiful, despite the various battle scars she acquired during her drug career, Deanna's platinum-blonde hair and piercing blue eyes stood out amongst her numerous track-marks, scrapes, and bruises. When people questioned why Dad was taking in his drug-addicted niece, he said, "You never turn away family, no matter how fucked up they are."

During the time Deanna stayed with us, she and I became very close. She was the older sister I never had. We stayed up late talking in my room, and she poured her heart out to me. When Deanna cried, I gently wrapped my arms around her petite, frail frame, and tried to console her. She was so painfully thin I felt every bone in her rib cage.

Dad had only one rule in order for Deanna to stay with us. She did not have to pay rent, cook, or clean. Nor did she have to chip in for food or utilities. All she needed to do was stay clean and sober. Deanna's solution to this little dilemma was she either did not come home for a few days (until she sobered up), or she opted to get drunk instead. Obviously, Dad approved of drinking alcohol, and she was over twenty-one. Deanna drank straight Bacardi like it was water. She could down a fifth within seconds.

Late one night, I was awakened by someone knocking loudly at the basement door. Dad was three sheets to the wind and happily passed out on the living room floor. I peeked outside to see who it was and, to my dismay, I saw a plainclothes police officer standing in our entryway. His hair was slicked back and he was wearing a pair of navy slacks, a button front shirt and a shoulder holster with his service revolver in plain sight. Quickly tiptoeing downstairs, I opened the basement door.

"Sorry to disturb you so late, miss. I am a narcotics officer with the Chicago Police Department. Your cousin Deanna was helping us with a drug sting this evening and was slipped some Tic (a potent form of Angel Dust). She'll be fine once it wears off, but I'm afraid she is a little out of it right now. Can I bring her in? I promise I'll be quiet. There's no need to wake your entire family."

Quickly contemplating my next move, I thought, *in Dad's eyes we have two strikes here. Deanna is high—strike one. A police officer is standing at the front door—strike two. If Dad wakes up and sees a police officer dragging his niece home in a drug-induced stupor, we most definitely have strike three.*

"We can't bring her upstairs. My father would be furious." I nervously blurted out. Then I paused briefly, regained my composure, and asked, "Um. Can you help me bring her into the kitchen instead?"

"No problem. I'll be right back."

The officer returned with Deanna draped over his right shoulder like a rag doll. I lead him to the kitchen where, under my direction, he propped Deanna up precariously on a chair between the table and the wall.

"Are you sure she'll be okay here?"

"Positive. Thank you for looking out for Deanna and for getting her home safe and sound. I really appreciate it."

"You're welcome. It's the least I could do, given she was trying to help us and all." Then he wished me good night and left.

Quietly shutting the door behind him, I scurried back to the kitchen and pondered the best way to get Deanna upstairs and into bed without waking anyone. Placing her arm around my neck, I foolishly attempted to carry Deanna upstairs by myself, but I only got as far as the kitchen door. For someone who weighed less than ninety pounds soaking wet, Deanna's dead weight might as well have been three hundred pounds. Sprawled out on the kitchen floor like a car crash victim, she was totally unresponsive. I tried waking her up by prying open her eyes, but they were bloodshot and dilated. Her beautiful blue irises looked as if they were floating in a pool of blood.

"Please wake up, Deanna. I need your help. I can't carry you upstairs alone," I pleaded.

Smacking her in the face and flicking ice-cold water at her did not make her flinch or even elicit one response. No matter what I did, I could not wake her. Clearly, Deanna was not going to make it upstairs on her own, and I certainly could not carry her. What was I going to do?

I thought all hope was lost until I noticed a deck of playing cards sitting on the kitchen table. I dragged Deanna over to the table, propped her back up on the chair and placed her head and arms on the table. Then I dealt the cards as if she were playing solitaire. To make it look good, I played a couple of rounds. Next, I took a cigarette and a lighter from Deanna's purse. I lit the cigarette, took a few puffs without inhaling, placed it in an ashtray off to the side, and let it burn. Then I took a glass from the cabinet, filled it halfway with pop, and positioned it on the table, out of Deanna's reach, so she did not accidentally knock it over.

When I was done I took a few steps back to admire my handy work and thought, *"It's perfect. Deanna fell asleep playing cards. Yeah, Dad will buy that."*

Pleased as punch with myself, I looked up at the clock and noticed it was three o'clock in the morning. I crept back upstairs and went back to bed. Fifteen minutes later, I heard a big crashing thud. Jolted awake, I sat quietly in bed trying to ascertain if anyone else was awakened by the noise. Not a creature was stirring.

I tip-toed back downstairs and found Deanna passed out on the floor. She did not even wake herself up. Exhausted, I placed her back into the chair and went back to bed. Less than half an hour later, I heard another thunderous boom.

I ran downstairs and whispered as loudly as I could into Deanna's ear, "Deanna I can't keep propping you back up into this chair. You have to help me out here. Please, wake up. Please." Tears of pure frustration streamed down my face as I did my best to put Deanna back into position. Fearful of what might happen to her if she were to wind up back on the streets, I wanted to preserve a safe, drug-free place for her to live with family who loved and cared for her.

It was nearly four o'clock in the morning when I crawled back into bed. I had Analytical Geometry exam first thing in the morning I could not afford to miss. I fell asleep before my head hit the pillow. The next thing I remember, Patty was yelling at the top of her lungs, "Hey, wake up! You'll be late for school!"

When I opened my eyes and saw how bright and sunny it was, I practically jumped out of bed. It was 7:15 a.m. and class started in half an hour. Frantically, I ran downstairs to see if Deanna was positioned properly at the table *and she was gone*. I could hardly believe my eyes. I darted back upstairs and there she was, sound asleep in the living room.

Dumbfounded, I got dressed and ran to school, the whole time wondering how the heck Deanna got upstairs. Did Dad find her lying on the kitchen floor and carry her up to the living room? I could not bear the thought. When I got home from school, I asked Deanna if she remembered what happened the night before.

She said, "I must have fallen asleep playing cards, because I woke up at the kitchen table in the middle of a game of solitaire. I put out the cigarette I was smoking, placed the glass of pop I was drinking in the sink, and went to bed."

Out You Two Pixies Go - Through the Door or Out the Window

It was a cold, rainy December afternoon back in the days of the "Great War," (the years after Mom's death when Patty and I were still in high school)—a war in which many battles were fought, no spoils won, nor victors did prevail. The temperature outside plunged as the gloomy gray skies turned into night, transforming the rain into an icy slush.

Patty and I were heavily engaged in hand-to-hand combat. I was doing my homework and wearing a T-shirt and shorts when the skirmish broke out. During the height of the battle, Patty pushed me out the back door and locked me out of the house. She barricaded the rest of the doors before I could reach them. I had no choice but to walk in bare feet during an ice storm, four city blocks to the neighborhood bar where Dad was watching a football game. Unfortunately, Dad left the bar before I arrived, and I was forced to walk back home—humiliated, freezing cold and soaking wet.

Dad was still missing in action when I returned home. Absolutely furious, I marched up the back steps, pounded on the back door, and demanded, "Let me in!"

"Fuck you!" Patty yelled then gave me the middle finger as she walked away.

Infuriated, I busted my way through the backdoor window with the heel of my right hand. Knocking shards of broken glass onto the floor, I unlocked the door, and let myself in. Although I received several nasty cuts, it was worth it to get back in the house.

As I meandered into the living room still numb from the cold, I saw Dad strolling up the front walk through the window.

"Dad's home. Oooooo you are in trouble now!" Patty shouted.

"I'm in trouble? You're the one who locked me out of the damn house!"

"No one told you to break the fucking window!"

Dad heard Patty and me bickering. He immediately did a one hundred eighty degree turn, got into his car, and drove back to the bar.

"Now look what you did. Dad's leaving!" Patty and I shouted in unison.

Dad told us numerous times, "I am not a goddamn police officer. If you two want to beat the shit out of each other, go right ahead. I, sure as shit, ain't going to stick around to watch you do it."

Sitting in for Santa

My best friend Allison's family gathered annually at her parents' house for a big Christmas celebration. Each year they decorated the tree, and one of Allison's brothers-in-law dressed up as Santa for the children. This year they asked me to do it. The kids were getting older, and they did not want the children to recognize them. I honestly did not think I could pull it off, but I gave it a whirl.

Allison helped me get dressed by shoving a mound of pillows into a Santa costume. "We've got to fatten you up, Mary. A skinny Santa will not do," she said with a smile.

"That's enough. I could fall down a flight of stairs right now and not feel a thing."

The bright white wig and fluffy red hat sat half-cocked on my head. The beard and mustache kept falling off my face. Allison and I were laughing so hard I could barely get out, "Ho. Ho. Ho. Merry Christmas!" as I walked into the living room and greeted the children who were eagerly awaiting Santa's arrival.

The most pathetic Santa I have ever seen, I pulled the piano bench out, and plopped my padded butt down. One by one, the kids sat on my lap, and I hollered jollily, "What do you want for Christmas?"

The children all spouted their little heart's desires to me. A couple of the older boys giggled as they sat on my lap, knowing full well I was an imposter, but they did not give me away. I smiled at them and gave them a wink.

I did not enjoy the holidays since Mom died. She always made them magical—even when we did not have any money. I had a lot of fun and it helped rekindle my love for the season.

When I returned back to the party wearing my street clothes, the kids could not wait to tell me how I missed Santa.

I sure did.

Footprints in the Sand

During the years of the Great War, Patty and I used any ammunition we could get our hands on to hurt one another. Nothing was sacred. Nothing was spared. I remember the following argument, not because of what we were arguing about—that was inconsequential—but rather for the cost of our pettiness and the total disregard for one another's feelings and belongings.

We were supposed to be sisters. We were supposed to stick up for one another. We were supposed to love and respect each other. We were not meant to be mortal enemies, but that is exactly what we became. We were completely different people when we were around each another. We were possessed—blinded by the ugly misdirected hatred which built up as a result of our serious lack of parental supervision. We would not treat anyone else in the entire world the way we treated one another. Peace treaties and cease fires were rare. Nothing was off-limits. If something had sentimental value, it became either a spoil of war (stolen) or a casualty of war (destroyed).

My parents gave me a music box for my eighth-grade graduation. It was a framed mirror with the poem "Footprints in the Sand" etched in it. When the key was wound, a magnetic dove swirled around the poem while the song "On Eagle's Wings" played softly. It meant a great deal to me, and I played it whenever I felt sad. It was one of the last gifts I received from Mom before she died.

In the heat of the moment, Patty stormed into my bedroom and destroyed my music box. Overcome by rage, I ran into Patty's bedroom and found the one thing my sister possessed that held equal sentimental value. It was a smoky-purple colored jewelry box that was made of plastic. It had a hinged-top with two bottom drawers. I grabbed it off her shelf, threw it on the floor, and jumped on it until it was in a million little pieces.

After the anger subsided, we both mourned our respective losses. Demolishing my sister's jewelry box did not make me feel any better. As a matter a fact, it made me feel worse. What the hell was happening to me? This was not who I was. It got to the point I did not recognize myself.

Chapter 17

Hi Dad

Dad was only out of surgery for a couple of hours when he was moved from intensive care to a recovery room. I took it as a good sign. Patty, Kathy, and I were at Dad's bedside, anxiously waiting for him to open his eyes. We all wanted to be present the moment he awoke.

Laboring to breathe from his mouth, Dad looked like he just finished running a marathon. He desperately gasped for air, exposing every rib in his chest. His stomach inflated like a hot air balloon and deflated as he exhaled. His mouth was dry, his lips were cracked, and he repeatedly struggled to moisten them with his tongue. The doctor informed us Dad's breathing would be like this for days. He was literally fighting for his life. The infection was still present in his body, even though they amputated his leg. Dad was receiving antibiotics intravenously and would for some time as part of his recovery.

Every so often, Dad opened his eyes and attempted to focus in on the three of us. Whenever he did, my sisters and I said in unison, "Hi, Dad!"

When Dad realized it was us, he closed his eyes in disgust. I think we were disturbing his beauty rest. It became a bit comical after a while.

Open eyes.
"Hi Dad!"
Look of disgust.
Close eyes.
Open eyes.
"Hi Dad!"
Look of disgust.
Close eyes.

This scenario went on entirely too long. It took a couple of weeks before Dad fully regained consciousness.

Stubborn as a Squirrel

A squirrel got caught in the chain-link fence between our house and our next door neighbor's house, because it refused to let go of the bright green crab apple it held in its mouth. Fearful it had rabies, Dad strictly forbade us from touching it. For two days, we helplessly stood by and watched as the squirrel desperately tried to break free, squealing feverishly, while it banged its head over-and-over again into the chain link fence, too stubborn to let go of that damn apple.

Against Dad's wishes, I took a stick and tried to pry the apple out of the squirrel's mouth, but it only dug its teeth in deeper, unwilling to let go of its prize. The squirrel died the next day—with the apple still in its mouth.

I never noticed the similarities before between the squirrel and Dad *until now*. The only difference is Dad's crab apple is in the shape of a Canadian Club whiskey bottle, and his fence looks an awful lot like the front door of Zosia's tavern.

Black Sheep

Technically, we have more than one black sheep in my family. The one who stands out the most is Uncle Kenny. He has, by far, spent the most time behind bars, has been shot and lived to tell about it, and has been addicted to heroin for most of his adult life.

My earliest memory of Kenny is from a visit to Grandma and Grandpa Velesovsky's flat on 18th Street when he was a teenager. Grandma was complaining to Dad, "Just look at what your brother has done to his bedroom. What will the landlord say?"

Patty and I quickly ran over to see what the hubbub was about. Kenny painted a huge psychedelic florescent mural with a jet-black background on his bedroom walls, which he illuminated with a black light. He was sitting on his bedroom floor with his legs crossed smoking pot from a four-foot-tall orange bong which he told us was filled with Kool-Aid.

The immigrant neighborhood my grandparents lived in changed drastically over the years. By the time Kenny was a teenager, they were one of the few white families left in the neighborhood. When Kenny was in his late teens, he attended a party held at a dance hall near his house and unknowingly danced with a gangbanger's girl friend. Even though Kenny apologized profusely for his error in judgment, the jealous boyfriend went ballistic and threatened, "I'll kill you mother fucker!"

Thinking quickly, Kenny dashed out the back door of the dance hall and ran for his life. The jealous boyfriend, however, saw him fleeing and chased after him. He followed Kenny into the alley and shouted "Hey, Pollock (Kenny's nickname)!"

Kenny turned around, saw the gun, placed his arms in front of his face and pleaded, "Don't shoot!"

The gangbanger pulled the trigger and shot Kenny in the heat of the moment. The bullet shattered the bones in Kenny's left forearm. The doctors removed the bullet and placed several stainless steel screws in the bone to hold it in place. He has a huge scar to this day.

The very first time Kenny tried heroin, he was hooked, and his life was never the same. His heroin addiction quickly grew into an expensive habit. At the height of his addiction, Kenny would do anything for money to buy heroin. Being a family of enablers, we were more than willing to oblige him. Unfortunately, Grandma and Grandpa could only give Kenny so much of their life savings, and Dad was often jobless or broke.

One time Kenny borrowed our Atari game system and all our games. He never returned them to us. Another time, I was on summer vacation and was watching my favorite soap opera. It was cliff hanger Friday, and the villain on *General Hospital* was about to be revealed when Dad and Kenny entered the living room, unplugged the television set, and carted it away. I never saw it again. Dad did not have any money to give Kenny, so he let him sell our Atari and color TV instead. Dad's excuse was, "What could I do? He's hurting, Mary."

Since Kenny was unable to quit and could not hold down a steady job, he did what every other drug addict has done at one time or another—he stole to support his habit. Kenny may be an amazing artist, but he is a terrible thief—which, by the way, is the reason why he has spent so much time in prison.

I was in high school. A couple of friends and I were walking down the street when I spotted Kenny coming up an alley with a shopping cart full of miscellaneous stolen items. He was ripping off people's garages like he was shopping at a department store. When the shopping cart overflowed, Kenny took it to the bar Dad was drinking at to sell the stolen items. One of the patrons looked at Kenny's stash and said, "Hey, I've got a drill just like that. I could always use a spare. I'll buy it." You guessed it. Kenny sold the items he stole back to the man he stole them from.

On one occasion, the police approached Kenny as he stood on a neighbor's porch with a crowbar in his hand. One of the officers asked, "What do you think you're doing?"

Reluctantly, Kenny answered, "I was going to use this crowbar to break into this house."

Back in jail.

Once, Kenny was high and broke into a house while the occupants were still home. The doctor who owned the house bellowed, "Don't move. I am going to call the police."

"You can't see me. I am invisible." Kenny proclaimed.

Then, thinking he was freaking the homeowners out with his invisibility ability, Kenny danced around the room while he held the stolen items in his hand, making them look as if they were magically flying through the air.

Even more time in jail.

Same Bat Time, Same Bat Channel, Part II
The Day Mary Grew Balls

Over two years passed since Mom's death. It was winter. The dry, dusty smell of the heat rushing out of the vent in my bedroom filled the air. I snuggled under the covers with my history book propped up on my chest, trying to study for midterms. I was having a difficult time concentrating. Patty and Dad were fighting again. The muffled sounds of their voices echoed through the vent. Once in a while, I could almost make out what they were saying. I turned my radio on soft enough not to break my concentration but loud enough to drown out their screams.

Their screams grew louder and clearer as their argument intensified. Defiant and unafraid, Patty pushed Dad passed his limit. Blowing his top, Dad cleared the kitchen table with one fell swoop, sending dishes and silverware crashing onto the floor. A few seconds later, a loud thunderous clap rang out, as his fist hit the wall. I turned off the radio. I usually did not get involved in their disputes, but I could not help this agonizing feeling I should go down to the kitchen and stop them before someone got hurt.

Only one thing was holding me back. I was afraid. Paralyzed by fear, I sat on the edge of my bed, in ready position. Kathy burst into the room and begged me to go downstairs, "He's hurting her!"

I could not refuse Kathy's pleas. It was the final straw. I allowed Dad's abusive behavior to rage out of control unchallenged for too long. Someone had to stop him, and this time it was my turn. I grabbed my "lucky" bat and ran downstairs. As I rounded the corner, I saw Dad hitting Patty's head repeatedly against the wall. Standing six-foot tall, he was very threatening and towered over my sister.

Then he grabbed Patty's hair, pulled her face close to his, and bellowed, "You are a worthless, good-for-nothing ingrate. If you don't start listening to me, I'm going to fucking kill you! Do you understand?"

"Leave her alone!" I shouted and held the bat up high to show Dad I meant business.

"You are not going to use that bat, and you know it, kid."

I slammed the bat against the kitchen door jamb as hard as I could and shouted, "I said, leave her alone!"

Calling my bluff, Dad lunged toward me. I swung the bat and narrowly missed his head. With that, Dad let go of Patty. At first, she stood there and gave me an "I am not taking orders from the likes of you" look. Then the reality of the situation hit her and she slowly made her way toward the front door.

"Patty, Kathy, run! Get out of here now!" I yelled holding the bat threateningly at Dad. "Just leave us alone."

The most frightening thing, when Dad was drunk like this, was his eyes. It was as if he was possessed. They were beet-red and bugged out of his head. His irises turned from a serene blue to an evil, glowing green. There was no reasoning with him, no negotiating, and he was completely unpredictable.

Once Dr. Jekyll reared his ugly head, my sisters and I could not stay home that night. We sought refuge elsewhere or we might get hurt—and not always with a fist, either. Dad's words lunged upward into my heart like a dagger. As he ripped the dagger out, my self-esteem and self-worth rushed out like blood from a gaping wound, leaving a scar that would never heal, and damage that could never be undone. A part of me would die.

I took the bat with me and ran like hell. The sober father would never consciously hurt us in this way, but his drunken counterpart most certainly would. Unfortunately, we rarely got to see the sober Dad after Mom died.

Put a Fork in Me, I'm Done

When we were growing up, Patty's demeanor could switch from "happy go lucky" to "just let me kick your ass" in 1.2 seconds. Her temper was almost as unpredictable as Dad's behavior was when he was drunk. At least with Dad, I could usually sense if he was going to be a mostly happy drunk that night, or a frightening keep-your-mouth-shut kind of drunk. With Patty, I was never really sure what set her off.

One particular battle took place in the kitchen—not a safe place for a battle to occur. There are plenty of sharp objects in a kitchen. Patty was digging her nails into my arms, punching me, and pulling my hair while I was doing my best to defend myself.

Here is where my confusion lies. The part of the story I will never understand. Kathy ran into the kitchen and saw the two of us entangled in yet another brawl. Even though I was obviously losing, Kathy assumed, because I was older, I must be hurting Patty. She shouted, "Leave Patty alone!" and came to Patty's defense by yanking my hair out.

As if Patty beating the crap out of me was not enough, we had to go and throw Kathy into the mix. What the hell did I do to deserve this? Why me? After five grueling minutes of this incomprehensible situation, with nails digging, fists flying, and hair pulling, we finally broke apart—panting, red in the face, with fists full of hair.

My gym teacher thought Dad was the one who was beating me. Upon seeing my numerous scratches and bruises, she pulled me into her office once to talk about it. I can count on one hand how many times Dad beat me. Patty and I fighting— well, that was practically an everyday event.

I honestly do not know what I did to set Patty off this time. My not knowing why she was pissed at me pissed her off even more. I could not win. Since I did not have that edge, that instantaneous rage Patty possessed, I never had a chance. The only weapon in my arsenal was words. Saying biting things I knew were not true was the only way I could think of to hurt her back. I deeply regret doing that now. Patty lashed out at me because of the anger and frustration she felt toward our parents. She had unresolved issues with Mom and was angry with Dad for not being there when we needed him, and she transferred her pent-up rage onto me.

Unfortunately, this fight was not over yet. Kathy grabbed the closest weapon she could find—a fork. She threw the fork at me with all her might and yelled, "Stop it! Why do you guys have to fight all the time? I can't take it anymore."

Do you know Kathy threw that fork so hard it landed in my arm? I was battered and bruised, and now I had a fork with all four prongs jabbed into my upper-left arm. It stood there, mocking me. "Oh, my God. I cannot believe you threw a fork at me. Look at this. I'm bleeding."

We all laughed. Then Kathy said, "Well, what the hell are you waiting for? Pull it out."

Same Bat Time, Same Bat Channel, Part III
The Breaking Point

I was sitting in my lovely shit-brown bedroom studying for a U.S. History exam I had the next day. (My friend's family let me tag along with them on a trip to Kings Island amusement part in Cincinnati, Ohio, during spring break. When I returned home, I discovered that Dad painted my bedroom this unbelievably hideous dark brown color in my absence. When I asked Dad why chose to paint my room such a dark color he said, "Well, at least it won't show any dirt". The problem was I could not see the words on the page I was reading, even with the lights turned on in broad daylight.)

Patty was at her boyfriend's house. Cousin Deanna was staying with us and was passed out in the living room, with the television blaring and the stereo turned way up. Kathy was playing in her bedroom, listening to records on her record player. As I adjusted my ears to the barrage of multimedia outside my room, Dad came home belligerently drunk. He was yammering on about our ridiculously high telephone and utility bills. Yelling at the top of his lungs to whoever would listen, Dad went from room-to-room shutting off lights and electrical appliances, and threatening to disconnect the telephone. Deanna, who constantly talked on the telephone, mistakenly thought we had an unlimited call package, and ran our telephone bill up to $250, ten times its normal balance.

"The only time I use the goddamn telephone is to call for

pizza!" Dad shouted, as he stepped into my room.

I was frustrated. Sick and tired of the constant interruptions while I tried to study, I snapped. When I was not at school or studying, I spent all my spare time babysitting a houseful of kids for less than a dollar an hour. I babysat over fifty hours a week that summer in order to earn enough money to pay for my advanced placement tests and senior prom. Dad did not believe in using banks, so, at his insistence, I gave my wages to him to "hold onto" for me. Earlier in the day, I learned Dad spent every penny I ever earned. There was not a red cent left. No doubt I could smell on his breath where he spent the money. I could not take it any longer.

I knew I could not reason with a drunk. I knew better, but I could not help myself. Normally, I could tune out Dad's ranting and raving, but I had had it. How was I ever going to leave this place if I could not study?

I let him have it. Everything I bottled up over the previous couple of years came pouring out. It may have been a low blow, it may have been kicking a man when he was down, but it was truth— every word of it. I let Dad know what a huge injustice I felt he cast upon me. It was very much a "look what an asshole you have been to me" kind of speech.

As anticipated, my disclosure was not well received. I have never seen Dad so angry before. Not only did I push him over the edge—I drop-kicked him over. The rage that ensued can only be compared to someone who is about to commit murder. He was furious with me. Dad lunged toward me with a closed fist and screamed, "Who the hell do you think you're talking to kid? I'll bash your fucking skull in and knock your ass into next week."

Then he knocked over the dresser and tried to hit me with it. I quickly darted out of the way and noticed my Louisville Slugger leaning up against the headboard of my bed but Dad snatched it out of my hands before I could use it to defend myself. I hunched down and placed my hands above my head as he cracked the bat against my back. My Louisville Slugger had a crack in it, and it split in two when it made contact.

The shock of the baseball bat disintegrating in Dad's hands stunned him briefly. I hurdled around the war zone that was once my bedroom and made a beeline for the front door. Dad was hot on my trail and hollered, "Hey, come back here. Wait until I get my hands on you, kid!"

I sprinted out the door and slid down the front stair rail with my hands, never touching a step. My gym shoes splashed hard against the wet pavement when I landed and my heart practically pounded out of my chest as I ran for my life. As I made my way to the end of our walkway, I heard Dad fall down the stairs and land on the next door neighbor's chain-link fence. I kept running and never looked back. Thank God I did.

Fueled by pure rage, Dad got up and ran to his car. His engine revved, and his tires squealed as he drove up-and-down the streets of our neighborhood searching for me. I sprinted three full city blocks to a neighborhood hot dog stand. Since it was a public place I felt I would be safe there—that is if Dad did not find me first. When I reached the parking lot, I heard Dad racing toward me. Panicked, I twisted my ankle on the wet pavement and fell. Oblivious to the pain, I got up and quickly hobbled into the restaurant before Dad found me. I did not realize it at the time, but I sprained my ankle in my haste to get away.

It was late; almost closing time. I could not stay at the hotdog stand, and I could not go to any of my usual safe houses. Allison was getting ready for bed. Dee Dee's parents would not appreciate me coming over this late on a school night. Jason was out with the guys. I had no alternative but to go back home and try to study—if at all possible.

After scouring the neighborhood, unable to find me, Dad returned home. Kathy was about to leave the house when she heard Dad's car pull up. Thinking quickly, she jumped into her bed, pulled the covers over her head, and pretended to be asleep. Moments later, Dad, stinking of cigarettes and alcohol, meandered his way upstairs, and staggered into Kathy's room. Thinking Dad was still angry Kathy shook like a leaf beneath the covers, terrified of his reaction when he didn't find me.

Before Dad uttered a word, he vomited on the floor next to Kathy's bed, wiped his mouth with his shirtsleeve and said, "I am sorry, Kathy. I did not mean to fight with your sister like that. I love you guys. You know that, right?"

Then he gave my little sister a vomit-covered hug and passed out on her bedroom floor.

When I got home, I could not believe my eyes. If it was not nailed down, Dad knocked it over. The house looked like a tornado hit it. During all the commotion, Kathy tried several times to wake

Deanna to help me. Deanna woke up briefly, heard my father and me fighting, and said, "Oh, they're just having a little disagreement, sweetie," and then fell back asleep.

Black and White

Just a black and white photograph with shades of gray,
capturing a two-dimensional moment in time.
Ensuring your memory never fades away,
forever young—life's cruelest crime.
Time cannot erase,
your beauty or your grace.
Nor can it ease the pain I feel,
am I dreaming, is this real?
Regrets of things never to be,
and bittersweet memories.
Serve as a haunting reminder,
of how we should have been kinder
whilst you were here.

Chapter 18

Ill Tidings

I stopped by Dad's house on my way home from the hospital to update Grandma Velesovsky on Dad's condition. It was a chilly March day. As I stepped into the living room, the heat was stifling. Quickly unbuttoning my coat, I tried to strategize the best way to tell Grandma what happened. The living room was flooded with sunlight, and the smell of cigarettes, coffee, and pot roast whiffed through the air. From my vantage point, I could see Grandma was on the telephone in the kitchen. She was in full-panic mode when our eyes made contact.

"Oh, Mary. How is your father?"

"Who's on the phone?" I asked, trying to distract her. Grandma was a notorious worrier, and I did not want to elevate her blood pressure any further.

"It's Kenny. He called collect from jail. Here, fill him in on what happened with your dad," then she whispered as she handed me the telephone, "Keep it short, Mary. This telephone call is costing me a small fortune."

"Hi, Uncle Kenny."

"Hi'ya, Mare. How's your Dad doing?"

As soon as I heard my uncle's voice, guilt-filled tears burst from my eyes. The incessant beeping, letting me know our conversation was being recorded by Illinois Corrections, rang out like Dad's heart monitor, sending me into an emotional tailspin. Even worse than signing the papers for Dad's surgery was trying to explain to his brother the levity of what I did. He and Dad were very close. My update felt more like a confession.

"Dad had an infection in his foot he let go for months. By the time we convinced him to go to the hospital, it was too late. The infection became gangrenous, and he refused to let the doctors remove his leg. Patty convinced the staff psychiatrist to examine Dad; he found him incompetent and allowed me to sign the papers authorizing the surgery."

My heart pounded so hard I could feel it pulse in my neck.

"He's going to be all right. Isn't he?"

"The doctor said, even though they removed his leg, he may

not survive. The infection has spread past his hip. If he does survive, they'll have a hard time fitting him for a prosthetic leg, because they had to remove so much."

The words gutted me, and spilled out like acid—bitter and painful. Any brief feelings of relief I felt that Dad was finally getting the help he needed, were soon replaced by an enormous wall of regret. What have I done? Dad will never walk again, and he will never forgive me. Never.

Just Let Me Die

Mom's death shook me like a violent earthquake and destroyed the foundation of our family. The aftershocks rocked the core of my very being. Consumed by her death, it was as if a part of me died with her. I developed a morbid curiosity with death. Wanting desperately to be with Mom, I became comfortable with the thought of suicide. I even researched it. I convinced myself it was the answer I was looking for.

Then one night I had a dream. Dad, Patty, Kathy, and I were walking along a waterfront. There were boats and a pier. It was a beautiful, warm, sunny day. The sunlight sparkled as it danced upon the surface of the water. Savoring the fresh, clean air, I took a deep breath, and bathed in the warm glow of the sun. As I feasted on the beauty surrounding us, I spotted Mom in the distance. I could hardly believe my eyes. *She's alive! I knew she would never leave us. I knew it couldn't be true. She's alive!*

"Mom! Mom!" I shouted.

Mom turned around, looked toward me, and waved. Then she ran down the pier and dove off it like she was going swimming. My father, sisters, and I ran toward her. I was ahead of the pack. As I approached the end of the pier, I looked at the water below and saw Mom violently thrashing about. She lifted up one finger, then two. Before she could lift up a third finger, I yelled "I won't let you die again!" and jumped into the water to save her.

Mom struggled bitterly with me. I could feel her dragging me under with her, but I was determined not to let her go. With every ounce of energy I had left, I made one last attempt to get us both to the surface. When we broke the threshold of the water, I was overcome with joy and thought, *I did it. I saved her.*

As I pulled Mom's head above the water, I gasped for air.

Mom looked me straight in the eye and said, "Mary, let me die. Please, just let me die."

I could not let go of her until then. From that moment on, the melancholy that consumed me since Mom's death dissipated. I truly believe Mom came to me that night to save me from myself.

Don't Let the Darkness Consume You

Don't be scared, I see it in your eyes,
There is no need to fear the weather,
The sun has set but also must rise,
We can ride out the storm together,
Have faith the light will surely come,
You're not alone, fears—we all have some,
Please hold on a little longer,
Overcoming it will make you stronger,
Be vigilant and no matter what you do,
Don't let the darkness consume you.

Way More Than I Bargained For

Early one brisk Sunday morning, I convinced Dad to take me grocery shopping at the Way Low, a grocery store near our house. Unfortunately, he was still drunk from the night before. An evening of binge drinking and consuming dozens of White Castle hamburgers gave him incredibly bad gas.

"Hark, I hear an angel calling," Dad said then he let one rip.

I knew I was asking for trouble, shopping with Dad while he was still under the influence, but we were literally out of everything. Besides, I needed to go grocery shopping before he spent whatever money he had left at the bar.

Dad has always prided himself on the potency of his flatulence, but he is particularly proud of his killer stealth ability. By the time we pulled into the parking lot, I was anxious to get our little shopping excursion over with. I hurried into the store and grabbed a cart. From the corner of my eye, I saw Dad prancing about ahead of me. As I placed a couple of boxes of cereal into the cart, he appeared next to me, giggling wildly and whispered, "Watch-this-kid!"

Then he skipped toward a poor, unsuspecting Hispanic woman in the fruit and vegetable section. Her shiny black hair was twisted up into a bun, and she was wearing her Sunday-best beneath a chocolate-brown wool coat with a *faux*-fur collar. The brown pumps she wore echoed in the practically empty store. In her hands, she held a large cantaloupe, which she checked for freshness by squeezing and shaking it.

As the woman put the cantaloupe up to her nose to smell it, Dad stood next to her, stuck his ass out in her general direction, and detonated a lethal silencer. Then he scurried away, laughing uncontrollably. The look on the woman's face was priceless. One whiff of Dad's potent brand and she grimaced like she bit into a sour dill pickle. The woman immediately placed the cantaloupe back on the display stand, with her nose facing the opposite direction. Then she grabbed her purse, left her cart, and quickly ran toward the exit. Dad was in tears. I did not know whether to laugh or reprimand him.

Purple Rein

As a rule, Dad never kept any alcohol at home when we were growing up. He preferred to drink at his favorite watering holes instead. During my junior year of high school, however, the owner of one of the bars he went to gave him a bottle of Crown Royal for Christmas. It came in a heavily jeweled, clear-glass bottle which was placed inside a royal-purple velvet bag with a shimmery gold drawstring. It was terribly fancy. Dad only drank it on special occasions and kept it in our kitchen above one of the upper cabinets, out of our reach.

One day, when no one was home, curiosity got the best of me. I climbed up on a dinette chair, uncovered the unique-looking bottle, and took a sip. As the caramel-colored whiskey scorched past my lips, mouth, and tongue, the intense smell flooded my sinuses, made my eyes water, and my stomach churn. Feeling like I drank the dry heat of the Mohave Dessert, I put the bottle down, ran to the kitchen sink, and dowsed the liquid fire in my mouth with cold water from the tap. Much to my dismay, the taste was equivalent to drinking gasoline or battery acid—not that I have ever drank gasoline or battery acid before. Feeling lightheaded, confused, and nauseous, I struggled to understand why my parents drank at all. It was awful. What was the appeal?

Got Milk?

We rarely had friends over. Dad had a rather strict policy against having anyone in the house when he was not present. In other words, we were never allowed to have anyone over. Since Dad was rarely home to enforce this rule, however, we broke it whenever possible.

On one of the few occasions my best friend Allison came to visit our humble abode, Patty and I were barely speaking to one another. We were eating cookies and milk in the kitchen, when Patty and I exchanged a few verbal blows. Sensing I did not want to fight in front of Allison, Patty egged me on by calling me several derogatory names.

Embarrassed, humiliated, and intensely angry—all at the same time, I was unable to ignore the gauntlet Patty laid before me. I grabbed the closest weapon I could find before she exited the room—a large glass of whole milk. Aiming for the back of her head, I flung the glass of milk toward Patty. As the Molotov milk cocktail hit Patty's backside, milk exploded upward into her hair and drenched the back of her shirt. An all-out milk fight ensued, as Patty grabbed the gallon of milk from the table. Allison quickly dashed for cover. Before long, the room was whitewashed with milk, and an occasional cookie crumb tossed in for good measure.

As the tsunami of milk came crashing down, Allison jumped up and screamed, "What are you doing? Sisters don't fight like this, and they certainly don't throw milk at one another, especially in front of company."

Reason was so out of place in our twisted world.

Surely, you must be joking, I thought. "Believe it or not, this is us being on our best behavior. You should see what we are like when we don't have company over." I said laughingly.

Chapter 19

Don't You Make My Brown Eyes Blue

After spending several hours in recovery, Dad was moved to a room on the fourth floor. To be honest, it was more of a ward than a room. It had three-quarter high cinderblock walls, a curtain where the door should be, and was void of any warmth.

Since Dad was vehemently against having his leg removed, we all feared what his reaction would be when he regained consciousness. Kathy made a poster for his hospital room thinking he needed to be reminded of what mattered most. She decorated it with several pictures of her daughter Brittney and it read, "Get Well Soon, Grumpy! We love you!" Kathy hung it on the wall at the foot of Dad's bed so he could wake up to Brittney's sweet face smiling at him.

I truly believe the poster Kathy made is what got Dad through his worst moments in the hospital. Knowing his little Brittney was at home, waiting for him, gave him the will to live.

Music Day

Music Day, a self-proclaimed holiday Dad declared whenever the mood struck him, was celebrated both at home and while cruising around in his car. We listened to loud music and sang our hearts out to The Beatles, Fleetwood Mac, Roy Orbison, ELO, Billy Joel, and Pink Floyd. Fun and completely participatory, it was one of the few ways my family bonded besides telling family stories and playing catch.

Our family anthem, "Paradise by the Dashboard Light," by Meatloaf, is a Music Day favorite and is traditionally played at most family gatherings. A great song, it ends with the line, "So now I'm praying for the end of time, to hurry up and arrive. 'Cause if I got to spend another minute with you, I don't think I can really survive. I'd never break my promise or forget my vows, but only God knows what I'm going through right now. So I'm praying for the end of time, so I can end my time with you."

I could not help but wonder if Dad felt the same way about his obligation to his three daughters after Mom died. Dealing with that much estrogen while under the influence of alcohol often proved to be a lethal mix.

Zosia, This Is Zosia

On any given day or night, Dad could be found patronizing Zosia's Tavern, near our house. It was owned by an old Polish woman named Zosia, who looked like Norman Bates' mother from the movie *Psycho*. Dressed in a dirty housedress and ratty pea-green wool sweater, her dingy knee-high tube socks slid down to her ankles and her grubby house slippers scuffed as shuffled across the floor. She seldom bathed and most of her teeth were rotted out of her head. The wig she wore was badly tangled, because she rarely washed or removed it. She even wore it to sleep. It was half-cocked on her head, and her long, thin, silver hair peeked out from underneath it as if it were gasping for air.

A cantankerous old woman, Zosia managed to scare away most of her regular patrons over the years. What was once a grand neighborhood bar her parents owned, deteriorated over the years like Zosia's mind. A diamond in the rough, the rich mahogany bar with brass footrests and leather barstools stood out amongst the dirt and clutter. The bar shelves once lined with bottles of top-shelf liquor, the beveled-mirror backsplash and arched stained-glass windows were hidden behind layers of filth and grime.

Zosia was not playing with a full-deck of cards by the time Dad joined her lonely-hearts club band. Her parents and husband long since passed, leaving her to run the bar alone.

Dad liked to patronize her establishment. I think it was the lack of foot traffic that attracted him to it. He could listen to whatever he wanted on the jukebox, watch whatever he wanted on the television, and play pool anytime his heart desired, plus he did not have to put up with the typical drivel like he had to at other places—with the exception of Zosia of course. The booze was old, the service was lousy, and he was often forced to serve himself. The glasses were dirty, the bar was sticky, and the octagon tile floors were filthy, yet Dad spent hours-upon-countless-hours there.

One of Dad's favorite pastimes was teasing Zosia. She made an easy target and did not seem to mind him poking fun at her. Dad telephoned Zosia from the payphone in the back of the bar, imitated her shrill old ladies' voice and said, "Hello, Zosia. This is Zosia. Is

Zosia there?"

"Just a moment, I'll see if she is here," she said falling for it every time. Then she placed the receiver down on the bar and called out, "Zosia, you have a telephone call."

She paused briefly until she realized Dad tricked her yet again. Then she yelled, "Oh, damn it!" and slammed the receiver down in disgust while Dad laughed until he cried.

Pizza Dude How Rude

After Mom died, we ate a lot of pizza. It was cheap eats. With a family-size pizza, our local pizzeria, Just-A-Pizza, threw in free 32 ounce bottle of soda pop, and they delivered. Each time the doorbell rang or someone knocked on the front door, I cringed. Dad got into a really bad habit of ordering a pizza before he left the bar. Then, he stuck around for one more drink, which turned into two, then three—well, you get the picture. Before he knew it, the pizza delivery man was knocking on our front door looking for payment—except my sisters and I did not have any money to give him, and we had no way of reaching Dad, since we did not have a telephone.

One day, the doorbell rang. I opened the door and was greeted by an antsy pizza delivery man. He was carrying a family-size sausage pizza and a bottle of RC Cola. "That'll be $17.50, ma'am," he said.

"Can I help you?"

"You order a pizza?"

"No, but my Dad probably did. He's not home though."

"Can't you pay for it?"

"Nope. I don't have any money. Sorry. I think he's still at Zosia's Tavern. You can try him there."

"Can't you call him?"

"We don't have a phone."

"Oh, I see."

It got to be such a common occurrence several of our regular pizza drivers went to Zosia's Tavern for payment first, before they dropped the pizza off at our house. Unfortunately for us three girls, there was always a new guy to break in.

The Fugitives

Early one evening, Dad and Uncle Kenny came home after a day of drinking and mayhem. They were covered in mud, dripping wet, and panting heavily.

Suspicious, I asked, "What have you two been up to?"

"Shhh!" Dad hissed loudly at me, as he placed his index finger up to his puckered lips. "We're on the run."

"You're what? Why?"

"We were on our way home from Zosia's when we spotted a cop giving a guy a ticket. The cop had his ass sticking out. Honest, Mary, he was begging for it."

"What did you do?"

Dad became very animated and loud.

"I inched over to the right, so Kenny could smack him in the ass, but he missed. So, I went around the block and lightly tapped the cop in the ass with my car, instead. Oh, I wished I could have seen the look on his face," he laughed hysterically, wiping the tears from his eyes.

"That's when the chase began," Kenny said.

"Chase?"

The policeman, quite understandably, did not find the humor in Dad's mischievous prank. He immediately jumped into his squad car in hot pursuit. Luckily, it was dark, and the officer was unable to make out Dad's license plate number. Dad and Kenny drove up and down nearly every side street and alley in our neighborhood avoiding arrest. Flashing lights and screaming sirens filled our otherwise quiet neighborhood while the police hunted for them. They ditched Dad's car and crawled through several back yards to escape capture. It was raining pretty heavily, and they were covered in mud from head-to-toe.

"Dad, you assaulted a police officer!"

"I didn't *assault* him Mary. I *accidentally* bumped into him with my car which caused him to lunge head first onto the lap of the guy he was writing a ticket to."

Dad and Kenny tossed their dirty clothes in the washer. Then they quickly washed up, changed into clean clothes and left, but not before they gave me explicit instructions.

"If the police come to the house while we're gone, tell them you haven't seen us," Dad instructed.

"Yeah. You know nothing. We haven't been home all day. Got it?" Kenny added.

"I got it."

And with that, they were off again, into the night from whence they came—another typical night in the Velesovsky household.

And the Ants Go Marching On

It was early May. Dad and Uncle Kenny were at Zosia's discussing our annual ant problem. Dad concocted yet another brilliant plan to eradicate our residence of this yearly nuisance. It did not involve calling the exterminator or investing in a can of Raid. No, Dad's ingenious idea called for pouring gasoline around the perimeter of our house. He was under the delusion gasoline would eliminate our ant problem once and for all.

Notorious for eavesdropping, Zosia proceeded to ask Dad and Kenny twenty questions after overhearing their discussion. She was very confused.

"Ronnie, how are you going to use gasoline to get rid of the ants without destroying the entire house along with them?" she asked, presuming Dad was going to ignite the gasoline.

Dad got annoyed with her constant interruptions and decided to toy with her.

"Zosia, these ants are so bad they are taking over the house. I came home the other day, and they were carrying the refrigerator out the front door."

Every time Dad and Kenny came to the bar after that, Zosia asked Dad how his ant problem was and Dad told her a different lie, each one more farfetched than the last. Several weeks later, Dad told Zosia, "The ants are still there, but the house burned down to the ground."

Cops & Robbers

Uncle Kenny slept on the floor in the living room along with his girlfriend Cindy and their son, "Little Kenny." My bedroom was next to where my uncle and his family slept. Cindy worked nights at a factory in Cicero while Kenny watched their son. Little Kenny was two years old and still in diapers.

It was late. I overheard my uncle playing with his son. They were playing cops and robbers—except the robbers were the good guys in this psychotic scenario. I could not believe my ears. This poor kid already had the odds stacked against him. Hell, his dad was a heroin addict, and his mom was sixteen when she gave birth to him, for goodness sake. I could not imagine how much damage this little game was causing.

I sat up in my bed and asked accusingly, "Uncle Kenny, what are you doing?"

"I'm playing with my son."

"By pretending the cops are the bad guys?"

"Well, what do you want me to do, lie to the kid?"

Chapter 20

On the Wagon Part II
Social Dis-Tortion

"Good morning. Thank you for calling. This is Mary. How can I assist you today?"

"Hello, is this Mary DeCraene?"

"Yes, it is. May I ask who is calling?"

"Mrs. DeCraene, my name is Lynette Jackson. I am a social worker with Cook County Hospital. You are listed as Ronald Velesovsky's next of kin. Is that correct?"

"Yes, ma'am, I am. Is my father okay?"

"He is as well as can be expected at this point in his recovery."

"Did you say you were a social worker?"

"Yes. It is customary for a social worker to be assigned to cases like your father's, in which an individual has been deemed mentally unfit to make medical decisions for himself. I am your father's case manager. My main role is to assess his needs and coordinate his overall care. The reason I am calling is I need your help determining what kind of help your father requires. Since he has been admitted, he has been unconscious, and I have been unable to interview him."

Mrs. Jackson proceeded to ask me a series of questions about Dad's mental and physical health, as well as questions about his ability to pay for treatment, and what living arrangements he had, if any. After I answered her questions to the best of my ability, she asked if I had any questions for her.

"I have visited my father every day since he was admitted to the hospital. Since his surgery, he has been having hallucinations, and he drifts in-and-out of consciousness. Before my father was hospitalized, he consumed a quart of whiskey and smoked three packs of cigarettes a day. This is the first time he has gone without drinking or smoking in many years. Do you think that might be the reason why?"

"Is he an alcoholic?"

"Yes, he is."

"According to your father's medical file, he is not currently

being treated for DTs (delirium tremens, more commonly known as
alcohol withdrawal) which may account for the issues he appears to
be having."

Mrs. Jackson assured me she would speak to Dad's doctors
and request he be given drugs to counteract the effects of his alcohol
withdrawal.

Dr. Dogdish

Our dog, Blacky, ran away often, but he always came back
the next morning, begging us to let him back in the house. This time
Blacky did not return. My sisters and I were heartbroken.

Whenever Patty, Kathy, and I so much as mentioned how
much we missed Blacky, Dad and Uncle Kenny laughed aloud and
said, "I guess it's time to see Dr. Dogdish again." I assumed they
were joking about Dr. Daudish, our family physician. I was sick
recently, and Dad took me to see Dr. Daudish. He was an older
gentleman with a thick German accent, who worked out of a small
office in Lyons, IL. We visited Dr. Daudish whenever one of us was
ill. He was inexpensive, did not require health insurance, and gave us
free samples so we did not have to pay for a prescription.

It did not take us long to figure out there was a connection
between Dr. Daudish and our missing dog, Blacky. Patty, Kathy, and
I confronted Dad. "What did you do with our dog?" we demanded to
know, as my sisters and I took turns punching Dad in the arm.

"All right. All right. I'll tell you. Uncle Kenny and I took
Blacky for a little ride to North Riverside (a suburb near Dr.
Daudish's office)."

"And then what happened?"

"Then we took him to a park and let him run around. He
seemed to really like it, so we left him there."

"You did what?"

We punched him even harder.

"But we went back there the very next day, because we felt
guilty for leaving him. Didn't we Kenny?"

"We sure did." Kenny said, nodding his head up-and-down in
agreement like a delinquent sidekick.

"Sure enough, we saw Blacky. He was wearing a leash made
out of a rope and was as happy as a pig-in-shit jogging through the
park with some rich broad who was wearing a pink jogging suit."

National Dishonor Society

My senior year of high school I was inducted into National Honor Society. We were given a white satin gown to wear to the ceremony and a beautiful invitation to give to our parents. It was the culmination of twelve years hard work, and I looked forward to sharing it with Dad.

Dad never put any pressure on me to do well in school like my friends parents did. His only requirement was I try my best. Even if I received a failing grade in every class, he would still be proud of me, so long as I gave it my all.

On the day of the induction ceremony, I got ready then took the robe out of its package. It was completely wrinkled. Dad was not home yet, and I only had a few minutes left before I had to leave. I never ironed anything before. Our crappy old iron never fully heated up. I did my best, but the loose rust from the iron discolored my robe and I was wrinkled from head-to-toe.

I waited as long as I could for Dad, but he never showed. I ran to school and made my way towards the auditorium sweating, panting heavily, and on the brink of tears. Arriving in the nick of time, I entered the auditorium and was greeted by rows of my classmates' ecstatic family members who were brimming with pride and snapping pictures.

My fellow inductees looked so polished, confident, and happy. I felt frumpy, insecure, and miserable in my wrinkled, white satin gown with iron-shaped rust stains. Dad never made it to the ceremony. I was the only inductee without my own private cheering section. Yet another one of my accomplishments that went unnoticed.

Who was I working so hard to impress? That is when it became abundantly clear to me. I was doing it for me. If I wanted to break free and stand on my own, it was crucial I do well in school. All my hard work would pay off—someday.

Kiss Me—You Fool

Patty's boyfriend Eddie and his family threw a huge Christmas party. All of our friends were invited. Eddie's mother, Diana, preferred to have her children party at her house so she could keep an eye on them and ensure they did not get into any trouble. I had to work. By the time I arrived, the party was in full swing.

Diana greeted me at the door and handed me a bottle of red wine.

"Come on, dear. You have to catch up. Everyone has a couple of hours on you."

"Oh, I don't know if I should. I am not much of a drinker but thank you," I said and gave the bottle of wine back to her.

"It's easy. You don't even need a glass."

Not wanting to seem impolite, I took a swig of the wine straight from the bottle and immediately grimaced wildly from the taste. Afraid I might get sick if I consumed any more, I handed her back the bottle.

"Thanks for the wine, but I haven't even eaten dinner yet. I don't think it's a good idea to drink wine on an empty stomach."

Diana handed me back the bottle along with a plate full of fried chicken.

"Here, eat this, and then drink up."

Not wanting to offend my hostess or appear rude, I ate a piece of fried chicken and reluctantly drank more wine. Diana grew increasingly impatient with me taking small sips of wine and suggested I chug it instead, so I did. Big mistake.

After I consumed an entire bottle of wine in less than twenty minutes, Diana sent me downstairs to join my friends. The wine made me very dizzy. I sat down on the couch next to my boyfriend, Mirek, and watched the room spin. Mirek was not much of a talker, but he sure liked to kiss. It was a party, after all, so I thought, *why not?* The longer we kissed, the sicker I felt. I excused myself and stumbled to the bathroom.

"Look at her, she's a lightweight!" I heard one of my friends shout as I opened the bathroom door. I was barely able to close the door before I puked into the bathroom sink. Projectile vomit came spewing out of me like a volcano. The sink overflowed with the fried chicken and wine which ran forth from my gut. The room spun violently, as I frantically tried to clear the drain of debris. Obviously concerned, my friends pounded loudly on the bathroom door and asked, "Are you okay?"

I nervously blurted out, "I-I-I'm okay. I-I'll be right out," as I held onto the sink for dear life. Desperately trying not to pass out, I feebly attempted to clean myself up before anyone came storming into the powder room and saw me in my current state of disarray.

The knocks at the door grew louder and the pleas for me to open the door intensified. Then Diana threatened, "If you don't open this door right now, we're going to call the fire department, and have them knock it down."

Alcohol poisoning successfully averted by the mass exodus of my stomach contents, bathroom sink overflowing with puke chunks, reeking of vomit and wine, opening the door, sitting back down on the couch, and trying to continue where I left off with Mirek by slurring, "Kiss me." Priceless.

Busted: From the Frying Pan and Into the Fire

Dad was out drinking. He got tired of my sisters and me constantly interrupting him at his usual haunts and told us he was going somewhere new to get away from us for a while. He needed peace and quiet. We needed supervision and a sense of security.

It was a cold and snowy night. Kathy was anxious for Dad to come home. She needed money for a school fieldtrip the next day. I was broke, and Patty did not have any money, either. We could not find Dad anywhere. Patty and I checked every bar within walking distance of our house. Kathy grew increasingly upset, because we could not find him.

"Don't worry, Kathy. Stay home and finish your homework. Patty and I will find Dad."

Patty, her boyfriend Eddie, and I set out in search of Dad. The wind whipped up and the weather turned from flurries to a full-on whiteout. Traipsing through six-plus-inches of snow, we spotted Eddie's friend Kasey, who was cruising with his friends near Kathy's school. We flagged them down and asked them for a ride.

We climbed into the car before we realized Kasey and his friends were drunk and had open containers of beer in plain sight. I immediately asked Kasey to drop us off at the next corner and thought to myself, *this is great. We're with a couple of drunken teenagers looking for my drunken father. What else could possibly go wrong?*

As the car approached the corner, the guy sitting in the passenger seat rolled down his window, hung his head out, and bellowed the words to the song playing on the radio, while he waved his arms up in the air. Smooth move. A couple of undercover cops witnessed his gallivanting and pulled us over. I was so upset.

It did not take long for the police officers to notice the beer in the car. Everyone was taken to the police station. The guys rode in the back of a paddy wagon, while Patty and I were afforded the honor of riding in the back of the undercover police officer's car. Patty and I tried to explain what happened. I could not help but think our babbling sounded like a poor excuse they probably heard a thousand times before. Despite my doubts, the police officers believed us, especially since Patty, Eddie, and I were obviously the only ones who were sober. However, I think it only made them lecture us all the more.

"What the hell were you thinking? Do you have any idea how lucky you are? You could have been killed or worse. Promise me you'll never get in a car with someone who has been drinking again," they pleaded. If they only knew how many times my sisters and I drove with our father when he was drunk.

The police department contacted everyone's parents. Luckily, we did not have a telephone, and Dad was not home. Not so lucky, however, for the driver of the car, Kasey, who was the son of a Chicago police officer. His father was absolutely furious and made him wait in jail for a couple of hours before he came to pick him up. The detectives let Patty and me off with a warning and released us into Kasey's father's custody.

As it turned out, if we were patient and simply waited at home, Dad eventually would have turned up. I could have studied, and we would have avoided this entire situation altogether.

Cold Shower

In April 1985, the utility company turned our natural gas service off at the street due to lack of payment. As a result, we had no heat, hot water, or gas to cook with. Being a teenage girl, I was rather concerned about my appearance and personal hygiene. Despite the obvious discomfort, I religiously took a cold bath every day (the house we lived in did not have a shower). March went out like a lion and the temperature hovered above freezing at dusk. It was far too cold out to be submerging myself in ice water daily. As a result, I caught a nasty cold.

Dad's parents lived within walking distance of us. After explaining my dilemma to Grandma Velesovsky, she invited me to use her shower any time I needed. I immediately took her up on her offer. The hot water lovingly embraced me and instantly opened my sinuses. It felt so good to be able to breathe again through my nose.

My grandparent's apartment was spotless and I made every effort to be neat and tidy, putting everything I touched back where I found it. While I was getting dressed, I overheard my grandparents arguing in the kitchen.

"Who the fuck is in the bathroom now? I gotta take a piss."

"Mary is in there taking a shower. She'll be out in a minute."

"Bern, I don't want these goddamn kids coming over here whenever they damn well please and leaving a fuckin' mess in the bathroom."

"George, keep your voice down. She'll hear you."

I loved my grandfather, but I had a gut feeling he would not appreciate me using his shower and what he perceived to be as an invasion of his privacy. As a rule, Grandpa did not mind my sisters and me coming to visit, as long as we did not stay long. The truth is he was an impatient old fart who did not have much tolerance for noise, and after all, a man's bathroom is his castle, right?

As much as it hurt my feelings, I understood. We were not his children. We were not his responsibility. We were not his problem. I never asked to use my grandparents' shower again. I only took one warm shower during those long six months. I felt as though I had no place to go, and my sisters and I were all alone in our misery.

The Department of Children and Family Services

Kathy was in fifth grade. Her homeroom teacher pulled her aside after class one day and asked, "Where is your homework?"

Kathy replied rather matter-of-factly, "Oh, my Dad was drunk last night. I didn't do it."

Obviously concerned, her teacher contacted the school counselor. They took Kathy into a private room and asked her what she meant by the comment she made. Kathy told them the truth. She filled them both in on what was happening at home and held nothing back. In response to Kathy's disclosure, the school contacted the Department of Children and Family Services (DCFS). DCFS interviewed Kathy. When Kathy did not deviate from her original statement, agents from DCFS went to our high school and interviewed Patty to verify Kathy's story. Patty denied everything.

Absolutely furious, Patty had a complete meltdown when she got home from school. Poor Kathy. She thought she was doing the right thing, and I could not help but think she was, too. Patty accused Kathy of breaking up our family and getting Dad in trouble.

"Are you completely nuts? Do you know what they will do? They'll put Dad in jail. They will split us up and make us live with people we don't know. You'll never see me or Mary again. Is that what you want?"

Things got sticky once the authorities became aware of Dad's drinking problem. DCFS conducted a formal inquiry and requested an interview with Dad. He was less-than-enthused to be placed under the scrutiny of a government agency. Paranoia quickly set in. We started using the back door to avoid running into anyone from DCFS. Whenever we heard a knock at the front door, we hid, pretended no one was home, and then peeked out the front window to see who it was before we answered the door. With every letter of inquiry we received from the agency, it reopened the wound, and Dad and/or Patty went berserk all over again.

Kathy was crushed. She thought she was getting us the help we needed. I wish I could have stood up to Patty and protected Kathy like an older sister should have—but I was too afraid. What if Patty was right? I promised Mom I would keep the family together.

Chapter 21

Secret Mission

For every good day with Dad at the hospital, we had a bad day. One day when I visited Dad, he was fully aware his leg was amputated. The next day, he was in total denial and lectured me about how all he needed was antibiotics.

Each day it took six doctors and orderlies to hold Dad down while they changed his dressing. Dad particularly disliked one resident, because he refused to give Dad a sedative before he cleaned his wounds. One time, the doctor's face got a bit too close to Dad's fist, and Dad gave him a black eye.

Dan and I visited Dad one Saturday afternoon shortly after his dressing was changed. We heard him swearing loudly from down the hall. When we entered Dad's room, he was out of breath from fighting with the doctors.

"I have an important mission for you Dan!"

Then Dad looked both ways to make certain no one was listening and motioned Dan to lean in close to him like he was going to whisper in his ear.

"Bring—me—a—bat!" He demanded loudly, in a menacing voice.

"What?"

"I said, bring–me—a—bat."

Dad grabbed Dan's shirt, pulled his face up close to his, and said with conviction, "You don't understand. The doctors here are trying to kill me. The next time those bastards try to hold me down to change my bandage I want to be ready for them."

Dad let go of Dan's shirt, slammed his hand down hard onto the railing of his bed, and yelled, "Bam! They won't know what hit 'em! Get the picture?"

Dad already gave one of the residents a black eye. Can you imagine what kind of damage he would inflict if we gave him a bat?

Serfectly Pober

One brisk spring evening, Allison and I went for a ride downtown with Dee Dee and her boyfriend Kasey. We cruised up and down Lake Shore Drive and wound up at the planetarium. Parking near the lake, we sat in the car watching the waves break upon the shore, while we jammed to Lou Reed's "Walk on the Wild Side." Shortly after we arrived, Dee Dee pulled out a bottle of ginger ale she altered earlier with contents from her parent's liquor cabinet. She claimed it was ginger ale with a splash of whiskey. I took one whiff and realized it was whiskey with a splash of ginger ale.

At everyone's insistence, I took a swig and grimaced wildly. I immediately handed the bottle back to Dee Dee and said, "Oh, my god. That is so strong. I can't drink another drop."

Dee Dee wanted me to have fun and insisted I drink more of her twisted cocktail. Kasey threatened to take me home unless I did. Even Allison dared me to try it. I took a large gulp and handed the bottle back to Dee Dee again. It was horribly unpleasant tasting, burned my mouth and throat, and instantly made me nauseous.

"Drink to the top of the label. You can do it," everyone urged.

Falling victim to peer pressure, I took a deep breath and gulped down the tainted concoction until I reached the top of the label. That was the last thing I remember until Kasey dropped Allison and me off at Allison's house. One of my shoes fell off between the curb and the street as I exited the car, and I could not find it. It took a long time for me to make it to Allison's front door, which was literally four feet from the curb.

Allison's family lived on the second floor of a two flat. Allison laughed hysterically as I struggled to negotiate her front steps. I eventually quit trying to walk up them and opted to crawl up them instead. This worked quite well until I reached the top.

Allison tiptoed over to where I was sitting on the landing, cupped her hand on the side of her mouth, as if she was going to whisper, and shouted slowly, "My parents are in the living room watching television. Try to act like you are sober."

Of the hundreds of times I visited Allison, her parents were never in the living room. They were always in the kitchen, their bedroom, or downstairs in the shop they owned. I was utterly ashamed.

"I can't. There is no way. I can't do it. Look at me."

Then I slumped down on the landing in defeat, while Allison begged me to sober up.

"All you have to do is walk past them and into my room. It is ten little steps. They'll never know you've been drinking."

"Allison, I crawled up your stairs. How am I going to make it to your room?"

"You can do anything you set your mind to, Mary."

Before I could protest Allison opened the door and went inside.

"Hello. How was your evening?" Allison's parents asked. Allison blurted out something about going for a ride to the planetarium and darted into her room, leaving me standing in the front doorway, all alone. I avoided eye contact with her parents as I struggled to look sober and walked in slow motion toward Allison's room counting aloud to ten. My long purposeful steps looked about as natural and relaxed as a soldier marching in the Third Reich. The moment my foot made it past the threshold of Allison's room, she slammed the door shut. I took one more step and happily plopped face first onto Allison's bed, which was full of clean clothes and linens.

"Allison, do you think they noticed I was drunk?"

"Not a chance. I told you, you could do it, Mary."

The room was spinning violently, as Allison insisted I partake in the White Castle hamburgers she purchased during our little drunken escapade.

"Come on, Mary. Have a hamburger. They're delicious."

"No thanks. I am not hungry. I think I am going to be sick." Then I let out a sour burp.

Allison kept waving the onion-encrusted hamburgers under my nose like they were smelling salts. Moving my head away, I warned her, "Stop! I am going to be sick." But, she insisted I try to eat something. The more Allison persisted, the sicker I felt. Before I knew it, I threw up all over her bed and rug, like a volcano, until all the toxins I ingested vacated my body.

I awoke the next afternoon on Allison's couch, terribly hung over from the night before and unable to move for fear my head might explode. Desperately wanting to go home and sleep in my own bed, Allison insisted I stay until I rehydrated myself.

Moments later, Allison's sister, brother-in-law, and nephews came to pay a visit. I was beyond humiliated as they piled in one after another. I welcomed them wearing one of Allison's old T-shirts, my hair standing up on end, and reeking of whiskey and vomit from the night before while I sipped ice water from a jelly jar.

Wicked Hot Sonnet

We were studying William Shakespeare in my English Literature class. The teacher asked the class to write a sonnet for homework. Almost everyone in class wrote a love poem. Here is what I wrote:

Fire

Ideas flicker in the mind of man,
Burning images ignite his future,
Through the hazy horizon his thoughts ran,
Death and destruction stand not for the cure,
Curiosity conceals temptation,
Through the evil eyes of hell's son Satan,
Beware of forbidden exploration,
For the apple of Eve has been eaten,
Take heed dear child; touch not Pandora's Box,
Smother those of weak heart and mind with love,
Open not the door to those evil knocks,
Be guided only by faith's light above,
Strike the tongue of the eternal liar,
For man's soul is doomed, he plays with fire.

May I Speak with You After Class?

"Mary, may I speak to you after class?" asked my homeroom teacher, Mr. Kowalski.

"Sure," I said hesitantly.

I had a sneaking suspicion why Mr. Kowalski wanted to talk to me. My grades were slipping. I was working thirty hours a week as a cashier at a department store after school. When I was not working, I babysat for several families in the neighborhood. Dad was getting worse, and our gas was shut off. I will admit it—I may have been a bit distracted in class.

After the bell rang, Mr. Kowalski approached me and asked, "Mary, do you know who I had lunch with yesterday?"

"No."

"Mrs. Meyer *(my Speech teacher)*, Mrs. Piazza *(my Advanced Placement Calculus teacher)* and Mrs. Shaughnessy *(my Marketing teacher)*."

A meeting of the minds as to why my grades were slipping. Oh, no. Here it comes, I thought.

The week before I brought Mrs. Meyer to tears during class. We were supposed to give a speech on a moment that changed our lives. Seriously, how many life changing events does the typical American teenager have? Most of the class discussed things like getting their driver's license, their first job, or falling in love. I had nothing prepared, so I spoke about the first thing that came to mind, Mom's last time home. I totally winged it. No outline, no cue cards. After I finished speaking, I sat back down in my seat, fully expecting to get reprimanded for delivering such an ill-prepared speech.

Mrs. Meyer was sitting in the desk behind me. She liked to get the same perspective as the class while her students were giving their speeches. Plus, she thought it would make us less nervous if she was not right on top of us. Complete silence. *Oh, no. I am in trouble now.* Then, I heard a soft sob and sniffling coming from behind me. I slowly turned around to see my teacher in tears. It took her almost five minutes to regain her composure. As it turns out, Mrs. Meyer loved the speech I gave and was touched by my ability to convey a heart-wrenching story with such detachment. I felt terrible. I did not mean to make her cry.

Between school, work, and home, I simply did not have the time required to dedicate to my A/P Calculus class. I was having trouble keeping up and I feared I may not pass.

Mrs. Piazza recently gave us a take home test. Pressed for time, I took the test with me to a hot dog stand after work to complete while I grabbed a bite to eat. Panic set in shortly after I reviewed the test questions and realized I was completely lost. The owner's son, a senior in college, saw the look of dread on my face and offered his assistance. He helped me understand a few of the concepts I was struggling with and I was able to complete the rest of the test on my own by following the examples in the book. I received a 92% and nearly blew the curve.

Mrs. Shaughnessy moonlighted at a teacher's credit union and asked me if I might be interested in a part-time job. Based on her recommendation, I was hired and was scheduled to start work come mid-May.

"We all took turns bragging about the most amazing student each of us has in class. After a while, it occurred to us we were all talking about the same student—you. I thought you should know how special we think you are."

I politely thanked Mr. Kowalski and rushed to my next class, wiping tears away from my eyes. Funny, I did not feel very special.

The Garden of Evil

Since they were underage, my friend Jason and his buddies found several creative places in which they partied. Jason dubbed one of their favorite spots the "Garden," because it was surrounded by a cluster of trees and bushes, and was nestled between a large industrial park, Interstate 55, and a junkyard. Jason and his friends "borrowed" a couple of vinyl car bench seats, a couch, and several large rocks from the junkyard next door. They placed the newly acquired seating in a circle, built a fire in the middle, and drank beer all night long. It was the closest thing to having a forest preserve in the middle of the city, and it was far enough away from the road it was rarely disturbed by security or the police.

It was an unseasonably cool spring evening when I went to the Garden in search of Jason. It was one of those nights I needed to get out of the house. Although I was not looking for trouble, it found me anyway.

Jason went on a beer run and was not there when I arrived. Only a couple of his friends, Ted and Drew, remained to keep an eye on the fire. The fire was warm, and the air was thick with the smell of hickory and beer. I sat down on one of the benches and waited for Jason to return. Even though there were easily twenty available seats for him to sit at, Ted chose to sit on the bench next to me. Before I knew it, he was making-out with me. Drew, feeling out of place, left. The kiss caught me off guard. I had no idea Ted was remotely interested in me. It was not a romantic kiss by any means. It was very forceful.

I immediately felt uncomfortable and tried to push him away, but he pulled me closer, and kissed me even harder. The more I resisted, the more aggressive he became. He knocked me down and pinned me on the bench while he groped me and sucked hard on my neck. I said no, and begged him to stop, but he would not let me go. Ted was a weight lifter, and was much stronger than me. I felt completely helpless and was terrified at the prospect of what might happen next, when I heard Drew shout, "Hey, what the hell are you doing, man?"

Thankfully, Ted let go of me. Tears of relief welled up in my eyes, as Drew offered to walk me home. Only a hushed whimper and an intermittent sniffle broke the silence on the way to my house. As we approached the front stoop, I uttered, "I don't know what would have happened if you didn't come along when you did. Thank you," then I ran into my house.

I rushed up to the bathroom and feverishly washed the smell of Ted's cologne off me. Unable to get what happened out of my head, I looked into the mirror in horror. For the first time, I witnessed the numerous hickeys which covered my neck. They were dark purple and bruise-like. I never received a hickey before and was mortified. It was May. Wearing a turtleneck was out of the question, and would only draw more suspicion. What was I going to do?

The next day, my friend Dee Dee tried several home remedies to remove the hickeys including applying ice and rubbing them with toothpaste but it only irritated my skin. She even attempted to camouflage the hickeys with cover up, but it was futile. They were simply too dark, and there were far too many of them. As a last ditch effort, she leant me a bandana to wear around my neck.

When I went to gym class, my teacher made me remove the bandana, because it was not part of the gym uniform. The look of disappointment in her eyes said it all. I felt like I was branded a slut against my will and what was worse—I could not say anything in my own defense. I was so worried about what my teacher thought of me, I almost forgot how lucky I was Drew happened along when he did. No one would have heard my screams.

Moment of Clarity
(We Aren't Like Other Families)

Early one Sunday morning, Patty and I took Mom's rickety old shopping cart to the Way Low to go grocery shopping. On our way home, we discussed our family. A harsh realization hit us simultaneously. We were not like other families.

When we compared ourselves to our friends' families, it occurred to us most of our friends came from normal families. Most of our friends did not have to work to support themselves, and did not have to track down their father at the bar for lunch money. Most of our friends had two parents who were living and happily married. Even our friends whose parents were divorced appeared to be in a much better place than we were.

None of our friends' families had a host of alcoholics and drug addicts living with them on and off. They all had furniture in their living rooms and color television sets. They had working telephones, heat, and hot water. Our friends did not have to worry about working two jobs and going to school. They did not have to worry about how they were going to pay the rent, do the laundry, and go grocery shopping. Why us? What did we do to deserve this?

Please Don't Go

Patty and I had a huge argument with Dad. The next day we decided enough was enough. Seeing Dad drowning in despair and rapidly deteriorating into a self-induced ticking time bomb took its toll on all of us. If we stayed, he undoubtedly would drag us under with him.

We got to talking. Both Patty and I were working two jobs, and I was graduating from high school soon. If we pooled our money together, we could afford to rent an apartment, take Kathy with us, and have a shot at living a semi-normal existence. We needed to be realistic though. Money was tight, extremely tight, but it was better than dealing with the daily turmoil we were being exposed to.

Feeling like we had no alternative, Patty and I agreed to move in together. We found an affordable apartment to rent and eagerly packed our bags. It was exhilarating and absolutely terrifying all at the same time. A morsel of hope riveted through my veins intermixed with waves of doubt and remorse. Patty and I could not get along to save our lives even though we had Dad to police us, albeit sparingly. What made us think we could get along without any supervision whatsoever? The answer was quite simple—survival.

As we finished packing, Grandma Velesovsky dropped by to see how we were doing. When she learned what we were planning, she begged us to reconsider. "You girls are all your father has in this world. If you leave him, there is no telling what it will do to him. Please don't go."

Pangs of guilt tugged at my heart strings. It did not take long before Grandma's guilt trip took hold. Dad was all we had left. How could we live with ourselves if anything were to happen to him? Bitter tears of disappointment streamed down my face as I slowly put my things away.

Chapter 22

You're Shitting Yourself

Dad refused to eat hospital food, surely a sign the man was feeling better. The problem was he was not eating anything at all, and, as a result, he developed chronic diarrhea. Since he was unable to get out of bed, he either used a bedpan or shit himself.

The sound of Dad's voice yelling obscenities echoed down the hallway, as I rounded the corner from the elevator. My heart began to race, as I anticipated yet another bad visit with him.

Dreading the confrontation surely to follow, I took my time walking to Dad's room. I prayed the non-stop plethora of vulgarity erupting from his mouth would stop. Although I was tempted to turn around and go back home, I forced myself to wait outside his room until the nurses finished cleaning him and his linens. Feeling anxious, I slowly sank to my knees and wished I had a pillow to block out Dad's rant.

"What the hell do you fucking niggers think you are doing? Get your goddamn hands off me!" Dad shouted.

The nurses and CNAs who took care of Dad at Cook County Hospital were incredibly resilient women who tolerated Dad's brazen, abusive behavior with nothing but grace and dedication. They took excellent care of him, despite his ornery disposition, and never once lost their temper with him, no matter how many curse words or racial slurs he spouted at them. You honestly could not pay me enough money to deal with the man—and he is my father. I simply do not know how they did it. He was merciless.

As the nurses exited Dad's room, he shouted, "You no good mother fucking, cock sucking niggers better stay the fuck away from me!"

I briefly made eye contact with one of the women in passing, then immediately looked down in shame. Taking a deep breath, I entered Dad's room, knowing full-well what a foul mood he was in.

"What the hell do you want?"

"Great to see you, too, Dad. I see you are in a lovely mood today."

"Fuck you and the horse you rode in on! These fucking niggers are trying to kill me!"

"I sincerely doubt they are trying to kill you Dad. Those nurses just finished wiping your ass. I think you need to show them a little goddamn respect. Not to change the subject, but the doctor said you are not eating."

"The food in here sucks. I can't eat this shit," Dad professed, as he pushed a tray of uneaten food at me.

"The doctor said if you ate solid food, you would take a solid shit and then the nurses wouldn't have to change your linens all the time."

"The doctor said. The doctor said. Fuck the doctors! They don't know what the hell they are talking about!"

"I love you, Dad. You know that, don't you?"

"Yeah, yeah, yeah. I love you too."

Then I bent down, kissed Dad on the cheek, and headed toward the elevator. On my way, I ran into one of Dad's doctors in the hallway. He was very concerned.

"Your father is refusing to eat. Therefore, he is not receiving the proper nutrients he requires, and it is hindering the healing process."

"I am so sorry. My father can be very stubborn. I'm at a loss as to what to do, doctor. As you are probably more than aware, it is very difficult to make the man do anything he doesn't want to do."

The doctor checked to see if anyone else was in the hallway, then he whispered to me, "I don't care what he eats, so long as he eats something. Please bring him whatever he wants, but, remember, you didn't hear that from me."

From that point on, I took orders for what Dad wanted to eat the next day. Some days he wanted Burger King, other days he preferred McDonalds. At least he was eating, and, thankfully for his and his nurses' sakes, his digestive tract gradually returned back to normal.

On the Wagon Part III
No Money, No Funny

Our natural gas service was shut off at the street because Dad refused to pay the bill for over a year-and-a-half. He used the money to pay for more important things, like rent, groceries, and *booze*. Even though our telephone was disconnected, it did not prevent the bill collectors from calling.

Late one afternoon, the next-door neighbor angrily pounded on our front door and shouted, "You have a telephone call."

Horribly embarrassed, I avoided making eye contact with her as we walked to her house in complete silence. She stomped into the kitchen, snatched the telephone from the table, and handed it to me, "Here!"

Not knowing what to expect, I timidly took the telephone from her, and said, "Hello?"

A collection agency representing the gas company had the audacity to call the next-door neighbor looking for Dad. The gentlemen (I use the term lightly), yelled and screamed about the eighteen hundred dollars *I owed him*. The man was so loud and obnoxious, the neighbor lady heard every word he said—and she was standing five-feet away from me. Even though I told him I was under eighteen years of age and insisted he speak to my father not me, the bill collector persisted on barraging me with his incessant demands. I was humiliated. The utility company already shut off our gas, what else could they possibly do to us?

After hanging up the telephone, I profusely apologized to the neighbor for the intrusion, and held my head down in disgrace as I walked back home. I was torn. I knew I had to tell Dad, but I could not bring myself to do it. His world was falling apart. He lost his wife. He lost his job. We did not have a telephone, heat, hot water or gas to cook with. Nor did we know where our next month's rent was coming from, let alone eighteen hundred dollars to get the gas turned back on—and the cupboard was bare. The worst part was Dad was completely sober. He fell into an awful depression after Mom died, and was certain he had cancer and was going to die. It was more difficult than dealing with the Dr. Jekyll/Mr. Hyde character that emerged when Dad was drunk. He could not eat or sleep and was melancholy all the time. He even threatened suicide.

My sisters and I knew, for the most part, how to handle angry and drunk, but we had absolutely no idea how to handle sad and sober.

No One Said Life Was Fair

Things were looking up. Uncle Bob paid our gas bill. Dad got a job. The DCFS dropped their investigation of our family. Then, the morning of my high school graduation, Dad found out he lost his new job. My graduation ceremony was a melancholy bag of mixed emotions for me, even before I realized Dad was not there. How drastically my life changed. Only four years ago, I was the valedictorian of my eighth-grade class, and had a complete family unit—albeit lovingly dysfunctional. I watched Mom fall victim to a vicious unrelenting disease, watched Dad crash and burn in the throes of alcoholism and depression, and I still managed to graduate in the top five percent of my class, as a member of the National Honor Society, and an Illinois State Scholar.

Yet I did not feel the same sense of pride or accomplishment as I did when I graduated eighth grade. My grades slipped, and it was a miracle I passed my advanced placement Calculus class. My heart was no longer in my school work. I was so disillusioned by the reality of life I had no desire to pursue my own dreams. It took everything I had to keep my family together, and there was nothing left for me.

I was already working two jobs during my senior year to help pay for AP classes and prom. It did not feel like too big a sacrifice at the time to postpone going to college for a year, while I helped pay the bills and raise my little sister. Mom's words echoed over and over again in my head, "No one said life was fair."

Winning the Lottery
(Easy Come, Easy Go)

Late one hot summer evening, my sisters and I were watching the Chicago Cubs game with Dad. He handed me his lottery tickets and told me to check the numbers as they appeared on the screen. I wrote the numbers down on a piece of scratch paper and then compared them to the tickets Dad purchased.

Dad played the Illinois State Lottery religiously. He purchased his tickets daily at a local grocery store called 7-9-11 on Archer Avenue, across the street from the American Legion hall he drank at occasionally and the funeral parlor where Mom was laid out. He played the same numbers for the Pick-3, Pick-4 and Lotto games every day, without fail for as long as I can remember. However, on this particular day, Dad tried something new. He let everyone at the bar pick his numbers for him.

As I checked the numbers, I laughingly said, "Hey Dad, one of the numbers you picked matches. No wait—two numbers. Oh, my

186

God. You've got three—no four and you match the lucky number too."

"You're shitting me. Stop lying!"

"I'm totally serious, Dad. Oh, my God. You won! You won!"

"Let me see that damn ticket, Mary."

Dad grabbed the stack of tickets and scrap piece of paper from my hands. Nervously, he checked the numbers and, before long, began to dance around.

"We won. We won the lottery. Woo! Hoo! Our ship has finally come in."

Dad, my sisters, and I all jumped up and down in the living room in celebration.

"How much do you think you won, Dad?"

"Well, it's not the big prize, you need to match all five numbers and the lucky number for that, but I'll bet it's substantial. And, it couldn't have come at a better time."

Dad was broke and was seriously hurting for money. He never won anything before. We were so excited we called all our extended family members from the payphone at Zosia's Tavern to let them know Dad won the lottery.

The next day Dad went back to the store where he purchased the ticket to claim his prize. He won sixteen thousand dollars. That may not be a lot of money to most people, but, for us, it was enough to pay our rent, food, and utilities for an entire year.

Well, that is, it seemed like a lot of money at first. Our celebration, however, was short-lived. After taxes, the money Dad owed Uncle Bob and the money we were behind on utilities and rent, there was nothing left. Dad shook his head and said, "Mary Kathrin, if we didn't have bad luck, we'd have no luck at all."

Is the Bottle Half Empty or Half Full

It was the summer after my high school graduation. I was working in the mailroom of a credit union by day and as a cashier at a department store by night. I stopped home briefly in between jobs to change clothes and ran into Patty. She claimed I gave her a dirty look and refused to let me leave the house.

Patty's favorite war cry was, "Just let me kick your ass!" As if kicking my ass would cure whatever she thought was ailing me— the be-all to end-all. When I heard those all too familiar words spring forth from her lips, I knew I was in trouble, but I honestly did not have the time to deal with her. I was running late for work.

As anticipated, we got into a scuffle. Patty pulled my hair with one hand, while she repeatedly punched me in the face with the other.

I pleaded with her, "Please leave me alone. I have to go to work."

No matter what I did, she would not relent, and charged toward me like a mad pit bull. Once her jaws locked down, there was no escaping her wrath. I looked around the basement for anything I could fashion a weapon out of. When I realized there was nothing within reach, I kicked her to get her away from me. Furious, she pushed me, and sent me crashing into the built-in wooden shelves which ran along the outside of the kitchen. They were butter-yellow and had matching floral cotton curtains draped in front of them to hide the clutter. We amassed quite the collection of empty thirty-two ounce glass bottles of RC Cola on those shelves, from all the pizza Dad ordered over the years.

I grabbed an empty glass bottle, waved it threateningly above my head, and screamed, "Leave me alone. I have to go to work. You can kick my ass later."

Patty leaped toward me and let out a blood-curdling scream, indicating the fight was far from over. I took the bottle and slammed it against one of the wooden shelves. It bounced back at me and nearly took off my face in the process. Patty laughed and lunged toward me yet again.

"Why can't you leave me alone?" I shouted, as I swung the bottle down with all my might against a corner of one of the shelves.

This time the bottle exploded in my hand. Glass shattered everywhere. *Now I had Patty's full and undivided attention,* I thought to myself. She was stunned silent while I grabbed my purse and sprinted out the front door, tossing what was left of the broken bottle onto the basement floor.

All I wanted was for Patty to stop hitting me long enough for me go to work. Patty interpreted what I did as a threat to her life. She seriously thought I was going to kill me with that broken bottle. I swear that was never my intention.

Punch Anyone?

Uncle Kenny was living with us for a few months and witnessed firsthand my daily confrontations with Patty. He asked me several times if I wanted his advice—self-defense, that sort of thing. I always declined. I wanted to keep the promise I made to Mom. Most of the times Patty and I fought, I was on the defensive. My forearms were riddled with wounds from blocking her punches and scabs from my sisters digging their nails into my arms. I even got my hair cut short to avoid losing fistfuls of hair, but it did not make a bit of difference.

One night after a particularly brutal fight, Kenny took me aside and said sternly, "Mary, you have got to fight back. By not hitting her back, you are giving her license to do this to you over and over again. Aren't you tired of this already?"

"Uncle Kenny, you don't understand. My mom said—,"

"Your mom is not here, and even if she were, I'm certain she wouldn't want you to keep getting hurt like this, day in and day out. Please let me help you. I have been in a lot of fights, and I can give you some excellent pointers."

Reluctantly, I agreed.

"You never make the first move."

It was true. I never made the first move.

"The next time your sister comes in here with an attitude like she was sporting today, give her a good sock in the puss. She'll be so caught off guard; she won't know what hit her."

"I can't hit like she does. Patty's been in plenty of fights. She is the only person I have ever been in a fistfight with. I don't usually hit her unless it is to get her off me."

Kenny showed me how to make a fist and then let me practice hitting him. I was timid at first, but he kept pumping me up.

"Harder, Mary, give me all you got!"

It took a long time to build my adrenaline up to the point where I hit Kenny hard enough to satisfy him.

"That's it, Mary. Hit Patty like that, and you'll never have to fight with your sister again."

With Kenny's encouragement, I was convinced I could defend myself.

The next morning, Patty started in on me while I was leaving for work. Before we came to blows, I pretended like I was going to walk past her. When Patty was within range, I let her have it with all my might. Unfortunately, it was not the power-packed punch I hoped for. I did not feel the same passionate fury I did the day before, when I was practicing with Kenny.

Now I know how the Japanese must have felt after they attacked Pearl Harbor. All I did was wake a sleeping giant. Patty was stunned for a millisecond. "Don't e-v-e-r touch my face again." she growled then charged toward me like a crazed Tasmanian devil.

I never struck Patty first again.

Take-ed Easy Labor Day

The Sunday of Labor Day weekend, a few of my friends and I went to the woods for an impromptu end-of-summer bash. It was a beautiful sunny day. The sky was blue, the temperature was in the upper seventies, and a gentle breeze made the trees rustle. Dee Dee parked the car, and we found a nice, sunny spot to toss a Frisbee, while the guys set up the grill and lugged a cooler full of beer and burgers to the picnic area.

After a couple of hours of direct sunlight beating down on us, I became very thirsty. Dee Dee and I went in search of washrooms and a water fountain while the guys grilled the burgers. Terribly weathered and foul-smelling, the outhouses we found left little to be desired. Luckily, one contained a roll of toilet paper and was void of hornets. The water fountain we found spouted rusty hard water that smelled like rotten eggs. Unable to bring myself to drink the well water and getting dizzy from the heat, I opted to drink the cold beer my friends brought. Unfortunately, by the time Dee Dee and I returned, all the burgers were gone.

The afternoon flew by. We packed up before the sheriff cleared out the woods at sunset and headed home. I jumped in the back seat of one of the cars and tried to stop the sky from spinning. The combination of the heat, hunger and drinking nothing but beer all afternoon caught up with me. My lips were completely numb. I kept biting them, but I could not feel a thing. *Uh-oh,* I thought to myself. *I do believe I am a bit tipsy.*

Dad was watching the *Jerry Lewis Telethon* when I got home. I tried to act sober in front of him, but he knew I was drunk. I grabbed a blanket from my bedroom, lay down on the living room floor, and watched the telethon with Dad.

"Hey, I know it is Labor Day, and you were just hanging out with your friends, but take it easy kid," Dad said.

Now, if a raging alcoholic takes you aside and tells you to ease up on your drinking, it's time to stop drinking. I had an epiphany that night. Something had to change.

Chapter 23

Cigarette Syndicate

A month after Dad was admitted to the hospital he regained enough strength to resemble a shadow his former ornery self. His incessant demands for contraband became unbearable. Every day he ordered me to bring him cigarettes and whiskey.

"This is a hospital, not a bar, Dad," I scolded him.

Irritable and suffering from nicotine withdrawal, Dad took his pent up frustrations out on the hospital staff and pretty much anyone he came in contact with, including me.

Every time I visited Dad, I spent over forty-five minutes looking for parking, fighting my way past the front guard, and waiting for the elevator. During one visit, he kicked me out of his room within one minute of my arrival because I did not bring cigarettes then he threw his food tray at my head as I left the room. Luckily, I ducked, and the tray crashed into the wall behind me. I left his room and immediately went in search of his doctor. He was standing near the nurse's station reviewing some test results.

"Excuse me doctor. My father smoked three packs of cigarettes a day before he was admitted to the hospital and he is absolutely miserable. Is there any way we can wheel him outside and let him have a smoke once in a while?"

"I don't see any harm in sneaking him a couple cigarettes once in a while. Everyone else on the floor smokes, even though it is strictly prohibited."

I was flabbergasted. I never expected Dad's doctor to give in to my request. Although, after getting to know Dad for the past month, I am certain his doctor figured out pretty quickly if Dad did not get what he wanted, his behavior only got worse.

The next day Dan and I paid Dad a visit with the sole purpose of smuggling him in a pack of his favorite smokes. The Chicago Bulls' game echoed down the hallway as we rounded the corner. Dan and I bought Dad a small black and white television set we picked up at a garage sale for $5 to help him pass the time. To our surprise, he was in his room watching the basketball game with half-a dozen people, including a Cook County police officer and a prisoner who was wearing hand cuffs, shackles, and a hospital *gown. Dad was charging a cigarette per person to watch the game. I did not have to sneak cigarettes to him. He was getting them on his own.*

After the game was over and his paid guests left, Dad revealed his secret stash to us. The nurses grew wise to Dad's previous hiding places and threw away any cigarettes they came across. This time Dad outsmarted them by placing the cigarettes in his electric razor case.

"But Dad, won't the cigarettes get crushed?"

"What do you think I am, an idiot? I tossed the razor out before I put the cigarettes inside.

"Oh, I thought you were looking a bit scruffy!"

Silent Screams

Sitting silently, thinking to myself, in an empty house, all alone—in a dungeon I have created for myself—I am my own worst enemy. Self-hatred, self-abuse has taken over where others have left off. I'm still the victim but now by my own hands.

I am in the middle of a vast whirlpool. I am drowning in despair. The current is great, and I fear I am going under. I search futilely for a life raft. Surely, someone must hear my cries for help. Why doesn't anyone answer me?

The silence is deafening. I scream, yet there is no sound. It is a nightmare from which I cannot awake. Someone is chasing me throughout a crowded department store. I run and run with all my might, and yet, he gains. I can feel his hands grabbing at me from behind.

I am so frightened when I try to scream for help, nothing comes out. A security guard is standing a few feet away from me, but I cannot scream to save my own life.

Please, someone help me. Please, someone, anyone, listen to me. Sympathize with me. Empathize with me. Tell me everything will be all right. Help me to see there is hope. Help me to stop this madness. What's the sense of drowning when there's no one around to throw you a life raft.

Experi-Mental

Helplessly standing by as Dad quickly unraveled made me

wonder. What power must this elixir possess that it hypnotizes its victims into abandoning everyone and everything they hold dear? I was unable to understand what made them want it so badly it clouded all judgment, voided all reason, and became more important than everything else. What was so amazing about this drug that it trumped everyone—including its victim's own children?

By my senior year of high school, most of my friends either drank alcohol and/or smoked marijuana, *some more than others*. One group of friends I hung out with did a variety of fun things, including playing miniature golf, bowling, and going to the movies and only partied on occasion. After graduation, they went from partying once in a while to all the time.

Although my firm anti-drug stance prevented me from trying marijuana, my morbid curiosity to understand why my parents drank got the best of me, and I experimented with alcohol. All alcohol ever did for me was to strip me of my self-control and make me vilely ill. What was the appeal? It certainly did not make the pain go away. Maybe I was missing something. Not being able to remember what happened the night before, puking my guts up, and experiencing the inevitable hangover that came the next morning, was enough to convince me drinking was not for me.

The summer after I graduated from high school, I was forced to make a decision I feel changed my life. If I stayed the course, I was powerless to escape the black hole of addiction, and would continue to spiral further out of control, unable to break free of its grip. My friends may have been able to say no and walk away before they crossed the point of no return—the blurred line where sobriety and addiction meet—but I did not have the tools or the ability to do so.

Allison went away to school. Jason met the girl of his dreams. Most of the friends I depended on were either growing up or moving on. Although it was a lonely decision, I severed ties with the friends I drank with. It was self-preservation. I simply stopped showing up. Since we did not have a telephone, it made the break easier. I felt awful, but if I tried to explain why I was not hanging out with them anymore they either would not understand or try to talk me out of it. Eventually, they stopped trying to reach me.

Bobbing for Apples
(a Heroin Trip)

Uncle Kenny was staying with us. He was battling a terrible addiction to heroin. I never realized how much watching my uncle self-destruct affected me. One night, after experiencing yet another drunken episode with Dad, I spent the remainder of the evening watching Kenny trying, unsuccessfully; to get up from the mattress he slept on in the living room near the front window. For two full hours, he attempted to get up from his mattress.

Kenny was nodding. He was tripping on heroin and was so high he could not function. All he could do was bob for apples, like a child who is up past his bedtime and is fighting sleep. They start to doze off, and then suddenly jerk back when they realize they are falling asleep—except with a heroin addict, it happens repeatedly.

The next morning, I fell apart at work when my boss gave me some constructive criticism. I apologized and confessed I was having trouble at home, but was too embarrassed to tell her what kind of trouble. How do you explain the day-to-day problems of an abnormal family to someone normal?

The Grinch Who Stole Christmas

Dad threw out our living room furniture and rug before Mom died, because the last time she was home she bled all over them. Our front room was bare, except for the television and VCR, the ivory Damask wallpaper, and the wood-plank subflooring. That was it.

Patty and I were both working two jobs to help ends meet. The week before Christmas, we came home to find someone, most likely one of our extended family members, stole the television set and VCR. All that was left on the metal faux-wood television cart was the ring of dust which once circled our television. I could not believe it. Our only form of entertainment was gone.

Who would do such a thing? The Grinch had more heart. It was obvious we had nothing. Not even a chair to sit on. All we had was that lousy television set and VCR. My sisters and I often joked if a thief ever broke into our house; he would leave us money along with a note which read, "Look, you need this more than I do."

My family was so depressed we decided to celebrate Christmas a week early. I went to the Swamp-O-Rama flea market and, for twenty dollars, purchased an old six-foot tall artificial tree and a dusty box of Christmas decorations. My sisters and I decorated the tree and exchanged presents to cheer ourselves up. My boyfriend Dennis' family, the only family I knew as poor as we were, lent us an old black and white television set until we could afford to purchase a new one for ourselves. It was the best and worst Christmas I ever had.

Send in the Christians

It was a bright and sunny Sunday morning and the house was full of activity. Dad was downstairs making breakfast. Patty and I were both getting ready for work, and Kathy was wishing she were anywhere but at home with her crazy family.

Dad looked out the window, and watched our neighbors as they went to church in their Sunday best. He opened the kitchen window and chanted loudly, "Send in the Christians. Let the games begin."

Patty and I heard Dad yelling and broke out in song.

"Would you be mine? Could you be mine? Won't you be my neighbor? Won't you please? Won't you please? Please, won't you be my neighbor?"

Kathy took her pillow, covered her head, and screamed, "Stop it. You guys are totally embarrassing me. This family is nuts."

Midnight Cruise

It was nearly midnight. Dad was sitting on our front steps, smoking a cigarette.

"Hey, kid! Pick up your shoes your pants are too short."

"These are capri pants, Dad. They are supposed to be this short."

"Oh, I thought you were preparing for a flood or something. What are you up to?"

"I was thinking about turning in. It has been a long day. Why do you ask?"

"Want to go for a cruise with your old man?"

"Gee, I don't know. It is getting pretty late. Besides, I've got to work in the morning."

"Come on, it's too hot to sleep. Let's go for a ride."

I could not say no to Dad. His enthusiasm was contagious.

"All right. Where to?"

"Nowhere in particular."

I got in the car and dug the seatbelt out from between the seats. As I reached over to lock the seatbelt into place, Dad asked, "What the hell do you think you are doing?"

"What does it look like I'm doing?"

"Take that damn thing off! What, don't you trust me? Let me tell you something. I was driving long before you were a gleam in your mother's eye."

Reluctantly, I unfastened my seatbelt and held on for dear life, as Dad peeled out of our neighborhood. He turned on the stereo and rummaged through his music selection in search of the perfect soundtrack. We got on the expressway and headed toward downtown Chicago. The night air instantly cooled me as it rushed by. Dad exited the expressway at Ashland Avenue and put on a tape by ELO. He cranked up the volume on a song called the "Jungle" which he loved to play whenever he drove through a bad neighborhood.

"Where are we going?" I inquired.

"I'm taking you for a little tour of the old neighborhood," Dad smiled fondly.

The old neighborhood changed drastically in the thirty-some odd years since Dad was young, and he and his friends roamed the streets. Eighteenth and Ashland, or the Pilsen neighborhood, as it is more commonly known, went from being a refuge for poor immigrants to a haven for gangbangers and drug addicts. It was a particularly scary place to be after dark—especially after midnight on a Saturday night. Dad and I stuck out like sore thumbs.

Pilsen is rich in architecture and diverse in culture. As we drove up and down the streets where Dad grew up, I was amazed by how ornate and colorful the old buildings and churches were. The sheer volume of graffiti that lined the homes, businesses, and garages was appalling. Even though it was very late at night, there was not a street we rode down without scores of people wandering about or sitting on their front stoops.

Dad insisted we stop the car in front of each house he lived in, every church his family attended, and all the playgrounds he played baseball at when he was a kid. He pointed out his car window, recalling stories of his glory days and exclaiming, "I lived there. I went there. I played there."

I can only imagine what the people sitting on their front porches must have thought as our junk heap slowly pulled up to their houses with its windows rolled down, radio blaring, and a stranger's finger pointing at them. Well, I know what I would have thought, if it were me—boom!

Chapter 24

Much Ado About Nothing
(Life Imitates Art)

The night we returned home from our honeymoon, Dan received a telephone call from Jacob, his brother's best friend from high school. Jacob was cast in a community-theater production of the Grapes of Wrath *and wanted to know if Dan was interested in trying out for the show. They were struggling to cast the part of Noah Joad, the odd, slower, older brother, and Jacob immediately thought of Dan. I agreed to let Dan try out, before I fully comprehended the time commitment involved. The next thing I knew, we were at the theater, and Dan got the part.*

Thus began our decade-long love affair with Community Theater, before long, we volunteered all of our spare time at the Oak Park Village Players. Dan liked acting and either worked with the construction crew or up in the light booth when he was not on stage, while I preferred to work behind the scenes with the stage crew or dabbling with set design and decoration. I loved everything about the theater. It was magical to witness how every show came together. There is nothing like watching a disastrous dress rehearsal transform into a stellar performance on opening night. Working at the theater was a great distraction and gave me a much needed creative outlet.

We were heavily involved with the theater, enjoying our third consecutive season, when Dad was admitted to the hospital. My life was perfect up until that moment. I had a loving husband, a beautiful new home, a fantastic new boss, and best of all, a new-found passion I shared with Dan. That is until I got sucked into Dad's drama vortex.

Dad was like the mafia. I kept trying to get out, but he kept pulling me back in. Each morning I went to work trying my best to carry on like nothing was wrong. After work, I visited Dad at the hospital, and then drove straight to the theater, often working until midnight. Then I went home, fell asleep, and did it all over again the next day.

While Dan acted in the main theater's production of Much Ado About Nothing, *I worked on the set. Dan played the part of*

Costard, who has one of my favorite lines from the play:

    "Remember that I am an ass. Though it be not written down, yet forget not that I am an ass."

    As part of the scenery for the play, I painted a trompe l'oeil mural on the back wall of the stage. It depicted a formal Italian garden which overlooked an iridescent-blue lake with majestic mountains and a faraway kingdom in the distance. The main theme for Much Ado About Nothing *is nothing is as it seems. How poetic, my life, imitate art. My whole life I led people to believe I was from a happy home and was raised in a normal family, when the complete opposite was true. I smiled when I was hurting inside. I said I did not mind, when I really did.*

Stop the Music

    Uncle Kenny, his girlfriend Cindy and their son Kenny moved to an apartment in Cicero leaving a vacancy at the Shangri-La Velesovsky. A few weeks later, my cousins Bobby and Jim moved in with us. Bobby is Uncle Bob's third born and Jim is Aunty Shirley's eldest.

    Unusually quiet, Jim kept to himself mostly, and was an oddity as far as teenage boys go. He was fanatically neat and clean. The obsessive-compulsive cleaning gene was definitely passed down from Grandma Velesovsky to Aunty Shirley and then onto Jim.

    Sounds like a model houseguest, right? Wrong. He may have been the most difficult person I have ever lived with. That is saying a lot, when you consider we harbored two known drug addicts and at least one alcoholic (besides my parents of course) over the years. Jim did not do drugs, drink or smoke. What offense did he commit? He played his music excessively loud late at night, every night, and had absolutely no consideration for anyone else in the house.

    We were on opposite schedules. While Bobby, Patty, and I were hard at work, barely making above minimum wage, Jim slept in and did not stumble out of bed until late afternoon. At night while Bobby, Patty, and I slept, Jim dee-jayed his own private house party. It never failed. The moment my head hit the pillow, he cranked up that damn stereo. The ceiling and walls vibrated so badly the windows actually rattled.

    There was one tune Jim was particularly fond of. It was called, "IOU" by Freeez. It is an extended dance mix and the only lyrics, "A, E, I, O, U, and sometimes Y" play repeatedly throughout the twenty-minute song. I swear Jim played that damn record over and over again until it warped. It sounded like a deranged *Sesame Street* song.

One night I came home late from work. As I walked toward the house, I heard the all too familiar beat Jim was so infamously known for reverberating between our neighbors' houses. He just stepped out of the bath. His thick, black hair was slicked back, and the water glistened off his naturally tan skin. The bathroom light highlighted his naked silhouette dancing in the front room like a scene out of the movie, *Flashdance*. As he danced, you could see every muscle in his torso. I was tempted to laugh until I realized how good he was. Jim danced like he was a professionally-trained dancer.

When he spun around, I giggled aloud. As soon as Jim realized he had an audience, he ran up to his room. In Jim's mad dash, however, he left some blackmail material behind. I raced into the bathroom to play off witnessing him prancing around in the buff, and that is when I saw it—a *Playboy* magazine *and* it was opened to the centerfold. I could not wait to tell Cousin Bobby (who shared the attic bedroom with Jim) and Patty about my encounter. We all had a good laugh at Jim's expense.

The next day, while Jim was out with his friends, Bobby, Patty, and I formulated a plan of revenge for Jim's rude ways. Jim truly was a neat freak—which we discovered while snooping in his drawers for further evidence of pornographic material to use in our evil plot. Every drawer in his dresser was in perfect military order. His socks and underwear were painstakingly folded and arranged in order by color. He hid his stash of *Playboys* in his bottom drawer, which he neatly stacked in chronological order. He even folded his dirty laundry and placed it in a laundry basket next to his bed. It was maddening. This boy needed help.

He was unlike anyone I have ever met. I could barely get him to say hello, but he could easily drive me to scream at him at the top of my lungs every night to turn down his stereo. His room was like visiting the set of the *Odd Couple*. Bobby played the part of Oscar Madison, the messy roommate who slept on a pile of dirty laundry and last week's takeout dinner. Jim was Felix Unger, the anal retentive, compulsively clean roommate.

"I know what we should do!" Bobby exclaimed. "Let's TP Jim's half of the bedroom. The mess will drive him crazy."

"I don't feel right going through Jim's things or messing up his stuff. Seriously, what if he goes nuts? What if we push him too far, he goes ballistic, and winds up hurting one of us?" I asked.

"Don't worry Mary. It's all in good fun. Besides, I would never allow Jim to hurt anyone," Bobby assured me.

"Yeah, Mary. Jim needs to loosen up. Who knows, maybe this will motivate him to be more considerate of the rest of us," Patty added.

Reluctantly, I agreed to continue with our diabolical plot. The music from *Mission Impossible* played in my head as we tiptoed through Jim's room tossing rolls of toilet paper until the room was covered with white streamers.

Then Bobby had another brilliant idea. "What if we rearranged his drawers? You know, like put his shirts in his underwear drawer and his *Playboys* in his T-shirt drawer?" We giggled with delight as Bobby and Patty rearranged Jim's drawers and I unmade his bed.

Anticipating Jim's reaction was far worse than the fear of getting caught while we did this dastardly deed. Bobby and Patty went to work. I was off for the night and forced to face the music alone as Jimmy strolled up our front walk. Tempted to undo what we did, I realized it was too late and took the coward's way out. I quietly closed my bedroom door, and hid under the covers. *I will cop the "I was sleeping" defense. Yeah, that will work. He'll believe that,* I thought to myself.

Hidden safely under the covers, I heard Jim race upstairs and then stop suddenly, as he was greeted by our toilet-paper calling card. There was an unnerving silence for five minutes, as he assessed the damage. My heart raced as I anticipated the impending explosion to follow. Jim paced back and forth in his room like a caged lion. Then I heard him open one of his dresser drawers. Once he realized his privacy was breached, he rummaged through the rest of his dresser to see if anything was missing.

Slamming each drawer shut after he inspected it, he angrily stomped over to Bobby's side of the room, and feverishly ransacked Bobby's piles of clothes and other miscellaneous debris. Jim emerged from the attic moments later empty-handed. He huffed and puffed angrily, then marched out of the house, and took off with his friends, who were waiting outside.

Hardly a peep or the reaction I hoped for. I guess I wanted to hear Jim verbalize what he was feeling. At the very least, I wanted him to yell at me—call me an asshole or tell me to never touch his things again. Any reaction other than silence was acceptable—some small sign Jim was human. Nothing.

Have a Catch

Every week when they were young, Dad and his brother Bob stood outside of St. Vitas Church, wearing their Sunday best, impatiently waiting for Mass to end. As the congregation let out, they ran inside the church, grabbed a copy of the bulletin and pocketed the money their parents gave them to put in the weekly collection. They used the money to buy baseballs.

Dad's first passion in life was baseball. When he was a boy, he played every day, weather permitting, with his friends at Cooper School yard on the south side of Chicago near his home. During the summer, he played baseball, sunrise to sunset, breaking only to walk his blind Busha (his Grandma Bartoszek) home. Every penny he and his friends scrounged up went toward buying baseballs and, on occasion, a cold Pepsi during the hotter part of the day. Dad wanted to be where the action was. He loved playing shortstop and centerfield, but gladly filled any position, including pitcher.

Even though Dad was blessed with three girls, he did not let it stop him from passing down his love of the game to us. My sisters and I all know how to throw and catch a ball, and are well-versed in the fine art of pitching a knuckleball and a curve ball. Dad spent countless hours playing catch with us on the sidewalk in front of our house. We used whatever was available at the time to play with. Sometimes, Dad brought home a rubber ball from the store which resembled a baseball, other times we tossed around a tennis ball, and on rare occasions, when nothing else was available, we played catch with the bright-green crab apples which fell from the trees in front of our house.

Dad's silhouette as he pitched to me is forever etched in my mind—the warm glow of the sunset shining brightly behind him, a lit cigarette dangling from his mouth. He wore a frayed baseball cap, a grimy T-shirt with a front pocket for his cigarettes, and a faded pair of Levi's. The skin on his face was tanned and wrinkled, his laugh lines deepened. His five o'clock shadow had bits of gray emerging from it, as did his once light-brown hair, which was slowly succumbing to his receding hairline. His deep blue eyes still had a twinkle about them. His hands were calloused and weathered, like a worn pair of leather gloves, and heavily soiled with oil and grime from the cars he worked on. His pinkies were permanently bent, from numerous breaks playing baseball as a kid. God forbid a splint got in the way of his playing.

Taking a drag of his cigarette, Dad cocked his arm back and gunned the ball toward me like a shot out of a canon. We played catch so often I could practically grab the ball from thin air with my eyes closed. Never taking my eyes off Dad, I reached up over my head, and plucked the ball out of the air. Dad threw the ball so hard my hand stung. Despite the pain I felt, I held onto the ball with a vice-like grip. It was strictly frowned upon to drop the ball once you had it in the palm of your hand. Dad did not believe in baseball gloves. If you could not catch a ball of your own freewill, you were no baseball player.

Dennis, one of the guys I dated in my late teens, was particularly fond of baseball and spoke at great length about it to Dad. One afternoon, Dad asked Dennis to show him his stuff on the field. We hopped in the car and drove to Edwards School yard. We played baseball for a couple of hours on one of the open diamonds. Dennis pitched, and Dad hit one ball after another. Every once in a while, they switched positions, and Dad pitched to Dennis.

When Dad grew tired of playing, he pointed his finger toward the outfield like Babe Ruth. Dennis smirked at Dad's cocky gesture, wound up, and threw the ball with all his might. It was a fastball, low and inside—Dad's sweet spot. Dad's face lit up as he hit the baseball. That was the last we saw or heard of it. I swear that ball flew past the field, across the street, and straight to the other end of the alley, a full block away.

That is how we all knew Dad was done playing ball for the day. When he had enough, he purposely hit the ball so it was irretrievable.

Dad was one hell of a baseball player.

Raging Bull

Late one Friday evening while I was getting ready to go out with friends from work, Cousin Bobby came bursting through the front door. He was openly sobbing. I could smell the alcohol on his breath from across the room. It was the first time Bobby drank since he moved in with us. He had blood all over his face and shirt, and it looked like his nose was broken. I grabbed a towel from the bathroom and helped Bobby apply pressure to his nose to stop the bleeding.

Dad, who was sleeping in the living room when Bobby came home, woke up and asked, "What the hell happened?"

"Uncle Kenny and I were in front of Zosia's drinking a six-pack of beer. Kenny pointed across the street and said, 'Hey, what's that over there?' Then he sucker punched me." Bobby cried.

"Why would Uncle Kenny do that?" I asked.

"I don't know," Bobby shrugged his shoulders.

I was comforting Bobby when I heard the basement door fling open and what can only be described as the sound of a raging bull charging up the stairs. Kenny kicked open the living room door and stampeded toward Bobby, yelling at the top of his lungs, "How dare you call the cops on me, Mother Fucker! I am not going back to jail!"

As Kenny lunged for Bobby with a closed fist, Dad flew through the air from the other side of the living room trying to stop Kenny before he hurt Bobby, like a secret service agent taking a bullet for the president. I was smack dab in the middle of their fight. Within seconds, a fury of fists and curse words filled our empty living room. Terrified Dad or Bobby might get hurt, I tried pulling the three of them apart, and yelled, "Stop it!"

The fight came to a grinding halt when Dad barked like a junkyard dog, "Get the hell out of here, Ken. NOW!" Kenny did not say a word as he turned around and ran out the back door.

Bobby McGee

Cousin Bobby is Deanna's brother. Bobby's thin-build, medium height, shoulder-length, dishwater-blond hair, and blue eyes with a hint of teenage angst reminded me of a young Kurt Cobain. A diehard fan of Black Sabbath and Ozzie Osborne, he once took me to see them at concert at the UIC Pavilion. The best seats we could afford were smack-dab in front of one of the amplifiers. My ears rang for four days. I rarely saw Bobby wear anything other than a pair of faded Levi's, a rock concert T-shirt, and his black converse gym shoes. He was twenty-two years old and was recovering from a bout with alcohol abuse when he came to live with us.

Dad had the same rules for Bobby he had for everyone else who came to stay with us. The rent was free, as long as you were drug-free. Bobby was seriously working on his sobriety and wanted to make something of his life. More than anything, he wanted to be a musician. He played the guitar beautifully and loved to write songs. Bobby once played me a song he wrote about his sister Deanna's addiction. It had a haunting melody and compared kicking drugs to climbing a mountain.

I got to know Bobby quite well during the brief time he stayed with us. We were both working two jobs and got home about the same time. We stayed up late and talked for hours in the kitchen. I saved enough money to purchase a television and a VCR. Bobby and Jim helped me lug them home on the bus. Every morning, I set the VCR to record the soap operas on ABC. Every night, Bobby and I watched them together after we got home from work.

It was June. Allison came home from college for the summer. She stopped by early in the morning and convinced me to go shopping with her at the mall. I was reluctant to go at first, but it was ages since I last saw her, so I went. We had a ball. When I came home, Jim was standing in the kitchen staring blankly at the wall. He hardly ever said a word to me. I thought he was joking when he told me what happened.

Bobby woke-up with the worst headache he ever had. Jim witnessed Bobby take an entire bottle of aspirin and then collapse. At first, Jim thought Bobby was playing around with him. When he realized he was not, Jim panicked and ran to Grandma and Grandpa Velesovsky's apartment, four blocks away. Grandpa jumped into his car with Jim and rushed to the nearest fire department. Since neither Jim nor Grandpa could remember our address they drove with the paramedics back to our house. The fire department immediately transported Bobby to the hospital.

Bobby had an aneurysm. A weakened artery wall in his brain suddenly gave way without warning. The doctor compared having an aneurysm to a time bomb going off in your head. He said Bobby was probably born with it, and it could have happened at any time.

Dad took my sisters and me to Cook County Hospital to visit Bobby. We were grief stricken. I cannot even begin to imagine how his family must have felt. Bobby was in a coma. His face was unrecognizable, due to the swelling in his brain. That's when the levity of the situation hit me. This was serious. Bobby might not make it.

I fell asleep praying for Bobby's speedy recovery. I dreamed I had one last conversation with Bobby in which I tried to convince him all he needed was physical therapy, and with a little hard work he would be fine. In the dream, Bobby told me he experienced enough pain in his lifetime. Physical therapy was not an option. He was better off helping people where he was and felt he could do more good there than here. I woke up to the feeling of someone kissing me on the cheek and whispering softly in my ear, "Goodbye, Mary." But when I opened my eyes, no one was there.

Bobby died two days later. At his wake, a continuous line of people ran out the door, circled around the building, and down the street. The funeral home was huge, yet there was not an unoccupied seat. It was a testament to how many lives Bobby touched. Everyone who ever met him loved him.

It was a closed casket. An eight-by-ten-inch picture of Bobby was placed next to the casket, and several other pictures of him were displayed throughout the funeral home. Bobby was dressed in his favorite Black Sabbath T-shirt and a pair of faded Levi's. His family placed a six-pack of beer and a carton of cigarettes in his casket before we left for the burial.

The funeral procession was incredibly long. Thankfully, we were the last car in the motorcade. Dad's badly rusted 1979 red Toyota Starlet had no muffler or brakes, was extremely loud, and totally inappropriate for such a somber occasion. It sounded like an airplane was landing whenever we approached a stop light. When the street light in front of us turned from green to yellow, my heart sank. Dad geared down and the engine roared loudly. Then he pulled on the emergency brake and the car skid to a grinding halt. Closing my eyes, I braced myself in anticipation, praying we didn't hit anything.

After the funeral, Dad opted not to go to the restaurant with the rest of the family, thus sparring us any further embarrassment. Instead, he took us to where he said Bobby would have wanted to go. We went to Burger King and ate Whoppers.

The Bi-Bull Lady and Other Saviors of Soul

Mom and Dad were non-practicing Catholics. Both attended

Catholic grammar schools and told us stories of being physically abused by the nuns who either beat them with rulers across their knuckles until they bled, or whacked them in the back of the head with erasers thrown from across the room. The only time my family stepped foot in a church when I was growing up was to attend either a wedding or a funeral. Although we celebrated the holidays, my sisters and I never understood the meaning behind them.

I only remember having one theological conversation with Mom. We were watching an old black and white movie, *The Song of Bernadette*, and I asked, "Mama, why do people pray to God?"

"They pray for all kinds of things, Mary. Some people pray for things they need, like food, water or shelter, while others pray for sick loved-ones to be well."

"What do you pray for?"

"When I pray, I thank God for my blessings. Everyone asks God for something when they pray, but people rarely take the time to thank him. We are very lucky. We have many things to be grateful for."

Once Mom died, Dad became a self-proclaimed atheist. He often proclaimed, "If there was a God, he never would have let your mother suffer like that."

Word got out pretty quick we did not go to church. We had literally every denomination trying to convert us. Well-dressed men and women smelling of sweet perfume and cologne, carrying and quoting the Bible, all came by in an impassioned effort to save us from a life of sin. They represented the Jehovah Witnesses, to the Baptists, to the Church of Jesus Christ of Latter-day Saints, and God-only-knows what other churches—all vying for our eternal souls.

One well-meaning, petite, four-foot ten-inches tall, gray-haired lady with black eyebrows and a thick French accent, made it her mission in life to personally save me from what she described, at excruciatingly great length, as an eternity of damnation. She told me in vivid detail about doomsday and how those without faith would perish as the fires of hell consumed the earth.

It seemed like I was always the one who answered the door, when the Bi-bull Lady paid us a visit. It became a bad joke after a while. If, by chance, Patty or Kathy happened to answer the door when the Bi-bull Lady came to call, they'd excuse themselves and shout, "Mary, there is someone at the door for you."

I honestly did not have the heart to tell the Bi-bull Lady we did not want anything she was selling. As a result, I was forced to listen to her ramble on about how the world was going to come to an end soon, and if she did not save me I would burn in the fires of hell for all eternity. She did not have to tell me the world was ending soon I was witnessing it crumbling down around me every day.

Chapter 25

Ms. Amelia Visits the Hospital

In my spare time, when I was not visiting Dad at Cook County Hospital or working, I volunteered with Dan at the Oak Park Village Players. They were a community theater group that performed main stage and children's theater productions. Before Dad was admitted to the hospital, I landed my first on stage role since the eighth grade. I was cast to play the part of Ms. Amelia in the children's theater production of The Little Princess.

Knowing Dad would never get the chance to see me on stage, I thought I would bring the theater to him. Shortly after a Saturday matinee performance, I drove to the hospital to visit Dad wearing my full 1900's costume and makeup. My hair was pulled up into a bun. I was wearing a white ruffled shirt which was tucked into a full-length, royal-blue skirt. A pearl necklace, cameo broach, and black leather boots completed the look. Strange as it may sound, I did not get many stares at the hospital. Apparently, the unusual is the norm at Cook County Hospital, and I went relatively unnoticed.

Never Forget I How Much I Love You

For a moment in time, the lines between sobriety and intoxication became blurred for me. I could not separate the things Dad said and did when he was sober from the things he said and did when he was drunk. I began to believe he never loved me, and that my sisters and I were a burden he was forced to deal with because Mom died.

Living with Dad was like living with Dr. Jekyll and Mr. Hyde. One day he was a madman with his hair standing on end and his nostrils flaring threatening to kill me; the next day he had no memory what transpired the night before, and we carried on like nothing happened. After a while, it all became routine. Forgive and forget. The most horrendous things occurred, and the next day we started over with a clean slate. But for a small period of time, I became disillusioned with the constant denial. How could Dad love me, when he said the most hateful things to me on a routine basis?

Dad and I had a huge fight the day after one of his drunken

rampages. Dejected, I yelled, "You don't love me. All you care about is your booze." Then I ran off and escaped to the comfort of friends. When I returned home, I found the following handwritten note from Dad.

"Mary Kathrine,

I have always loved you and always will. Don't get it? I will always love you no matter what.

Always, Your Dad."

Unpaid Debts

Some debts you can never repay and some debts you have to pay the piper. I knew Dad was guilty of many things, but I never thought in a million years …

Let me explain.

We did not have a telephone for a number of years. Dad ripped the telephone out of the wall and refused to pay the bill after Deanna ran it up. I was working regularly and tried to pay off the remaining balance. Illinois Bell told me they did not keep records for more than two years. Since the old telephone line was in my deceased mother's name and the record was no longer on file, they suggested I put the telephone in my name. So I did.

Shortly after the new telephone line was installed, I was barraged with a variety of collection calls for Dad. One call was from the funeral home where Mom's wake was held. The owner called me personally.

"Hello. Are you related to Ronald Velesovsky?"

"Yes, he is my father."

"Your father has an outstanding balance from your mother's funeral. In the history of our family-owned business, no one has ever not paid their bill. No one. We tried several times to set up a payment plan with your father, but he simply refuses to pay."

"How much does he owe?"

"The original balance was $3,500 but with interest and penalties, he now owes over $5,000."

My jaw hit the ground.

Overwhelmed by what he said, I blurted out, "Oh, my God. I don't know what to say. I am so sorry. To be honest, I'm a student. I simply don't have that kind of money, sir."

He apologized to me saying it was Dad's debt, and told me

not to worry about it. I was stunned. How could Dad not pay the bill? Was it too painful? What happened to all the money our family and friends gave Dad for the funeral? Part of me could not help but think it was Dad's final parting shot to Mom for leaving us.

Interstate Porn

Dad came home one day from the bar and announced we were moving in with one of his drinking buddies, Gene. Gene was a recent retiree, a lifelong bachelor, and to be honest, a bit slow. He wore thick, Coke-bottle lenses which made his eyes all but disappear. His gray five o'clock shadow and wild hairs which stuck out of his ears and nose made him look old and scruffy. He wore a plaid button-down shirt with a white T-shirt beneath, polyester pants that did not quite match, and a thick, black leather belt.

Dad called him, "Gene, Gene the Dancing Machine" because his black leather steel-toed shoes shuffled as he walked. Gene's breath smelled of cheap whiskey and cigarettes. His hair was greasy and brushed forward. He had a childlike quality about him which was reflected in the collection of cherub wax candle figurines he proudly displayed throughout the house. He spoke with a slight lisp, sounded like a drunken Winnie the Pooh, and his loose, upper false teeth whistled when he spoke.

Gene's family took care of him most of his life. When Gene was of working age, his stepfather got him a job at his company. Gene worked there for forty years. The last couple of years Gene worked, however, he was not making the cut. His co-workers took up the slack, ensuring Gene retired with full benefits. After Gene's sister died, no one was left to look after him. For some reason, Dad was more than happy to fill the role (with the assistance of my sisters and me of course).

Gene's home had not been cleaned in years and was absolutely filthy. My sisters and I went from room-to-room cleaning and disinfecting every surface, including the floors, walls, and ceilings. It took the better part of a week for Gene's place to resemble a house again.

We were living with Gene for a couple of weeks. It was Wednesday and I was home from work. I was in my bedroom studying, when Gene unexpectedly came home early from the bar. Not knowing Gene well, I did not feel comfortable being around him without Dad present. Luckily, Gene usually did not stay home long.

Gene turned on the television in the front room and slipped a video tape into the VCR. Since he was hard of hearing, he had the volume turned way up. I was about to open my bedroom door to go to the washroom, when it became abundantly clear Gene was watching a pornographic movie. It was the incessant moaning, the crack of a whip, and a dominatrix yelling, "You've been a naughty, naughty boy!" that clued me in.

Gene obviously doesn't realize anyone is home, I thought. I banged my dresser drawers open and shut loudly, and slammed the closet door closed to let him know I was home. Unfortunately, Gene did not hear me over the dominatrix yelling at her willing victim.

The urgency of my overflowing bladder, however, overrode any embarrassment I felt. I turned the doorknob and that is when I heard it—the sound of a whip smacking Gene's derriere. At first, I thought I was hearing things. I quietly opened the door a crack and peered into the living room. Gene was standing smack-dab in the middle of the room, stark naked, watching a pornographic movie, and shouting, "You're a bad boy!" as he spanked himself.

I immediately closed the door and freaked out. Just when I thought it could not get any worse, I heard the buzz of a vibrator snap on. I was a prisoner in my own bedroom. How could I get to the bathroom without disturbing Gene or witnessing what I am sure was a bad amateur porno? I paced back and forth to help me think and to relieve the urgency I felt. Climbing out the window was not an option—we were too high up. Calling Dad was out of the question; the telephone was in the kitchen. What was I going to do?

Because Gene was drunk, it took him an extraordinarily long time to—well, let's say, finish what he started. As soon as Gene was—done, he turned off the television, put the video tape away, and left. As he slammed the front door closed, I ran into the bathroom and happily relieved myself.

I thought, *What if Kathy came home from school during Gene's porn fest?* For the love of Pete, we had no living room curtains. Anyone walking by undoubtedly witnessed Gene's bare ass and x-rated behavior.

Compelled to find Dad and tell him what occurred, I tracked him down at one of his new watering holes, the Chateau. Dad was surprisingly calm when I told him what happened. He did not utter a single word. He simply put on his baseball cap, grabbed his jacket, and left the bar. His silence unnerved me. The next thing I knew, Dad was back at the house packing Gene's pornographic tapes and sex toys into a large cardboard box. It easily amounted to a couple thousand dollars' worth of materials. Dad grabbed the box, placed it in his car, and drove down Interstate 55. He pulled over to the side of the road and waited until a large semi-truck approached. Then he tossed everything into the truck's path—video tapes, butt plugs, vibrators, and whips went flying up into the air in a million little pieces. Problem solved.

The Drunk Gourmet

From time to time, when Dad is under the influence, he craves comfort foods from his past. He tiptoes into the kitchen with a grocery bag full of secret ingredients and blocks the window to prevent us from seeing what he is up to. When Chef Ronnie is cooking his covert culinary concoctions, we are not allowed in the kitchen until his monster-piece is complete. Grinning from ear to ear, Dad happily announces, "Dinner is served," then he herds us into the kitchen and forces us to taste test his experimental fare like guinea pigs.

One day I came home after school and heard Dad singing a song by Frank Sinatra in the kitchen.

"Fly me to the moon, and let me swing among the stars..."

"Hi Dad! Whatcha doing?"

"Making dinner. Want to try some?"

My senses were on high alert as I struggled to ascertain the ingredients Dad used to produce his latest creation by smell alone. This particular day's offering delved into the staple of Italian cuisine—spaghetti. I peered skeptically into the pot. At first glance, the cooked pasta and red sauce appeared normal however, upon further inspection; I noticed it had an orange hue.

"I don't know. Something doesn't seem right, Dad."

"Try it. You'll like it. Your sister Patty loved it."

I grabbed a bowl of Dad's experimental pasta and sat down at the kitchen table.

"The sauce is thinner than Mom's."

"Just try it."

Suspicious, I twirled the spaghetti onto the prongs of my fork and slowly raised the pasta to my mouth.

"So what's the verdict, kid? You gonna shit or get off the pot? Take a bite already."

Then I tasted it. As the altered tomato sauce hit my palate, I instantly knew what Dad's secret ingredient was.

"This tastes like it has alcohol in it, Dad!"

"Wow. Your sister Patty asked for seconds, and she didn't even notice. There are two full bottles of beer in that sauce. The beer gives it great flavor. Don't you think?"

"Um, no. No, it doesn't."

One cool fall evening, when I was a sophomore in college, Dad came home hammered with a hankering for ribs. He put the ribs into a roasting pan, slathered them with a combination of grape jelly, maple syrup, and mustard, and then placed them in the oven at 500 degrees. Ravenously hungry and rather impatient, Dad mistakenly thought the ribs would cook quicker at a higher temperature. Unfortunately, he failed to close the oven door all the way before passing out on the couch in the living room.

Four hours later my boyfriend Dan drove me home after a night out with friends. I invited him inside for a pop before he headed home. When we opened the door a hideous burnt-food smell permeated the room. We stepped into the kitchen to investigate further and were overcome by a wall of heat so intense it melted all the wax figurines Gene stored on the shelves above the sink. Dan placed the ribs outside which were reduced to a smoking, charred, gelatinous mess as I ran around the house opening all the windows in an attempt to air out the house.

Now what have we learned from this little lesson kiddies? There are certain things you should never do if you have been drinking including but not limited to—driving, dialing or cooking. Words to live by.

Chapter 26

Pins and Needles

During the brief moments Dad was conscious during the first couple of weeks he was in the hospital, he yanked out every IV he was given and disconnected every monitor he was hooked up to. Each day when I came to visit, he looked like he was in another bar fight—bruised and bleeding, with additional bandages on his arms and an IV sticking out of a new site. Naturally, I attributed Dad's combative behavior to his alcohol withdrawal. I was wrong.

When I was little, I thought Dad was invincible—that he was made of steel or something. He was Superman. After all, he even told me so. The man was fearless, confident, and incapable of being afraid of anything. As I grew up, it came as somewhat of a shock to me that Dad was human. I never would have guessed the reason he refused to go to the hospital was because he was afraid.

It was what he was afraid of that did not compute. It was not a rational fear, like being afraid of what the doctors might find was wrong with him, or being afraid of being admitted to the hospital for an extended period of time, because he could not afford the bill—no, nothing reasonable like that.

He was afraid of needles. Needles. A tiny, insignificant little pinch. He survived dozens of bar fights, abscesses, and gout. He sneaked past armed National Guardsmen—twice. Yet, the prick of a needle is what frightened Dad. His fear was so great he avoided going to a doctor for six months and literally risked life and limb— all because he had a paralyzing childhood fear of getting a shot. Seriously? You have got to be kidding me!

The Ugly Drunk

We should have listened to Dad when he said he did not want to go to Cousin Annemarie's wedding. He hated dressing up and was not much a fan of public family events, especially ones involving Mom's side of the family. Dad attended begrudgingly.

Once he learned there was free booze, however, he was a bit more agreeable. It did not take long before Dad was stinking drunk and obnoxious. As the priest said grace, Dad announced rather loudly, "I've gotta take a piss."

You could have heard a pin drop, as he staggered his way toward the men's room. I was so embarrassed I could have slipped out of my chair and hidden under the table for the remainder of the evening. It took everything I had not to start bawling.

Dad returned to the table with another drink in his hand shortly after the priest concluded his prayer. Throughout dinner I prayed Dad would stop drinking, but he did not. With every drink he downed, Dad became more belligerent and confrontational.

When the deejay played our family anthem, Meatloaf's "Paradise by the Dashboard Light," Patty saw the opportunity to take Dad's keys and seized it. She dragged Dad out onto the dance floor and convinced him to dance with her. As Dad twirled around, Patty stole his keys from his pocket. Then she spun around, nonchalantly bumped into Dan, and dropped Dad's keys into Dan's pocket.

After the song was over, Dad left the dance floor, and headed for the bar. He came back to the table with another drink in his hand and announced, "Well, it's been a slice, but I've had about enough fun for one evening. It's time to go."

We were miles from home. There was no way in his present condition that we could allow Dad to get behind the wheel of a car. My sisters and I played it off like Dad lost his keys, but he knew one of us took them. Dan and I drew the short straw and ended up driving Dad home. Incessantly grumbling on and on about what assholes we were for taking his keys, Dad's confrontational behavior made for an arduous ride home. I thought the trip home was painful until the next day when I took Dad back to fetch his car. Dad did not say a word to me the entire time we were in the car, but his silence spoke volumes. The tension was so fierce it caused my hands to shake uncontrollably. I was barely able to grasp the steering wheel or concentrate on the road. Dad wanted to drive home when he was too drunk to even walk, but we were the assholes. Yeah, right.

After the War

Was it motherhood or absence that made Patty and my hearts grow fonder? I would like to think it is a bit of both. Patty ran into an old schoolmate from grammar school, fell in love and got married. Our lives were never the same after Patty's son, David Anthony, was born. The years of Patty and me bickering and fighting seemed to melt away the moment I looked into his big blue eyes. David was the spitting image of Dad and had his personality to boot.

Sure, Patty and I had brief reconciliations over the years and there were rare occasions in which we were both on the same side. But those times were few and far between. David changed everything. He was the cement that bonded my sisters and me together. He was what was missing in our lives. It did not happen overnight. Old habits die hard. Trust me. But he was the catalyst. I actually enjoyed spending time with my family again, and I loved watching my nephew grow up. He was as smart as a whip, and Dan and I found ourselves quoting every word that came out of his mouth.

The bitter cold war between Patty and me was finally over.

Water Caddy

Gene had a mild stroke. When he was released from the hospital, he insisted Dad take him to the bar for a beer. Dad reluctantly agreed. While they were at the bar, Gene had another stroke. It left him completely incapacitated, and he was placed in a nursing home. No longer able to drive, he gave Dad his beloved Cadillac Eldorado. Dad never owned a new car before, let alone a fully loaded one with real leather seats and air conditioning. He absolutely loved the car and drove it everywhere.

I was looking out the plate glass window in our front room admiring the sunset as it cast an orange glow on the warehouses across the street. Out of the corner of my eye, I spotted Dad pulling up. He came in hard and failed to engage the brake in time. His Cadillac jumped the curb, tore up the lawn, and ran full-force into the fire hydrant on the corner. Water shot high up into the air like a cartoon. It is one thing to spiral out of control in private agony. It's another thing to completely melt down publicly for the whole world to see. We could not hide or sweep this under the rug.

He Did It His Way

A month before our wedding, Dan and I rented a garden apartment in Cicero, near his parent's house. Even though I was twenty-five years old, I felt guilty leaving home. So much so, the first night we were in the apartment, I drove back to Dad's and spent the night on the couch. Dad could have cared less I was leaving the nest. The next morning he woke me up shouting, "What the hell are you doing here? I thought you moved out."

A week later, Dan and I were unpacking boxes at our apartment when the telephone rang. It was Grandma Velesovsky, and she was hysterical.

"He's not breathing!"

"Who's not breathing? Grandpa? Did you call 911?" My heart began to thud hard.

"Yes, I called 911. I tried calling your father, too, but I can't reach him. Can you please come here, Mary?"

"Of course, Dan and I will be right there. Don't worry. Everything will be all right."

No sooner did I hang up the telephone, Dan and I were on our way. The paramedics were already on the scene when we arrived.

Grandma's muffled cries spilled into the hallway as Dan and I made our way up to her apartment. She could hardly breathe, she was so upset. Grandma embraced me tightly and cried, "Oh, Mary. He can't die. What will I do without him?"

As I attempted to comfort her, the paramedics worked feverishly to revive Grandpa. I was so scared, I began to cry too. Grandpa survived a heart attack a couple of years before, but not before he gave us one hell of a scare. To everyone's surprise, he heeded his doctor's advice, had an angioplasty, stuck to a strict heart-healthy diet, and drastically cut down on his drinking—only indulging in a beer once in a blue moon.

My grandparents were married for fifty-two years. Although they had their share of heated arguments and disagreements, they loved each other very much. I did my best to calm down Grandma long enough to find out what happened.

Uncle Bob and Grandpa got into a terrible argument. Uncle Kenny's drug habit and legal expenses were quickly depleting my grandparents' life savings. Deeply concerned for his parent's welfare, Bob was vehemently against Grandpa bailing Kenny out of trouble again. Grandpa felt he must use whatever means necessary to help his son. Bob felt Kenny required more of a "tough-love" approach. Grandpa and Bob never saw eye to eye where Kenny was concerned. The argument ended with Bob tearing the telephone out of the kitchen wall and angrily storming out of the apartment.

Grandpa laid down on the couch and called out to Grandma, "Bern, get me a glass of water, I'm thirsty."

By the time Grandma returned to the living room with the glass of water, Grandpa was no longer breathing. Grandma plugged the telephone back into the wall and frantically dialed 911.

The paramedics put Grandpa on a stretcher, placed him in the back of the ambulance, and transported him to Holy Cross Hospital. Dan and I gathered Grandma and sped toward the hospital.

When we arrived we went to the front desk to inquire about Grandpa's condition. The clerk told Grandma she needed to check Grandpa into the hospital first before she could release any information to us. Grandma was too distraught to answer her questions, so I jumped in on the questions I knew, like his name and address.

Then the clerk asked, "What *was* his birthday?"

What was his birthday? Oh, my God. Grandpa died and they haven't had the decency to tell Grandma yet, I thought to myself, as Dan and I exchanged a knowing glance. Thank goodness Grandma was too hysterical to realize what was happening. After I finished answering the clerk's questions, she sent us to a tiny waiting room and closed the door.

A representative from the hospital met up with us a half an hour later.

"Excuse me, are you relatives of George Velesovsky?"

"Yes, I am his wife. How is my husband?"

"I am sorry to have to tell you this but, he did not make it."

Grandma was inconsolable.

After the initial shock wore off Grandma asked, "Can I see him?"

"Of course, you can, ma'am. Please wait here, a member of the hospital staff will take you to him."

Five minutes later, an orderly escorted us to Grandpa's remains. Guiding us through the emergency room maze, he led us down a long corridor, and then stopped briefly in front of a room. He double-checked the name on the chart before he parted the curtains and let us in. As he pulled back the sheet, revealing Grandpa's lifeless body lying on a hospital gurney, I wanted to bolt.

Surely, Grandpa would not want Grandma to see him like this, I thought. During their efforts to revive Grandpa, the paramedics removed his false teeth. He looked like he fell asleep with his mouth open. He had a three o'clock shadow and the hairs on the sides of his head, which he normally kept slicked back, were standing up wildly like a bad case of bed head. I could no longer fight back the tears as I watched Grandma sorrowfully say her final goodbyes.

As much as I dreaded having to do it, I called Dad to let him know his father died. His reaction shocked me. Surprisingly calm, he said, "I can't believe he is gone. My best friend died today. I am really going to miss him." Then he paused briefly and cried, "Oh, no."

"What, Dad?"

"I was supposed to take Pa over to Patty's house to meet his great-granddaughter for the first time this weekend. He never got the chance to meet her. When was Amanda born?"

"October eighth. Ten days ago."

Dan and I considered postponing our wedding, but Grandma would not have any of it. She said Grandpa would want us to be happy and go on with our lives.

The Brady Bunch Meets the Addams Family

November 7, 1992. Dan and my wedding day. I had such high hopes for a smooth sailing event, but instead of getting a good night's rest the night before, I stayed up late attempting to clean our apartment. As a result, I overslept and missed my hair appointment.

I took the quickest shower of my life and raced to the beauty salon where I begged them for mercy. Luckily, they took pity on me and had enough time to do a quick wash and set. After the beautician sprayed my hair with a can of hairspray, I was on my way. The photographer was waiting for me outside the apartment when I came home. My father, sisters, and other bridesmaids arrived five minutes later.

Dad was drunk and reeked of cheap cologne, alcohol, and cigarettes. On the plus side, he was in great spirits. I breathed a sigh of relief, as we posed for pictures in the makeshift studio the photographer created in my living room. Every time the photographer took a picture, Dad stuck up his middle finger or made bunny ears behind my head. He could not behave himself for one second.

I thought to myself, *If we can make it through the church*

service without any drama or shenanigans from Dad, we're golden. I hedged my bets on Dad remaining relatively sober until there was an abundance of free alcohol available at the reception. By then, he would blend in with the rest of the wedding party, and no one would notice he was stinking drunk. I never anticipated Dad greasing the wheels before he arrived.

Dan's mother saw Dad standing at the back of the church, came up from behind him, and patted him on his shoulder. Dad, in classic Ronnie-style, turned to her and said, "Pardon me, but is that your tit in my back?" Oh, how I hoped Dad would wait until after Dan and I were married to insult my mother-in-law.

Chapter 27

Thera-spa

Convincing Dad to go to rehab after being released from the hospital was nearly next to impossible. He spent two and a half months at Cook County Hospital and was anxious to go home and sleep in his own bed. I cannot say as I blamed him. After much urging, however, he reluctantly agreed to go to physical therapy—but not before he put up one hell of a fight. The doctors and nurses surely rejoiced the day Dad was discharged from the hospital. I swear I heard the Hallelujah chorus playing as he left the building.

The rehabilitation center was directly across the street from a beautiful park. Spring sprung, and the park was full of life. The trees were covered in delicate pink and white blossoms. Bright green blades of grass emerged from the ground, colorful flowers perfumed the air, and the birds sang their song of hope eternal.

The first time I visited Dad at Schwab Rehabilitation Center, I was pleasantly surprised. Parking was readily available. Checking in at the front desk was a breeze by comparison. The center was much cleaner and more modern than the hospital. Plus, Dad had his own private room. What more could one ask for?

By the time I made my way up to Dad's room, however, he was nowhere to be found. I inquired at the nurses' station as to Dad's whereabouts. The nurse behind the desk put on her black-rimmed reading glasses, flipped through the chart and said, "According to the schedule, he is at water therapy, but he is due back any minute. You can wait for him in his room if you'd like."

"Thank you!" I exclaimed, as I walked back to Dad's room with a spring in my step. Optimistic we were finally approaching the end of Dad's arduous journey, I breathed a sigh of relief as I entered his room. Refreshingly bright and cheery, the sun streamed in from a huge picture window with a view of a park. There was a working color television, a telephone on the table next to his bed, and a couple of cozy chairs for visitors to sit on. I took a seat and admired the artwork on the wall as one of the attendants delivered Dad's dinner.

Tentatively lifting the cover, I took a peek and thought to myself, "He might actually eat that." Then I heard a familiar voice call out from behind me, "Hey kid, what's the good word?"

"Hi Dad! How was therapy?"

"This place is like the Taj Mahal. They had me in what they call 'water therapy.' It is a Jacuzzi the size of a swimming pool. When they turn the jets on, it feels like you are getting a massage from head to toe. It was awesome. I tell ya, I could get used to this, kid."

"Is it better than being at the hospital?"

"Much."

St. Valentine's Day Massacre

Dad fell down the basement stairs and broke his right leg. He waited an entire week to seek medical attention, despite Patty, Kathy, and my pleas. Of course, he insisted Dan and I take him to Cook County Hospital on Valentine's Day, during the worst blizzard the Chicago area has seen in over a decade. So much for the romantic evening Dan and I planned.

The twenty-mile journey from our home in Romeoville took us nearly two and a half hours. The heavy snow fall, which pounded the Chicago area during rush hour, brought the Stevenson Expressway to a grinding halt. By the time we arrived at Dad's house to pick him up, he was completely furious. I grabbed Dad's jacket while Dan helped him up the stairs. Once we were all safely in the car, Dan drove us to the hospital as quickly as he could.

The emergency room entrance was practically deserted when we arrived. As I helped Dad swing his legs to get out of the car, Dan convinced an orderly to bring a wheelchair out to us. The orderly suggested we park the car and wait in the waiting room while he escorted Dad to triage.

I will never forget the horrible night we spent in the waiting room at Cook County Hospital. Besides the uncomfortable chairs, lack of entertainment, and an undesirable, scary element, the low light of the evening was watching the security officers kick the homeless out into the cold snowy night. It was nearly sunrise by the time the doctors took x-rays of Dad's leg and placed him in a full leg cast.

Dad's car was a stick shift. He did not let a broken leg stop him from driving it, however. Driving with his left foot, Dad rested his right leg across the passenger seat and used his crutches to engage the clutch.

From Mexico with Love

Kathy fell in love and moved to Mexico for about a year with her boyfriend Hugo. Dad was gutted. He walked around in a perpetual fog, like a lost puppy. Every day he asked me, "Have you spoken to Kathy?"

Kathy and Hugo lived with Hugo's parents in a remote part of Mexico, two hours south of Mexico City. Hugo opened a pizza place in a nearby town called Atlacomulco. When Kathy was not gathering supplies or working at the pizza place, she taught English at a local language center. Needless to say, she was rarely home, and it was difficult to reach her.

Six months after moving to Mexico, Kathy found out she was pregnant. Dad, Patty, and I worried about Kathy living in a foreign country even before we found out she was pregnant. After we learned she was pregnant, we worried nonstop. Kathy saw a doctor regularly in Mexico and had an ultrasound performed. She was having a boy. We were all beyond excited.

Dad constantly probed me for information about Kathy. How is she doing? Is she going to her doctor's appointments? How is the baby? When is she coming home? He was completely miserable without her. After all, Patty and I were both married. Kathy was the last to leave the nest, and her moving so far away tore Dad apart. He missed her terribly. Fortunately for Dad, Kathy decided to have her baby in the states. When she called to ask me if I would pick her up at the airport, I was elated.

I'll finally get Dad off my back, I thought.

Dan drove me to O'Hare Airport. I walked to where the international flights were landing. Kathy appeared from within a crowd of people walking toward me. As soon as I saw her round, pregnant belly, I started to cry. I know I am only seven years older than her, but I felt like a mother looking at her daughter.

Time flew and before we knew it, Kathy was ready to give birth. I could not believe it when she called me at work. She asked Patty and me to stay with her until her boyfriend Hugo was able to make it to the hospital. Kathy insisted Patty and I come directly to the hospital from work. She was certain she was going to have the baby right away refused to let us go home to change first.

I was completely caught off guard when Kathy called me. Although it meant a lot to me, I am certain her preference was to have Hugo by her side. Hugo promised Kathy when she went into labor he would hop on the next available flight. But he never came.

Each time the doctor came into the room to examine Kathy, she asked Patty and me to leave. But by the time she was ready to give birth, all modesty went out the window, and she demanded Patty and I watch as the baby crowned. When Kathy pushed, I saw a head full of black hair peek out.

Then the doctor said, "Okay, just one more push."

Patty and I looked intently as the doctor announced, "Congratulations, Mom! It's a girl."

A girl? But, wait. Didn't the ultrasound Kathy had in Mexico say she was having a boy?

My sweet niece, Brittney Angelica, came into the world with a full head of naturally curly black hair and the biggest brown eyes I have ever seen. Her rosy cheeks, fair complexion and sweet smile instantly captured my heart. She looked like Snow White.

Brittney and Kathy moved in with Dad, who happily filled the void left by Hugo. Dad was completely crazy about Brittney. How could you not be?

Chapter 28

How Bumpy Got His Name

After my nephew, David and niece, Amanda were born, we called Dad, "Grandpa." The name did not stick. Dad has never possessed the warm and fuzzy quality associated with the name. Then, early one morning, Kathy was babysitting David and Amanda. Dad was hung-over and in a foul mood. Unable to tolerate the children's laughter or them banging on their toys as they played, Dad bellowed, "Be quiet!"

Startled, both David and Amanda cried. Kathy did her best to console them and said sweetly, "Remember the story Snow White and the Seven Dwarfs? *Well, Grandpa is sort of like Grumpy." That made them both laugh. From that point on, Dad was known as "Grumpy."*

The day Dad was released from the hospital my family threw an impromptu welcome home party for him at his house. We gathered around Dad's daybed in the basement. Ecstatic to be home, Dad could care less he was still hooked up to an IV antibiotic drip and had to have his dressings changed twice a day.

Dad sported a wicked grin, the one he wore when he was up to no good (which earned him the nickname of "Little Devil" in Polish from his Busha Bartoszek) and said, "Hey, David, who stole my leg?"

David paused for a moment, lifted up the blanket on Dad's bed and said sternly, "Grumpy, what did you do?"

We laughed out loud.

After Dad's leg was amputated, all he had left where his leg used to be was a rather large—well, in Dad's words, "bump." Whenever Dad felt the phantom pain associated with his amputation, he complained, "My bump hurts." Kathy's daughter, Brittney, was learning how to talk when Dad came home from the hospital. Whenever she said "Grumpy," it sounded like "Bumpy." And the name stuck.

That is how Dad, aka Grandpa, became "Grumpy" and then "Bumpy." Sure, he has several other nicknames he goes by, too, like "The Bump," "The Bumpinator," and "Asshole," to name a few, but the grandkids call him "Bumpy."

Past, Present, Future

You cannot run away from your past, nor can you change it. Try as you might to forget it, it is there staring you right in the face every time you look in the mirror. Your past is your present, and it is your future. You cannot bury it, and you cannot ignore it because that would be like denying who you are. You cannot leave the past in the past nor should you dwell on it.

Embrace your past, the good, the bad, and the ugly. Make peace with it. The point is you survived it. Whether you realize it or not, you are better for it, because it has made you who you are today, and you are wonderful. Given the chance, you would not change a thing, nor would you choose to live it over again. Regret nothing. Appreciate everything. Live every day like it is your last.

The Truth

The truth is but the strike of a match away. It is the spark that ignites the flicker of thought swirling around you like smoke lingering from a lit cigarette—unearthing the key to your past, unlocking the door to your psyche, and unraveling the mystery of who you are. It lures you in with its promise of self, and entices you with its potential to expose your deepest, darkest secrets.

Tantalizing thoughts dance on the tip of your tongue, and emit sketchy details, gently awakening memories which slowly surface like old records playing in your head. Forgotten dreams and foolish notions wisp up like an intoxicating poison, gradually seeping into your subconscious. Hypnotizing, hauntingly familiar reflections emerge of who you were and what you have become.

As we grow older and face the uncertainty of what lies ahead, there is a longing for things familiar to us; to go down roads traveled before; to revisit the past and understand how it has made us who we are today. Your past is the ingrained yellow cigarette smoke that gets into your eyes and stains your soul. One need only look back to see what lies ahead.

When my sisters and I were growing up, everything was colorful and complicated, but in retrospect it was all black and white.

The End
(of the madness I hope)

Afterward

One More for the Road

I believe I inherited my sense of humor from Dad. Always the prankster, he teases the people he likes the most. In that way, I am much like him. Mom was always the serious one—the one who considered herself a realist. I can only remember her telling one joke, and I think it sums up our family quite well. It goes like this:

A man walks into a tavern and sees three guys sitting at the bar. He watches them intently for a while. The first guy is grabbing something from the air and putting it into his pocket. The second guy is taking something from the first guy's pocket and putting it up into the air. The third guy has two fingers extended and is running them along the bar over and over again.

Five minutes go by and the man asks the first guy, "What are you doing?" The first guy says, "There are too many stars in the sky. I am removing them."

Perplexed, he asks the second guy, "What are you doing?" The second guy says, "There are not enough stars in the sky. I am putting them back."

Stumped, he asks the third guy, "What are you doing?" The third guy says, "These two guys are crazy, I am getting the hell out of here!"

Family Tree

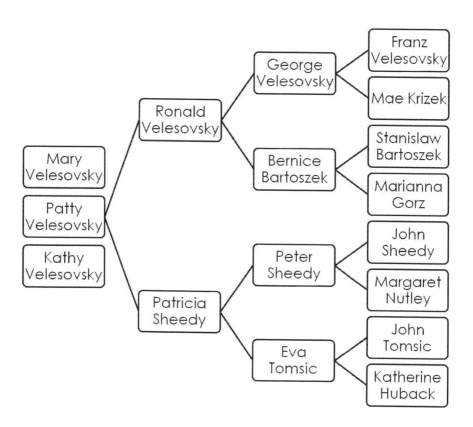

Index of Stories

28961951R10130

Made in the USA
Lexington, KY
08 January 2014